SKIN IN PSYCHOANALYSIS

SKIN IN PSYCHOANALYSIS

Jorge Ulnik

KARNAC

First published in 2007 by
Karnac Books Ltd
118 Finchley Road, London NW3 5HT

British Library Cataloguing in Publication Data
A.C.I.P. for this book is available from the British Library

ISBN-13: 978-1-85575-516-1

Edited, designed, and produced by
Florence Production Ltd, Stoodleigh, Devon
www.florenceproduction.co.uk

Printed in Great Britain by Biddles Ltd.
www.karnacbooks.com

I dedicate this book to Ester, Alejandra and Analía, who give me all the love and understanding I need to feel well.

．

"When I set myself the task of bringing to light what human beings kept hidden within them, not by the compelling power of hypnosis, but by observing what they say and what they show, I thought the task was a harder one than it really is. He that has eyes to see and ears to hear may convince himself that no mortal can keep a secret. If his lips are silent, he chatters with his finger-tips; betrayal oozes out of him at every pore. And thus the task of making conscious the most hidden recesses of the mind is one which it is quite possible to accomplish." (Freud, 1905d, pp. 77–78)

"In order to judge a man, we must know at least his secret thoughts, his doubts, his emotions; the wish to know only the material events of man's life is merely chronology, the history of fools." (Honoré de Balzac, 1831, p. 88).

This book was translated from Spanish by Valeria Muscio and subedited by Ben Weller.

CONTENTS

ACKNOWLEDGEMENTS

I would like to thank my Spanish friends for making it possible for me to visit their marvellous country every year: Dr Gerardo Gutiérrez, Dr Eduardo Chamorro, Dr Victoria Serrano Noguera, Dr Juan Rodado Martínez and Dr Lourdes Sánchez García (psychoanalysts); Dr José M. López Sánchez (psychiatrist); Dr José Zurita (psychotherapist); Dr Emilio Suárez Martín, Dr Enrique Herrera Ceballos and Dr Carmen Brufau (dermatologists).

I would like to thank Dr Javier Ubogui, an exceptional dermatologist, for his generosity, his intelligent advice, and his deep understanding. His help has been invaluable in every sense, but in particular with Chapter 11, which he helped write and for which he provided clinical material and photographs.

I would like to thank my parents, who set an example for me even today, and who were always supportive.

And I would also like to thank:

Dr Fernando Stengel, Dr Juliana Förster Fernández and Dr Miguel Fridmanis (dermatologists), because they have always trusted me;

the staff at Psoriahue, who share interdisciplinary work with me: Dr Miriam Saposnik, Dr Maria Laura Garcia Pazos (dermatologists), Dr Irene Dabbah (psychiatrist and psychoanalyst), Lic. Patricia Mirochnik, Lic. Mónica Czerlowski, Lic. Eugenia Melamed (psychoanalysts) and Professor Alicia Lago (eutonist);

my associate professors at the department of Psychosomatic Diseases of the UAI who helped me write the chapter about attachment: Lic. Alicia Monder, Lic. Mónica Czerlowski and Lic. Mónica Santcovsky (psychoanalysts);

the National Psoriasis Foundation (USA), who always support scientific work in order to help psoriasis patients;

Mariela Tzeiman and Dr Federico Bianchi, who helped me with charts and graphics, and Dr Silvio Litovsky, who gave me the translation of some medical words;

Vivian Gerome and Valeria Segura, who put a lot of effort to follow all my instructions and who helped me a great deal with this book;

Professor Vicente Galli and Dr Alcira Mariam Alizade (psychoanalysts), who support me with affection.

ABOUT THE AUTHOR

JORGE C. ULNIK, MD, has a PhD degree at the University of Granada, Spain, and at the University of Buenos Aires, Argentina. He is full member of the International Psychoanalytical Association and training and supervising analyst at Argentine Psychoanalytical Association.

He is Professor of Psychosomatics at the School of Psychology of Universidad Abierta Interamericana (U.A.I) and Staff Teacher at the Postgraduates Department of University Reneé Favaloro (Buenos Aires).

He got the position of Visiting Professor, earned by international competitive examination in the "Programa Cátedra Fundación BBVA" (2000). Since then, he has been invited annually to Spain and Portugal. In Spain he is Professor in charge of the Area of Psychosomatics at the Master Degree in Psychoanalytic Psychotherapy, Complutense University of Madrid; Professor of the Master Degree in Humanistic Integrative psychotherapy, Galene Institute, Madrid; Honorary Professor at the Unit of Teaching and Psychotherapy, Andalusian Health Service, Granada and he participates annually as a lecturer in the cycle "cinema and psychoanalysis", organized by Cajamurcia Foundation in Murcia. In Portugal he has been invited to give lectures at the Porto Psychoanalytical Institute, Portugal Society of Psychology, Lisbon University, and Lisbon Psychoanalytical Institute.

He organizes and participates in interdisciplinary teams, especially in the dermatology area. He is Medical Director of Psoriahue Medical

Center (Interdisciplinary Medicine for the comprehensive treatment of psoriasis and vitiligo). He is member of the Editorial Board of Archivos Argentinos de dermatología and Dermatología Argentina. He is the author of 22 published papers, 18 consulting university booklets, 5 book chapters and two books. The first one, Monográfico de Medicina Psicosomática (ed. Virgen de las Nieves, Granada, 2002) as co-author with José María López Sánchez and members of the staff of CEPA (Arg) and UDyP (Granada, Spain). The second one, El psiconálisis y la piel (ed. Sintesis, Madrid, 2004) is the Spanish version of this book. He is in the private practice of psychoanalysis in Buenos Aires, Argentina.

PREFACE

To write a few words about Jorge Ulnik's book, the book the reader is holding in his or her hands, is for me a pleasurable yet delicate task. I am not an expert in the subject the book deals with—the skin and its disorders—but on the other hand, brief yet true friendship bonds me to Jorge. I would not wish the former to discredit my words, and on the latter, I would not like to convey the idea that I am blinded by friendship (something I have never found to be bad in itself, except when it comes to writing an introductory-critical comment about a book).

Are we dealing with an introductory book on a relatively new and undoubtedly highly specific subject, aimed at people who know little about it? Or is it rather an advanced research project which will be useful above all to those professionals who already have some experience and familiarity with the subject of the skin? I can say without doubt that it is both. This book is a magnificent source of information and motivation for those who are starting out, as well as a well-documented, conscientious and complex study with abundant and varied clinical material for specialists.

While I was reading the book, I longed for a specific chapter regarding the psychotherapy of patients with skin diseases, with methodological and technical precision as well as extensive follow-up of some of the cases treated. It is very probable that Jorge's active mind has already dreamt and thought about such a chapter. If this were not the case, I set myself up as the spokesman of those who would like to find such a work.

And now I invite the reader on a quick tour of some aspects of the work and its author which, in my opinion, are worth emphasising.

Jorge's theoretical contribution is important: in the first place, due to the revision of authors he embarks upon, starting with Freud. We now rediscover in Freud multiple direct or indirect references—which are put in order and categorised—to the subject of the skin. In a conscientious and thorough way, he includes all that Freud says regarding the nature and function of the skin, which is spread all over his work, from the *Project for a Scientific Psychology*, written in 1895, to the *Outline of psychoanalysis*, dating from 1938. This important work is, above all, one which clarifies.

The book also discusses at length Anzieu's contributions (the common skin with the mother; the functions of the Ego-skin; the levels of symbolisation and its five corresponding logics, which Jorge begins to introduce and to illustrate in clinical practice as well as in works of literature and films; the importance given to masochism as "suffering covering", and so on) and a long list of psychoanalysts who have dedicated themselves to this subject with variable intensity.

The reader should then be prepared to go through several authors hand in hand with Jorge. I don't know whether they have all been included: probably not; however, I felt well-guided and well-informed. I was particularly impressed by the expressive function of the skin, proposed by Roberto Fernández, and the contribution—which in my opinion is fresh and up to date—of a well-known author as close to Freud as Max Schur is.

Regarding the interpretation made by Rosenfeld of the popular story *Donkey skin*, I find it complex, rich and interesting, though I cannot say the same about the methodology with which he approaches the story, which is a product of traditional culture and thus should have been studied in its own context. However, this subject; i.e. the methodology of approach to these treasures of our oral culture, is a completely different matter, and I have no doubt that Jorge will be able to find there truly valuable materials for his line of research.

We are likewise impressed by something the author himself announces: his honest revision of authors. He neither conceals his sources in any way, nor does he limit himself to literally mentioning these ideas; rather, he puts them forward while at the same time making them his own, including them within his system of thought and action.

Within this aspect of theory we find in the book a decidedly complex point of view regarding the skin: the skin as source, the skin as object, the skin as protection and as a way of entrance, as contact and as contagion, the skin "for two" within the relationship with the mother, the skin as envelope and as support, as a shell presented as "second skin", as demarcation of individuality, as a place of inscription of non-verbal memories, as a toxic envelope, and so on. In addition to this, an interesting idea is presented: the multiple influence of the psyche over the body has always been known, but what is far less known—apart from the inhibitive or depressive effects of serious somatic conditions—is the influence of the body over the psyche, in particular that of the skin over the psyche. This is an idea which is constantly developed in the book.

Still within the same arena of the author's theoretical contributions, what has impressed me most has been his constant interest in meaning. Important voices in the world of psychosomatics have introduced a structural point of view (psychosomatic structure) which, so to speak, "sentences" the patient—who is suffering from symptoms that are considered to be psychosomatic—to a diagnosis of psychosomatic personality, which has been previously constructed with a high level of generalisation and, I might add, of segregation.

Jorge does not belong to this group. Each patient attracts his attention because of their individuality, their history, the family sayings that have affected them, the material functionality of their symptoms, and so on. He is always interested in the meaning of each itch, of each spot, of each scale of epidermis. And perhaps in this way, and by going beyond the diagnostic method we were alluding to, he tries to introduce the patient to a symbolisation which has not only been suffered but also experienced and handled. Jorge's text is full of patients. We read a few paragraphs and a person appears, someone who is perceived from close range and about whom everything is interesting: his name, the nicknames by which he is known, his clothes, his representations in publicity products, his naiveté regarding possible remedies for his disease . . .

However, Jorge does not stop here. He goes out to find patients in the wider world: in children's drawings, in well-known cartoon characters, in popular stories, in literature and in film. And suddenly we begin to perceive these well-known characters from the perspective of the skin (armour-skin, the skin as the place of slight or brutal inscriptions, the skin used to display and to conceal things, and so on). We perceive this in Perrault, in Balzac, in Calvino, in Kafka. Indeed, we should notice the richness with which our vocabulary includes representations of the skin. This is obviously not a merit of Jorge's, but what is indeed his merit is to have compiled so many examples, to have obtained authentic treasures from our language. And we can easily see that constantly mentioning the skin through such well-known and familiar sayings of our language has the effect of putting us in contact with our own body.

Reading this book involves our own body. This is a very different effect indeed from the one I experience on reading authors who speak of a conceptual, faraway body, a body which is alien to sayings, jokes and children's songs, among other things. This sensation I experience, i.e. that my body is present while I am reading, is very curious. I am not certain whether this is an effect of what the author says or of how he says it. And I tend to think it has to do with his psychoanalytical way of talking to us which, in this case, is the body and the skin.

I would not like to avoid saying that I sometimes find the author's clinical examples somewhat disquieting due to the symbolic character he attributes to symptoms as well as to remedies. This is possibly due to the fact that I lack the enormous clinical experience he has. In any case, I am eased by the fact that through those daring interpretations and interventions both the symptom and the treatment are included within chains of meaning. We have already mentioned the author's repeated decision to name and to signify that which, for almost everyone, appears to be mute or incomprehensible (precisely due to its lack of meaning or, even better, of possible meanings).

The reader will discover in Jorge something that some of us already knew from his visits to Madrid and his involvement in the Masters in Psychoanalytical Theory and in Psychoanalytic Psychotherapy at the Complutense University: his qualities as a teacher. In relation to this, I would like to comment on the spiral movement with which the author presents his ideas. He progressively adds concepts, shows clinical examples, recalls previous concepts, adds more concepts, brings in more examples from other arenas, and so on. In this way he succeeds in introducing us to a world (the world of the skin, its nature and disorders) of remarkable complexity. We seem to perceive part of this teaching method already in the introduction, when the author lists the chapters which will be either theoretical or clinical. These chapters are not all grouped together, some at the beginning and others at the end; rather, they are strategically alternated.

I have always admired how the author presents, in an easy and understandable way, certain aspects of the *Project for a Scientific Psychology* which are not easy to grasp and which have thus caused a good number of psychoanalysts to criticise and reject it. Every time he mentions the Project, he manages to clarify it and to make it accessible to readers. I refer the reader, for example, to any of these comments throughout the text.

Another aspect of his teaching method is the use he makes of successful metaphors from the didactic point of view. I will merely quote two examples: one is the "tailor's mirror", which is put forward to illustrate the symbolic system through which the subject will imprint the image of the fellow human, thus having an influence upon the body image. Another example is the idea of mourning as a "tearing" of attachment, when he mentions that someone's hand slips, thus leaving the subject only connected to the image, or in contrast, the subject is alive only if he believes that he is seen by the other. I find this idea very suggestive not only for understanding those processes in which the body and the skin "must be given to be seen", but also for understanding aspects of the mourning process in general.

Regarding Jorge's abilities as researcher, I will only mention two things. On the one hand, as we have mentioned previously, we know that he always pays attention to the particular, to the singular circumstances of each observed subject, but at the same time he is always looking for links that will allow him to make generalisations. In this sense, for example, he puts forward typologies that will make knowledge, and the consequent intervention, easier. These typologies are present in each of the chapters, and what is more, they could even constitute a true taxonomy of skin diseases and of patients suffering from them.

Jorge's interest in research has led him to develop a conscientious method of test and assessment regarding the subject of somatic patients seen from the perspective of proxemics. Thus what he develops in Chapter Six regarding affective distance, the construction of a certain spatiality and the relationship of these with skin diseases has its empirical correlate in the research I mentioned, with which we at the Complutense University in Madrid hope to have the chance of collaborating.

I understand that one of the most important consequences of Jorge's years of work, as well as an important reason for the present book, is a serious proposal for interdisciplinary work between dermatologists and psychoanalysts. I believe that in our circle it is an original and promising proposal. There are many analysts interested in the heterogeneous field of psychosomatics, but only a few (in fact, I don't know if any) have referred to the convenience of establishing a close relationship between dermatologists and psychoanalysts. This aspect has been an important reason, in the last few years, for his presence in our country, where his help to different dermatology teams is highly valued. I believe that Chapters 11 and 12 (in particular the clinical case, its analysis and Jorge's interdisciplinary proposals) are an excellent display of this interdisciplinary interest.

I cannot finish this preface without mentioning the therapist. Based upon the admirable conjunction of gaze and listening in his clinical work, Jorge always tries to establish a connection between the patient's symptoms and the threads of meaning, thus promoting a process which, based on a solid theoretical foundation, has a clear therapeutic goal. If the reader has had the patience to follow me this far, he or she will now be able to verify that friendship has not been the reason for my writing this preface, and will enjoy, as I have done, a good book, written due to the interest aroused by the secrets, misfortunes and emotions of men, to put it in the words of Balzac which open the book.

Gerardo Gutiérrez
Director of the Master in psychoanalytical psychotherapies,
Complutense University of Madrid

Introduction

E ver since I decided to study medicine I was interested in its humanistic aspect. I was very lucky because when I began my studies, the authorities of the School of Medicine decided, for the very first time, to act on something which had always been spoken about but never corrected, i.e. that it was not right for medical students to begin studying anatomy with dead bodies.

As soon as we started our first year, they made us work at the hospital as nursing assistants, and in this way we were able to establish contact with patients from the very beginning. This is how I witnessed childbirth long before a dissection. I learned to give injections directly in the buttock and not in oranges or pillows. However, being near patients also made me feel close to human suffering, and made me aware that in the hospital wards the lungs are flooded with tears that go towards the interior, that patients' bodies are invaded by cells but also by invasive and evil relatives, and that patients' skin stings and itches, thus craving cuddles. I also realised that patients recover but then they relapse because although their livers—which had been destroyed by alcohol—can regenerate, their dismembered families, their dead relatives who have not been adequately mourned, and their neglected children can never regenerate. And then their livers are once again destroyed by alcohol.

The hospital is a place where both tragedies and miracles occur, where many people go to recover but many others go in search of punishment. It is a place where patients cannot, and should not, question treatment, because doing so would be interpreted as being "on the side of" disease. This is perhaps the reason why I have devoted my entire professional life to psychosomatics, trying to understand diseases as singular experiences which are inscribed as chapters in people's life story. By chance, or due to some unconscious determination, my interest in psychosomatics led me to the dermatology ward, where doctors asked for interdisciplinary consultations with greater frequency. And in the same way as the skin is the erogenous zone par excellence, it is also the entrance and the exit door for many emotions and situations which mark us.

This book is the result of more than fifteen years of work with dermatologists and patients with skin diseases, psoriasis in particular. As usually happens in interdisciplinary work, it is difficult to find a common language and to arouse homogeneous interest in colleagues from different disciplines. As a consequence, some of the chapters of this book will be of interest to psychoanalysts and psychotherapists almost exclusively. Other chapters, which are also directed at the field of psychology but are more easily readable and refer more to clinical work, will be more interesting for doctors and dermatologists.

In the first part of the book, which is similar to an essay, I have tried to investigate and summarise all the references I could find about the skin in the work of Freud, Didier Anzieu and other analysts. I am referring in particular to the first three chapters: The skin in the works of Freud, Didier Anzieu's *Ego-skin*, and Contributions from other psychoanalysts and psychiatrists to the subject of skin and psychoanalysis. These are not mere summaries, but "trips" along the paths different authors have traced. While I go along these paths, as though looking at a landscape through a window, I blend the trip with my own comments, I offer examples from my own clinical practice, and I attempt to illustrate and clarify the ideas of each author by means of figures, charts and pictures which I consider representative. In certain paragraphs I have found it difficult to separate my own interpretation of the authors' texts from my original contributions. Perhaps this is why the reader will find in non-textual quotations the bibliographic references normally used with textual quotations (author, year and page number). I did this so that the reader with a particular interest in a certain subject could easily trace the original ideas from which the contributions originate, which often go beyond what was said by the author whose work is being summarised.

The book has also a theoretical part in which I have tried to analyse in depth current theories about the skin from a psychoanalytical perspective, adding the contributions of other disciplines, such as the attachment theory and proxemics. This part can be found mainly in chapters 4, 6, 8, and 10: The skin and the levels of symbolisation: from the Ego-skin to the thinking-Ego; Reflections upon attachment; Body image and psychosomatic patterns in childhood. Medical publicity regarding the skin; and Franz Kafka's *In the Penal Colony*: Superego and the skin. The chapters dealing mainly with clinical cases also include a theorisation about the skin and the gaze, symbiotic relationships and many other interesting subjects.

Finally, the book has a clinical part, which is implicit in all chapters, but in particular in chapters 5, 7, 9, 11 and 12: "It works for me": symbolic efficacy and placebo effect; The case of Mr Quirón; Pathomimias: self-inflicted lesions on the skin; The relationship between what the psychoanalyst hears and what the dermatologist sees; and Psoriasis: Father, don't you see I'm burning? (The skin and the gaze). I consider chapters 5, 6, 9 and 11 particularly interesting for those who wish to work in an interdisciplinary way: whether clinicians, dermatologists or doctors who have dedicated themselves to other specialities.

I would like to emphasise that clinical work is my main objective. Nothing in my effort to write this book would be justified if it were not useful in order to understand, interpret, accompany and mitigate in some way the suffering experienced by patients in their souls, and which is displayed on their skin. This suffering, like psychic suffering, is minimised by all, and can only be understood by those who have experienced it, or at least by those who have analysed it with a not exclusively visual curiosity.

I hope the path I believe I am tracing will be useful for other "travellers", and if I have traced any paths that lead nowhere, we should bear in mind that the pleasure of travelling is not exclusively based on the final destination. Every year, when I visit Granada to give my seminar on psychosomatics, between one seminar and the next I like to lose myself within Albaicín, the old Arabian area, which is full of labyrinthine, narrow streets. Indeed, if it were not for the fact that I once got lost and could not find my way back, I would never have discovered a small park, the name of which I cannot recall, but which had a small balcony from which one of the most marvellous views of the Alhambra can be seen without tourists around.

CHAPTER ONE

The skin in the work of Freud

Although Freud expressly refers to the skin in several passages throughout his work, and even goes so far as to grant it the status of "erotogenic zone par excellence", referring to the skin in the Freudian work is not exclusively to speak of the skin as an organ and its eroticism, but also to speak about the functions and diseases of the skin, the drives which are originated in it, the action of touching and its consequences, as well as contact in general and its relationship with contagion, the relationship between the skin and identity, and lastly, about the Ego and the functions of boundary, surface, protection and perception. With this in mind, the references to the skin and its functions will be arranged into the following sections:

- The skin as an erotogenic zone
- The skin and its functions with regard to the unconscious
- The touching drive and the skin as the source and object of the drive
- Contact as a general idea. Contact and contagion
- The skin as a cortical layer: its functions of boundary, surface, protection and perception
- Mention of skin diseases and their interpretation or articulation with psychic facts

As is usually the case, these subjects are not mutually exclusive; certain quotations and reflections can be placed in more than one section. However, it can easily be seen that arranging this information into different sections is merely a teaching resource the aims of which are to clarify and make reading easier, as well as to enrich the analysis. In the development of each section, the subjects I have considered more important will be put forward, certain quotations from the work of Freud will be transcribed, and along with the theoretical development, certain reflections will be pointed out. In addition to this, I will discuss clinical cases and examples which in my opinion emerge from the application of these subjects to clinical practice and to everyday life.

The skin as an erotogenic zone

For Freud, the skin is the erotogenic zone par excellence (1905a, p. 169). This hypothesis emerges from psychoanalytic clinical practice, mainly from the study of hysteria, although Freud also makes reference to this subject in his analysis of everyday life as well as in dealing with obsessional neurosis and psychosis. In everyday life, the idea of the skin as a privileged erotogenic zone comes from the study of infantile sexuality and the expression of affect.

STUDY OF INFANTILE SEXUALITY

On studying infantile life, Freud discovered that the skin could be stimulated or could be the source of sexual excitation as a result of different motives such as:

- Washing and rubbing in the course of a child's toilet (1905a, p. 187)
- The action of intestinal worms, fungus and wounds (*ibid.*, p. 188)
- Rhythmic mechanical agitation of the body (*ibid.*, p. 201)
- Romping or wrestling with playmates (*ibid.*, p. 202)
- The auto-erotic action of thumb-sucking (*ibid.*, pp. 179–180)
- The expression of the emotions (1905b; p. 286)
- Corporal punishment and painful stimulation (1905a, p. 193)
- The close contact of the mother's body (1909a, p. 111)
- Thermal stimuli (1905a, p. 201)

- The action of the eyes, which take the skin as an object (*ibid.*, p. 169)
- The constitutional disposition of pleasure derived from cutaneous contact, and because different zones of the epidermis generate a certain amount of pleasure due to the excitation inherent in affective states (1907, p. 133; 1909a, p. 111)
- The instinct of contrectation (impulse to establish contact with another, or need for skin contact) (1905a, p. 169 [footnote]; 1909a, p. 111)

For the reader unfamiliar with psychoanalysis, we should clarify that all the aforementioned experiences become a source of sexual excitement because they cause an increase in excitation that Freud called erotogenicity, which does not manifest itself in the exclusive domain of biological needs. Although this increase in excitation does not have a genital goal, it nevertheless participates in what Freud called the general current of the sexual impulse.

STUDIES ON HYSTERIA

The concept of the erotogenic zone stems from what Freud once called the "hysterogenic zone", a zone of the body which, on being stimulated, unleashed a hysteric attack. "The significance of the erotogenic zones as apparatuses subordinate to the genitals and as substitutes for them is, among all the psychoneuroses, most clearly to be seen in hysteria; but this does not imply that that significance is any the less in the other forms of illness" (1905a, p. 169).[1] In hysteria, the pressure or pain experienced by the skin can correspond to thoughts awoken or stimulated by physical contact. Either a feeling of contact or a part of the skin can be the focus and the starting point of hysterical pains by virtue of its association with memories and feelings "interpreted" (Freud, 1883–1895), that is, linked to a sexual desire which can be either the individual's own or someone else's. This could be one of the causes of its consequent repression. Owing to this "interpretation" of the feelings of contact which remain stored in the memory, an equivalence is established in the unconscious between contact in general and sexual contact or contact with the genitalia (Freud, 1883–1895). In this way an attack of hysteria seems to be the direct effect of contagion, because when we touch a hysterogenic spot we provoke an unintended reaction: we awaken a memory which can in turn evoke a whole series of events and ideas associated with sexuality (Freud, 1896).

Erotogenic zones, and in particular the mucous membranes which correspond to them, can behave like genitalia, and under sexual excitation can be the source of new sensations and "changes in inner-vation" or processes which can even be compared to erection. Although this can be better recognised in hysteria, the phenomenon is not exclusive to this neurosis and can also be seen in others; "it is only that in them it is less recognisable [than in hysteria], because in their case (obsessional neurosis and paranoia) the formation of the symptoms takes place in regions of the mental apparatus which are more remote from the particular centres concerned with somatic control" (Freud, 1905a, p. 169).

> María, a patient who had been admitted to a general hospital, was suffering from a chronic ulcer on one of her limbs. I was called on an inter-consultation because the doctors treating her were concerned at how badly her condition was developing. The patient was 46, a virgin, obese and had an infantile character. She had always wished to become a ballet dancer. Her father was a pharmacist who took care of her health, testing on her some of the new medicines that came onto the market. On one occasion, when she was 13, she hurt her leg while she was dancing and her father had healed the wound trying out new antiseptics and dressings on her.
>
> The nurse came into the room in the middle of the interview to apply a dressing, and I decided to stay and watch her do it. At the moment when she put on an antiseptic that stung, the patient threw her head backwards and with an evident expression of pleasure and pain exclaimed: "Ahhhh! What a thrill!" I then remembered Freud's definition of hysteria as a pathology in which the reversal of affect predominates. Although he was referring to the fact that revulsion appears where sexual excitation should, we could also consider the appearance of an orgasmic reaction in the place of pain as a reversal of affect. In other words, it was evident that the ulcer was a lesion on the skin which was behaving like the female genitals.

OBSESSIONAL NEUROSIS

In obsessional neurosis the importance of the erotogenic zones as surrogates for the genitals is not as evident as it is in hysteria. However, the anal zone has a preponderant role. Regarding the rest of the skin, the new aims created by the drives are the most singular. We know that the pain and cruelty components of the sexual instinct, for which the corresponding erotogenic zone is the skin (Freud, 1905a), are of the utmost importance.

PSYCHOSIS

Schreber finds in his own skin the smoothness and softness which are typical of the female sex and, by means of applying pressure to any part of his own body, he can feel the feminine "nerves of voluptuousness" under his skin, in particular if he is thinking about something feminine while he is applying the pressure. This means that by applying pressure or performing any other action upon the skin, that action can gain the significance of a change in gender. This is important as men with skin diseases have to apply creams as women do while women, in order to hide the lesions to their skin, tend to stop using feminine clothes and wear "men's clothes" (for example with psoriasis: trousers, long sleeves, collarless shirts, etc.).

EXPRESSION OF THE EMOTIONS

The skin is also intimately related to the expression of the emotions. Freud states that among other physical changes which are part of the expression of emotions, the ingurgitation of the skin is an example of the mind's action on the body (1905b, p. 286). Moreover, as can be seen in the following list, there are several expressions which allude to the skin in order to refer to emotions. Here multiple references to the skin or to the feelings caused by the skin to express ideas have been summarised:[2]
The skin used to express affective moods:

- *Fear, emotion or shock*: I got goose pimples (piloerection)
- *Perplexity*: "I was frozen", I was struck dumb (vasoconstriction and paleness)

- *Embarrassment*: I blushed (vasodilation in the face)
- *Rage*: I was red with rage (vasodilation)
- *Hypersensitivity and irritability*: To have a quick temper
- *Nervousness or fear*: My hair stood on end (piloerection)

The skin to express contact:

- *Abstract contact*: "To caress an idea", to cherish, or toy with, or relish an idea
- *Affective contact*: It touched my heart
- *Aggressive contact:* "Touché" (used in fencing); to lay a finger on somebody
- *Sexual contact:* To snog, to get off with someone, to make out with someone, to canoodle, to cuddle
- *Social contact:* To be tactful, to have social graces, to avoid any brushes (with the law)

Expressive function of sweat:

- To sweat over something (to work hard, or to succeed in doing something with a lot of effort)
- To sweat your guts out (to work very hard)

Expressive function of the hands:

- To have a firm hand (to control things strictly)
- A hand (as in a hand of cards)
- To get your hands on someone (catch someone you are angry with)
- Hand to hand combat (an encounter in equal conditions or when opponents are very close)
- To fulfil a wish, "to touch the sky with your hands", "it was a dream come true"

The skin as a symbol of identity:

- To like (or dislike) a particular person; to rub someone up the wrong way

- "To be the skin of Judas", a Judas; "He is the skin of the Devil"
- To be skin and bone (to be extremely thin)
- To save your skin (to save your life)
- To tear somebody to shreds (to gossip about someone in a very severe way)

The skin to express identification:

- "I would like/would not like to be in your skin", to be in somebody's shoes

Expressive function of the hair:

- "He loses his hair but not his tricks"; You can't teach an old dog new tricks
- "To throw a grey hair to the wind", to throw caution to the wind (to do something forbidden or dangerous as a treat, generally used in a sexual sense)
- It gave me a few grey hairs (something causes problems or trouble)

The skin to express protection and lack of protection:

- "One needs to harden", or "to tan" (to acquire experience, not to be sensitive or vulnerable)
- "She is so fragile that you can look at her but you cannot touch her" (to refer to someone who is fragile and always complaining about things, a highly-strung person)
- Near the knuckle, close to the bone (to refer to something the other finds very painful)
- To be devastated, "raw" (to be extremely sensitive, to feel skinless, to feel wounded)

To conclude, here are some quotations from Freud referring to the skin as an erotogenic zone and to the erotic function of contact, which may be useful to the reader interested in these subjects:

Thumb-sucking appears already in early infancy and may continue into maturity or even persist all through life. It consists in the rhythmic repetition of a sucking *contact* by the mouth (or lips). There is no question of the purpose of this procedure being the taking of nourishment. *A portion of the lip itself, the tongue, or any other part of the skin within reach—even the big toe— may be taken as the object upon which this sucking is carried out.* [1905a, pp. 179–180]

The sexual activities of this erotogenic zone, which forms part of the sexual organs proper, are the beginning of what is later to become "normal" sexual life. The anatomical situation of this region, *the secretions in which it is bathed, the washing and rubbing to which it is subjected in the course of a child's toilet, as well as accidental stimulation (such as the movement of intestinal worms in the case of girls),* make it inevitable that the pleasurable feeling which this part of the body is capable of producing should be noticed by children even during their earliest infancy, and should give rise to a need for its repetition. If we consider this whole range of contrivances and bear in mind *that both making a mess and measures for keeping clean are bound to operate in much the same way, it is scarcely possible to avoid the conclusion that the foundations for the future primacy over sexual activity exercised by this erotogenic zone are established by early infantile masturbation, which scarcely a single individual escapes. The action which disposes of the stimulus and brings about satisfaction consists in a rubbing movement with the hand or in the application of pressure either from the hand or by bringing the thighs together.* This last method is by far the more common in the case of girls. The preference for the hand which is shown by boys is already evidence of the important contribution which the instinct for mastery is destined to make to masculine sexual activity. [*ibid.*, pp. 187–188]

It is, however, a fact that a number of people report that they experienced the first signs of excitement in their genitals while they were romping or wrestling with playmates—a situation in which, apart from general muscular exertion, *there is a large amount of contact with the skin of the opponent.* [*ibid.*, pp. 202– 203]

The eye is perhaps the zone most remote from the sexual object, but it is one which, in the situation of wooing an object, is liable to be most frequently stimulated by the particular quality of excitation whose cause, when it occurs in a sexual object, we describe as beauty. (For the same reasons the merits of a sexual object are described as "attractions".) This stimulation is on the one hand already accompanied by pleasure, while on the other hand it leads to an increase of sexual excitement or produces it if it is not yet present. *If the excitation now spreads to another erotogenic zone—to the hand, for instance, through tactile sensations*—the effect is the same: a feeling of pleasure on the one side, which is quickly intensified by pleasure arising from the preparatory changes [in the genitals], and on the other side an increase of sexual tension, which soon passes over into the most obvious unpleasure if it cannot be met by a further accession of pleasure. *Another instance will perhaps make this even clearer. If an erotogenic zone in a person who is not sexually excited (e.g. the skin of a woman's breast) is stimulated by touch, the contact produces a pleasurable feeling; but it is at the same time better calculated than anything to arouse a sexual excitation that demands an increase of pleasure.* The problem is how it can come about that an experience of pleasure can give rise to a need for greater pleasure. [*ibid.*, pp. 209–210]

In obsessional neurosis what is more striking is the significance of those impulses which create new sexual aims and seem independent of erotogenic zones. Nevertheless, in scotophilia and exhibitionism the eye corresponds to an erotogenic zone; *while in the case of those components of the sexual instinct which involve pain and cruelty the same role is assumed by the skin— the skin, which in particular parts of the body has become differentiated into sense organs or modified into mucous membrane, and is thus the erotogenic zone par excellence.* [*ibid.*, p. 169]

The skin and its functions with regard to the unconscious

The relationship between the skin and the unconscious and its functioning can be analysed by following the path that takes us through the study of *The interpretation of dreams, Totem and Taboo* and the works on group psychology (in particular the phenomena of identification) and fetishism.

We know that the unconscious works by means of the condensation and displacement mechanisms which are produced between
thing-representations and word-representations, and we are used to
thinking that only those thoughts and fantasies which are articulated
can be worked through by the psychic apparatus. However, there
are many ideas within psychoanalytic theory in which Freud claimed
that the somatic could be intertwined with the universe of representations, using the same mechanisms that apply to representations:
for example, when he critically studies the scientific literature on
dreams due to somatic stimulus and the somatic sources of dreams;
when he describes the experience of satisfaction and the experience
of pain; when he develops the concept of drive; or when he describes
the Id. He also put forward these claims throughout his theory on
feelings which, although they cannot be unconscious, can have their
"innervation key" in the unconscious representations (Freud, 1900b;
Chiozza, 1980; Ulnik, 1990, 2002). We must remember that in a letter
to Groddeck in 1917, Freud said that "the unconscious action has a
profound plastic influence over somatic processes that conscious
actions never acquire" (1915b, note 6).

From this perspective, it could be said that the associative links
of the unconscious, despite having been described in order to make
reference to the relationship between representations, could also
include physical contact and make it form a chain with the thoughts.
This is the reason why two parts of a person's body, or of different
people, can be associated in thought after they have been in physical
contact. The associative laws by which they are governed could be
the same ones that stand for the unconscious representations. For
example, a girl can retain a narcissistic aura in front of her friends
merely by having touched the hand of their rock idol. She herself
might not want to wash the hand with which she touched him, as
if she wanted to turn that contact into an indelible tattoo.

Feelings of excitement, ideas and old memories, but also new
associations can be revived or awoken by a mere physical contact
with the skin. In the unconscious there could be equivalence between
innocent contact and sexual contact. Hence the expression "to lay a
finger on (somebody)", which literally mentions the contact of the
finger, could be interpreted as having an erotic intention.

THE INTERPRETATION OF DREAMS

The power to enlarge and deform with which the dreams "work on" the tactile stimuli are proof of what is unconsciously felt at the level of relationships when confronted with every stimulus of being brought closer together or of separation, and at the physical level before every stimulus of contact, caress, tickle, pinch, prick, pressure, pain, warmth or cold. In the examples put forward by Maury and quoted by Freud when studying the scientific literature on dreams, it can be seen that at the unconscious psychic level, the smallest stimulus to the skin can be considered equal to a complete separation; alternatively it can be considered homologous to cruelty, to coming closer, to cuddling, to holding, to intrusive invasion, etc. Maury's examples quoted by Freud are paradigmatic:

> *His lips and the tip of his nose were tickled with a feather.* He dreamt of a frightful form of torture: a mask made of pitch was placed on his face and then pulled off, so that it took his skin off with it.
>
> *He was pinched lightly on the neck.* He dreamt he was being given a mustard plaster and thought of the doctor who had treated him as a child.
>
> *A hot iron was brought close to his face.* He dreamt that the *chauffeurs* had made their way into the house and were forcing its inhabitants to give up their money by sticking their feet into braziers of hot coal. [Freud, 1900a, p. 25]

The simple stimulus of a tickle, a pinch, a feeling of warmth on the skin, the feeling of getting close to someone, separation or contact are retranslated or re-transcribed within the dream and are interpreted as estrangement, cruelty, getting close, cuddling, aggression or detachment of the skin. This could be explained by the link between touching and the cruelty drive, by experiencing the feeling of contact as the loss of the protective barrier against stimuli, and also by experiencing separation as the loss of a skin shared with the significant other which wraps the bodies of both.

In "Infantile material as a source of dreams" (1900a, p. 189), Freud relates a dream of his own which leads him to associate the scales of epidermis with death. In this dream, which he himself called "the dream of the Fates", he is putting on an overcoat lined with fur, after which he meets three women. One of the women is rubbing her hands, as if she were kneading dumplings. The analysis of the dream reveals that she is a representative of Freud's mother, who tried to speak to him about death when he was a boy. Rubbing her hands, she showed him the blackish scales of epidermis that came off, as a symbol of the fact that we are made of dust, and confirmation of the fact that "you are dust and to dust you shall return", and that after all "You owe nature a death".[3]

On associating the elements of this dream, dealing as it does with such critical issues as identity, sexuality and death, Freud claims that we feel in as close a union with our own name as we do with our own skin, implicitly emphasising the indissoluble relationship between the skin and identity. In the dream the skin is represented by the hands and the mother's blackish scales of epidermis as well as by the overcoat.

The words of the mother activated the filial complex within Freud because she spoke about the human origins and death. Freud was influenced by a series of events linked to jokes about his name, which worked as residues of the day. His filial ties had been questioned and made fun of, and this issue was being mobilised.

Although his mother had wanted to explain a theory of the origins to him with an example, it is evident that as a child, Freud was not yet ready to assimilate this explanation. On the contrary, the image of the scales of epidermis worked as what Nasio calls "anticipatory images", that is, images which make an impression on the child that is beyond his receptive capabilities of assimilating and compre- hending what he sees. These kinds of experiences work as a "calling from the Other", because they invite the individual to respond despite the fact that he has no means to do so. When we lack the words or representations to respond to this kind of "calling", an organic lesion could appear, as happens for instance when we receive an unexpected and unfair redundancy notice, when we are called upon to fulfil a role with which we cannot cope, or when we discover a dramatic piece of news which we did not see coming.

In this dream the scales of epidermis (which is what Freud himself calls them) generate a bridge with psychic representations through contact. They are transformed into a symbol of castration and of death (1900a), because each object which is separated from the body brings up once again the fact that we are incomplete, and hence sexuated and mortal at the same time.

Although this dream could well be called the "dream of the dumplings", because Freud's mother was kneading dumplings and Freud associates that word with the last name of a university professor called Knoedl ("dumpling") to whom he owed his histological knowledge of the epidermis, he himself calls it the "dream of the Fates" because that is more appropriate for the uncanny effect it produces. Representatives of destiny, the Fates are the three mythological sisters who spin and through whose hands the lives of mortals slip. They respectively receive birth, matrimony and death, and they measure the life of each human being with a thread which the first sister spins, the second winds and the third, when the time comes, cuts. These three divinities are called Clotho, Lachesis and Atropos. Daughters of the night, they grant mortals possession of good and evil, and punish the wrongdoings of men and the gods. Hesiod claims in *Theogony* (Bozal, 2002) that the goddesses' wrath is terrible before they impose their bitter punishment on all wrongdoers. The appearance of three women is frequent in Freud's dreams, as for example in the dream of Irma's injection.

Feeling his identity questioned and investigating the origin of man, it is probable that his mother's explanation as well as the exhibition of her hands with blackish scales of epidermis might have made Freud feel anxious, and also feel that his life was in the hands of his mother, who thus appeared as Clotho in Goya's picture, who has a small man with his hands tied in her own. The destiny which awaits this man is held in store by Atropos and is irretrievable because "you owe Nature a death". It is probable that if Freud had not produced this dream, he would have suffered from a lesion to one of his organs.

This is a critically important issue in dermatological clinical practice, because it could explain an anxiety, so typical of almost all people, over the scale of epidermis that has been shed. This anxiety could be related not so much to a "borrowed" significance of the kind that equates the skin which has been shed with the faeces or any other pregenital object, but rather to a proper significance in which the quality of coming off and falling, the shed skin's status as a "lost object", plus its implicit biological reality (the last layer of skin is formed by dead cells) give the scale the value of a drive object, with the same symbolic and erotogenic level of the faeces, the breast or the urine.

> This is the issue which filled a patient who had psoriasis with anxiety: she was driven to desperation when she noticed that an ant colony had developed in her bathroom, where the ants were feeding on her scales of epidermis, as if she was dead inside. She felt as though she was watching how the insects were devouring her body, because her scales of epidermis accounted for her condition of "remainder".
>
> Another patient had an anxiety attack and a fit of crying when he came into the consulting room where he received photo-therapy sessions three times a week and saw scales of epidermis on the floor, testimony to the presence of a previous patient. The nurse who usually saw him was absent that day, and hence his anxiety and his complaint about the substitute nurse's lack of hygiene were initially interpreted as a reaction to the abandon-ment he suffered as a result of the absence of the nurse-mother who always saw him. The patient strenuously denied having been affected by that fact, and attributed the traumatic effect he had suffered to the scales of epidermis themselves. To everyone's surprise, he came to the following session with very serious conjunctivitis, which he attributed to the vision of the scales of epidermis. When it was admitted that there probably was something in the scales of epidermis that was affecting him, he remembered that his mother, who suffered from psoriasis, would not let herself be helped; she refused advice and treatment and used to leave scales of epidermis all over the house as a testimony to her presence and to her disease. The vision of the scales was a stark testimony to the presence of the wounded body of his mother, who would not let herself be repaired (this example is mentioned again in Chapter 11).

TOTEM AND TABOO

The study of *Totem and Taboo* allows us to go deeper into the psychological mechanisms of magic and of mythological beliefs. It is precisely with these that we can appreciate most clearly that the contact between two people is equal to the contact between two representations, and that as such this contact is liable to be worked through by means of unconscious mechanisms. Just as the association or the "contact" between representations is of the utmost importance in psychic functioning, contact and contagion between people and things is of the utmost importance in the social field. Freud's work *Totem and Taboo* will be thoroughly analysed in dealing with the issues of contact, contagion and the touch drive. However, certain general ideas on the skin and the functioning of the unconscious will be developed in this section.

The reports and descriptions regarding the different actions that turn an individual into a taboo are based upon some sort of contact, whether of love or of aggression:

> Among the Monumbos of German New Guinea anyone who has slain a foe in war becomes thereby "unclean" (. . .) He may touch nobody, not even his own wife and children. [Freud, 1912–1913, p. 40]
>
> (. . .) anyone who touches a dead chief is unclean for ten months. [*ibid.*, p. 52]

The law which is obeyed in mythology, according to which what is at one time venerated comes to be rejected and despised when it is overcome (Freud, 1912–1913), can also be applied to the skin, because the atavistic rejection suffered by the patient with a skin disease and the characteristic of impurity attributed to him due to the visibility of his lesions is merely the opposite of the skin at a primitive time, with its characteristics of "immaculate", attractive and appealing: baby skin, skin of youth, skin of a woman, skin of nakedness. The more immaculate the skin is as an ideal or as a source of charm and sexual appeal, the more impure the disease becomes. In the contagious magic, based as it is on the association by contiguity, the following happens:

> Things become less important than ideas of things: whatever is done to the latter will inevitably also occur to the former. Relations which hold between the ideas of things are assumed to hold equally between the things themselves. Since distance is of no importance in thinking—since what lies furthest apart both

in time and space can without difficulty be comprehended in a single act of consciousness—so, too, the world of magic has a telepathic disregard for spatial distance and treats past situations as though they were present. In the animistic epoch the reflection of the internal world is bound to blot out the other picture of the world—the one *we* seem to perceive.

It is further to be noticed that the two principles of association— similarity and contiguity—are both included in the more comprehensive concept of "contact". Association by contiguity is contact in the literal sense; association by similarity is contact in the metaphorical sense. The use of the same word for the two kinds of relation is no doubt accounted for by some identity in the psychical process concerned which we have not yet grasped. We have here the same range of meaning of the idea of "contact" as we found in our analysis of taboo. [Freud, 1912–1913, p. 85]

The processes of identification by means of the skin in "Totem and Taboo" and in "Group Psychology"

Looking like somebody else is a primitive form of identification (Freud, 1921), and there is a relationship between the process of identification as a psychic fact and the material action of covering oneself with the skin of the object at which the identification is aimed. This is translated in the uses of the language: "To be in someone else's skin".[4]

Contact gains a close relationship with the idea of copy, imitation, contagion, and transmission of attributes from one ego to the other or from one body to someone else's. Hence the idea that the identification is a kind of contact just as contact is a kind of identification (Freud, 1912–1913). It all depends on the direction in which the vector uniting them is traced. In turn, the libidinal link, which in the case of the identification is reached by the introjection of the object within the ego, is reached in more primitive uses through the wrapping of the object around the ego, and in these primitive uses the skin is the covering factor, as it is also the receptor of the covering. This kind of copy or imitation could be conceived of as a special variety of identification which we could term mimetic. Several authors have described these kinds of mechanisms in different ways and under different names, but all things considered, they allude to similar phenomena.

Donald Meltzer calls it adhesive identification, and he describes it in a type of patient who has difficulties in configuring the notion of a closed space. These patients might have bi-dimensional object relations, that is to say superficial relations, without any spaces which can make projective identification (to get into the other) or introjective identification (with a space into which one can attract something) possible. They are characterised by the predominance of imitation, superficiality, the externalisation of values and the absence of time (for example, they live in a linear time or in a circular time without the idea of process). They do not have an internal source of values, a product of their own personal assessment. The identification they can carry out is not projective because these patients cannot distinguish between being inside or outside the object (Meltzer, 1975).

Jean Guir, in "The face and psychosomatic phenomena", Chapter 5 of her book on psychosomatics and cancer, says:

> [. . .] We notice that the mark on the face determined by the psychosomatic phenomenon frequently leads us to an as yet unsolved mimetic linking, which in turn leads to the face of one of the members of the patient's family. This "mimesis", so to speak, expresses itself in two ways: the face invokes another face, which presents a distinguishable mark in the same spot. [. . .] the spot on the other individual's face does not present anything legible, but we discover in the discourse of the patient that this part of the body has been mutilated. [. . .] This lesion-witness thus leads to an erotogenic drive zone of another body. [1984, p. 59]

David Liberman, drawing on Meltzer's concept of adhesive projective identification, develops in turn the concept of mimetic introjective identification. He proposes that these patients, who have suffered infantile experiences of lack of support, defend themselves from psychic pain by amputating their own internal life and developing a defensive organisation in which they become bi-dimensional to themselves. Deprived of the awareness of an internal life, physical as well as emotional, they stereotype the "flat" vision, the "façade image" and the contact with that "flat" object which they need and to whose external qualities they pay attention. They try to maintain an illusory union by mimetically incorporating the superficial traits of the object. They are prone to developing a fantasy in which they are "stuck on the outside like a piece of skin or a stamp", becoming part of the object (Liberman et al., 1982, p. 336).

FETISHISM AND THE SKIN

The skin and velvet can represent the pubic hair and can act as fetishes in the same way as underwear and clothes, because they are the last cover of castration. This cover would still allow one to consider the woman as phallic (Freud, 1927).

The organs have a sexual function as well as an "egoic" function. The latter (which, when we refer to the skin, includes irrigation, innervation, sensitivity, speed of cell reproduction, etc.) could become altered when the erogenicity or the sexual significance of an organ increases (Freud, 1926). The "fetishisation", so to speak, of the skin is closely related to the increase in its erogenicity.

In "Fetishism", Freud explains that faced with the traumatic effect caused by the perception of the woman's lack of penis, the child remains fixated on the perception immediately previous to this discovery. That is the reason why the underwear, the legs and most particularly the feet acquire such paramount importance as generators of sexual excitement in men, because during childhood they would look at a woman from the bottom upwards. The hands could acquire the function of fetishes because they are one of the means of contact with the genitals, by substituting looking with touching (brooding drive) and because "to go hand in hand" or "to be taken by the hand" are ways of contact with the mother previous to the discovery of castration.

The skin as a whole can be eroticised. And in addition, when (due to the mechanism of disavowal) the skin gains the function of a phallic representative and cover against castration, it can also work as a fetish: hence the frequency of animal furs, fur coats, etc. present in the fantasies and sexual scenes of certain perversions.

These considerations have an influence on the importance of the lesions' localisation in skin diseases. The sick spots can be fetishised, and when that happens, the evolution of the disease acquires such importance that the anxiety it generates is not entirely justified by the disease itself, but rather by the castration threat that the appearance of the disease (and at other times its cure) sometimes generates. For example, the appearance of erythema and inflammation can make a part of the body more important, more sensitive and even bigger, and from this perspective, the patient can "make it phallic", so to speak. In this case, healing could imply a castration threat. In contrast, sometimes the patient experiences his disease as a progressive loss of a part of his body, which cannot carry out its usual functions, or which has been "devoured" or "taken" by the disease. This is most especially appreciated when the disease is in the genitals, or when there are lesions to the hands and the feet which are so serious and difficult to cure in cases of eczema and psoriasis.

The touching drive and the skin as source and object of the drive

THE TOUCHING DRIVE

There is an apprehension drive or contact drive and touching can be a pregenital, provisional sexual aim. When it becomes an aim in itself, it "provides the purest cases of the neurosis" (Freud, 1894b, p. 101, 102). To Moll, the drive is divided into a contrectation drive and a detumescence drive. The former means the need for contact with the skin, an impulse to establish skin contact with the other (Freud, 1909a, p. 111). The latter means spasmodic relief of tension of the sexual organs (Freud, 1905a, p. 169, footnote 2). In sharing a bed with someone else, one of the essential erotic satisfactions is that of "the pleasure derived from cutaneous contact" (Freud, 1909a, p. 111), to which we are all constitutionally prone.

THE RELATIONSHIP BETWEEN THE TOUCHING DRIVE AND THE LOOKING DRIVE

Touching the sexual parts is a primary pleasure which can be substituted by the pleasure of looking at the genitals or "what is sexual". Looking is a surrogate or a substitute for touching (Freud, 1905c, p. 98). There could be a "visual libido" as well as a "tactile libido". Both of them could be active and passive, as well as masculine and feminine. The passive aspect of the visual libido is prone to the pleasure of exhibitionism, the dam of which is the feeling of shame. For women there are many ways of escaping from the feelings of shame, chief of which is fashion, with all its occasional "caprices" (Freud, 1905c, p. 98).

The same can be said about the pleasure of being touched, which finds in tattoos, medical examinations, massages or in the application of creams a disguise or a way of escape from the dams of revulsion, education and repression. It is very common to see that for some patients, making their spouses apply to them a cream which has been indicated as treatment, because the lesions are located on parts of the body where their own hands cannot reach, constitutes an excuse to receive at last the caresses they want and are afraid to ask for through fear of being rejected.

The relationship between looking and touching is linked to what Adler called drive intertwining, which is produced because the same object can simultaneously satisfy several drives. In the case of the skin, we know that it can be the object of the touching drive as well as of the looking drive. The displacement is also produced because the ways in which the drive's aim of cancelling the state of excitation in its own source is achieved can be diverse. The reason is that sexual drives can easily replace each other and have the capacity to change their object indefinitely, thus producing path changes (Freud, 1915a). This is the reason why they can carry out operations, by means of sublimation, which are far removed from their original aims. The issue of the path changes, the exchange of objects in order to fulfil an aim, and everything that could be considered drive intertwining, acts as basis for considering the value of bridge-words which synthesise two psychic processes in a superior unity, thus establishing identity between them, as in the word contact, for example (see Figure 1.1). This is what happens, for instance, between the physical contact established by contiguity, which is more related to touch, and the contact with ideas established by analogy, which is more related to looking.

The psychic apparatus has, according to Freud, a biological tendency to keep itself free from energy, or at least to keep energy at a constant level. In order to achieve this, it defends itself by trying to avoid stimuli or to discharge them when they have entered the psyche (Freud, 1895). The touching drive and the skin, which is its source, are closely connected with that biological tendency: in the

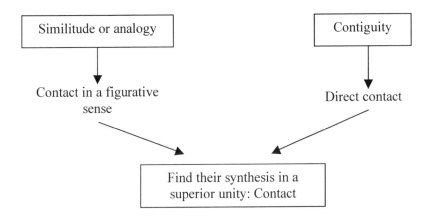

Figure 1.1 Contact and the two principles of association of ideas in contagious magic

first place because the skin is a protective barrier against stimuli and consequently avoids them; and in the second place because the touch transmits, transports, and ultimately discharges, as the last trans-mitter of a motor action, the "energy" which has already entered. However, the skin has a paradoxical function because at the same time as it discharges energy, it is also in charge of receiving it. This problem is related to the pre-repressive vicissitudes described by Freud for the drive (Freud, 1915a), because the skin can be a *source*, but it can also be a drive *object*; something which helps to clarify the paradox concerning the skin working as a barrier and at the same time as a receptor of stimuli.

Among the pre-repressive vicissitudes of the drive, Freud describes the reversal into its opposite and the turning onto the subject's own self. The reversal of an instinct into its opposite resolves into two different processes: a change from activity to passivity, and a reversal of its content. While the former affects only the aims of the instincts, an example of which could be the passage from scopophilia (pleasure of looking at) to exhibitionism, the latter involves a reversal of content, an example of which could be the transformation of love into hate. In the turning of an instinct onto the subject's own self the aim remains unchanged. This is the case when the drive originally stems from oneself and is directed towards another object (for example, touching someone else's genitals) but it turns back to oneself, which is why it includes the "self" element: to touch oneself, to look at oneself. The agent remains unchanged and the aim is still touching or looking at. What has changed is the object. The consequence of this is that the skin and the action of touching, the aim of which was the discharge on an external object, end up receiving the stimulus once again and incorporating it. The drive of touching or of looking at, when they acquire this reflexive function, by virtue of which they take the Ego as an object, maintain their narcissistic organisation.

THE DAMS AGAINST THE TOUCHING DRIVE

Freud says that certain feelings (disgust, feelings of shame) and certain ethical and aesthetic considerations (morals) are the dams which stop the flow of the drive. Among these dams, and very close to shame, is disgust. Disgust is a limitation imposed on the sexual drive of touching, in particular when it is dealing with touching the genitals with the mucous membrane of the mouth. "[. . .] the sexual instinct has to struggle against certain mental forces which act as resistances, and of which shame and disgust are the most prominent" (Freud, 1905a; p. 162). (For example, against disgust for the genitals or for sexual contact.)

In "Sexual use of the mucous membrane of the lips and mouth" (Freud, 1905, p. 151), Freud describes a struggle between the forces of the sexual instinct and the disgust to be overcome. This disgust is in close contact with the touching drive, either tactile or with the mucous membrane. Perhaps the disgust inspired by skin diseases might be related to the fact that they specifically threaten what the skin as an attraction awakens: the will to touch and to kiss, or its substitute: the will to look at it.

This is an important topic because one of the forces operating against the patient with a skin disease is the disgust of the other, and this disgust is perceived and measured in order to evaluate the other's love for him or her. Sometimes disgust is what puts a limit on these patients' exhibitionism; at other times it is what gives a context and a frame to exhibitionism, thus making it stand out.

THE SKIN AS AN OBJECT OF THE DRIVE AND THE MASTERY DRIVE

When the skin is the object of the drive, we come closer to auto-eroticism, exhibitionism and masochism, because for example the wish to master one's own skin as an object leads to the action of pinching it, sucking it or hurting it. These actions are mastery intents, either visual or even tactile, and usually have sadistic characteristics.

In early infancy there are many auto-erotic behaviours in which the skin is the object of the drive, among which sucking is critical. This is a sucking contact, and any other spot of the skin can be taken as an object of sucking. Thumb-sucking, defined as a sucking contact, is accompanied by a "grasping instinct [which] may manifest itself as a simultaneous rhythmic tugging at the lobes of the ears" (Freud, 1905a, p. 180). The infantile connection between the cruel and the erotogenic instincts is dangerous as it can be fixated for good. "[. . .] the painful stimulation of the skin of the buttocks is one of the erotogenic roots of the passive instinct of cruelty (masochism)" (ibid., p. 193). In Totem and Taboo, Freud claims:

> We cannot be surprised at the fact that, in the restrictions of taboo, touching plays a part similar to the one which it plays in 'touching phobias', though the secret meaning of the prohibition cannot be of such specialised nature in taboo as it is in the neurosis. Touching is the first step towards obtaining any sort of control over, or attempting to make use of, a person or object. [1912–1913, pp. 33–34]

The instinct of apprehension or mastery is related to sadism and cruelty. This is the reason why diseases which involve pinching and scratching (acne, psychogenic itching, self-inflicted dermatoses) could be considered taking into account this instinct of mastery, not only because of the "grasping" or "mastering" of the spot or the scale of epidermis, the skin or the pimple, but also because of the cruelty and sadism of the procedure (see Chapter 9).

THE SKIN, FORE-PLEASURE AND ITCHINESS

When Freud considers the relationship between the feeling of tension and pleasure, he encounters a theoretical contradiction, for if pleasure is equal to a diminishing of tension and displeasure is equal to its increase, he cannot then explain how it is that in sexuality certain stimuli which cause pleasure generate at the same time an increase in tension and sexual excitation or a "stimulus to it". As was noted earlier:

> If the excitation now spreads to another erotogenic zone—to the hand, for instance, through tactile sensations—the effect is the same: a feeling of pleasure on the one side, which is quickly intensified by pleasure arising from the preparatory changes [in the genitals], and on the other side an increase of sexual tension, which soon passes over into the most obvious unpleasure if it cannot be met by a further accession of pleasure. Another instance will perhaps make this even clearer. If an erotogenic zone in a person who is not sexually excited (e.g. the skin of a woman's breast) is stimulated by touch, the contact produces a pleasurable feeling; but it is at the same time better calculated than anything to arouse a sexual excitation that demands an increase of pleasure. The problem is how it can come about that an experience of pleasure can give rise to a need for greater pleasure. [Freud, 1905a, pp. 209–210]

The developments regarding fore-pleasure and the feelings of tension that generate pleasure, or at least a demand for pleasure—when, according to the pleasure-unpleasure series, it should generate displeasure because we are dealing with an increase in quantity— are linked to the phenomenon of itchiness, which is of the utmost importance in dermatology and psycho-dermatology.

Pichon-Rivière (1971) even said that itchiness was an equivalent of anal anxiety. An itch generates a scratching behaviour which produces a feeling of pleasure, but also a demand for more scratching due to a sort of increase in tension. Some patients can only stop this vicious circle when some liquid (serum, pus, blood) is exuded. The feeling provided by the itchiness-scratching cycle has a certain "voluptuousness", which is similar to that of sexual stimuli. Freud uses the term "itching" or the term "centrally conditioned itching" several times to refer to sexual excitation. More references on itching follow:

The state of being in need of a repetition of the satisfaction reveals itself in two ways: by a peculiar feeling of tension, possessing rather the character of unpleasure, and by a sensation of itching or stimulation which is centrally conditioned and projected onto the peripheral erotogenic zone. We can therefore formulate a sexual aim in another way: it consists in replacing the projected sensation of stimulation in the erotogenic zone by an external stimulus which removes that sensation by producing a feeling of satisfaction. This external stimulus will usually consist in some kind of manipulation that is analogous to the sucking. [Freud, 1905a, p. 184]

Further, the whole significance of the anal zone is reflected in the fact that few neurotics are to be found without their special scatological practices, ceremonies and so on, which they carefully keep secret. Actual masturbatory stimulation of the anal zone by means of the finger, provoked by a centrally determined or peripherally maintained sensation of itching, is by no means rare among older children. [*ibid.*, p. 187]

Return of early infantile masturbation. During the years of childhood with which I am now dealing, the sexual excitation of early infancy returns, either as a centrally determined tickling stimulus which seeks satisfaction in masturbation, or as a process in the nature of a nocturnal emission which, like the nocturnal emissions of adult years, achieves satisfaction without the help of any action by the subject. [*ibid.*, p. 190]

What the rat punishment stirred up more than anything else was his anal eroticism, which had played an important part in his childhood and had been kept in activity for many years by a constant irritation[5] due to worms. [Freud, 1909b, p. 213]

NEUROSIS DERIVED FROM THE FIXATION ON THE PLEASURE OF TOUCHING

On referring to the different ways in which obsessional neurosis can present itself, Freud proposes that there are brooding neuroses: those in which the actions of looking at, touching and exploring become excessively sexualised. This kind of neurosis could explain the importance of the fear of touching and the obsession with cleanliness as reactive formations to the brooding wish (Freud, 1916–1917, p. 309).

The brooding tendency is intimately linked to the search for dominion, control and the sadistic mastery of the object. We can see this clearly in the destructiveness that some children exercise over their toys, which starts with the objective of investigating and controlling their functioning, the parts that constitute them, and so on. This propensity to control and to mastery of a sadistic sort is typical of obsessional neurosis and is very close to the touching drive, as we have previously seen.

SUMMARY: AXES OF THE TOUCHING DRIVE

- The skin can either be a source or an object of the drive
- The drives which have a stronger relationship with the skin as a *source* are the touching drive, the mastery drive or apprehension instinct and the impulse to be in contact with another person, or "contrectation" drive. (Although they are mentioned separately, they could be viewed as different ways of referring to the same thing).
- The drives which a have stronger relationship with the skin as an *object* are the drive to look at and the sadistic drive. The skin as an object of the drive can play a fundamental role particularly in auto-eroticism, exhibitionism and in masochism.
- We can find relationships between drives which can substitute one another, or which are associated in a particular way. This is the case with the relationship established between the visual and the tactile (drive of looking at and drive of touching).
- Sexual excitation is associated with the feeling of itchiness, either exterior or "centrally conditioned".
- Like all drives, the drive of touching has its own dams, the most important of which is disgust.
- There are neuroses which are caused in particular by the predominance of the drive of touching: the brooding neuroses.

Contact as a general idea. Contact and contagion

Contact and contagion can be studied following Freud's ideas in the *Project for a scientific psychology*, in *Totem and Taboo*, and in his reflections on obsessional neurosis, which run throughout his work. While on the one hand the study of the *Project for a scientific psychology* is useful as a way of following the ideas of contact, contact barriers and facilitations as a kind of neuronal metaphor of what happens with psychic representations, on the other hand the development of *Totem and Taboo* provides us with a social or mythological metaphor of the same object of study. It is in the idea of contact that the hinge or the pivot guiding us through both domains is to be found.

CONTACT, CONTACT BARRIERS AND THE ELECTRICAL CHARGE ON THE SURFACE OF BODIES

In the *Project for a scientific psychology* (1895), Freud discovers something similar to the synapses between neurons at an earlier date than Sherrington in 1897, proposing the idea of contact between neurons through contact barriers and facilitations. The term "contact barrier" is very suggestive because it condenses within the same signifier two contradictory functions: the function of barrier and the function of contact.

This condensation of meaning expresses quite a critical idea in order to understand the functions of the skin as an organ and also to understand a certain paradox about the psychic apparatus: the need to protect itself from stimuli and the simultaneous need to incorporate them, or at least perceive them, as well as the need to eliminate them once they have been incorporated. Indeed, the contact barriers alternate the characteristics of permeability and non-permeability. They exercise a resistance to the passage of quantity, and by virtue of it they remain facilitated. The ideas of permeability and facilitation form the axis that divides neurons into different types (phi, psy and omega neurons) as well as classifying stimuli into endogenous and exogenous, thus providing a key determinant to the establishment of an outside and an inside.

The need of the psychic apparatus to fulfil the functions of reception, register, memory and incorporation, protection, exchange and elimination can only be met through the development of discrete but interrelated systems. This subject can be better understood by studying the *Project for a scientific psychology*. The exchange between systems is critical to the development of psychic functions and the construction of symbolic dimensions.

In *Totem and Taboo* (1912–1913) and also in "Psychoneuroses of defence" (1894a), Freud makes comments about contact between people which seem to be homologous to those concerning the transmission of quantity between neurons put forward in his first theory of the psychic apparatus. For example, he proposes that contact can generate a discharge with disastrous consequences, and that these consequences depend on the resistance and protection of the receptor as well as on the "electric charge" at stake, which is transmitted through the "surface of the body" (1894a, p. 60).

Both physical contact and its consequences are liable to condensation and displacement, as are representations. The "electric charge" to which he refers when he describes taboo people and things evokes in us cathexes, libido, neuronal quantity, affective value, and all those references to an energy that is transmitted to people and things in accordance with the laws of condensation and displacement. In the same way, the resistance and protection of the person who is acting as the receptor, as well as his or her investiture, reminds us of the resistance of the contact barriers, their permeability or non-permeability, or their "facilitation", which also depends on its level of charge at a given time.

The primary process in contact: when contact is contagion

The relationship between contact and contagion is closely related to the validity of the translation or application of the functioning of the unconscious to contact between people. *For the typical displacement of the primary process, contact is contagion.* To put it in a different way: contagion is a primary contact, that is to say a non-inhibited contact.

Anyone who has a dangerous and transmissible force transforms contact into contagion. All those who present the characteristic of being special ("kings, priests, newborns"), the exceptional states ("menstruation, childbirth, puberty") and the uncanny things ("illness, death") possess the inherent force that diffuses itself and is contagious by virtue of the transmission of contact (Freud, 1912–1913).

Following the primary process, not touching is like not thinking. That is why whenever it is forbidden to think about something, the prohibition of touching will also fall upon it. This explains why, in different taboos, what is mentally associated is also forbidden to be materially touched. For example, touching the dress of a woman, even if she is not wearing it, is equal to having touched the woman herself, since both she and her dress are associated in the mind of the person who has touched the dress. But following this same primary process, touching is the bridge to thinking, fantasising and imagining, or to awakening the mastery drive, because (as will be remembered) "touching is the first step towards obtaining any sort of control over, or attempting to make use of, a person or object" (*ibid.*, p. 34).

THE TABOO OF CONTACT, THE OBJECT CHARGE AND OBSESSIONAL NEUROSIS

The expression "taboo" can be translated in many different ways, but the best translation of all, according to Freud, is the one that considers taboo as what must not be touched because of its demonic power. "(. . .) it stresses a characteristic which remains common for all time both to what is sacred and to what is unclean: the dread of contact with it" (Freud, 1912–1913, p. 25). Touching and physical contact are the nearest objectives of the object charge, both aggressive and loving (Freud, 1926). That is why the taboo of contact is one of the oldest and most critical commandments of obsessional neurosis.

> As in the case of taboo, the principal prohibition, the nucleus of the neurosis, is against touching; and thence it is sometimes known as "touching phobia" or *délire du toucher*. The prohibition does not merely apply to immediate physical contact but has an extent as wide as the metaphorical use of the phrase "to come in contact with". Anything that directs the patient's thoughts to the forbidden object, anything that brings him into intellectual contact with it, is just as much prohibited as direct physical contact. This same extension also occurs in the case of taboo. [Freud, 1912–1913, p. 27]

In obsessional neurosis, it is contact that is forbidden, because it involves sexual contact or aggressive contact due to the ambivalence of feelings. From the same equivalence (between contact and aggression) comes the expression *touché* uttered by fencers, where *touché* means dead due to having been touched by the foil. The game of battleships, in which being "touched" is the previous step to being sunk, is also well-known. For the same reason electrical current is called "contact". When contact is either lacking or excessive, it seems to be felt as painful or mortal. It is as if eagerness or longing for contact has led to a search for pain, or as if it has simply made the simplest of contacts painful due to the hypersensitivity of the receptor, who, in order to receive contact, becomes hypersensitive by diminishing the threshold of his barrier of protection from stimuli. As a consequence, it is likely that a kind of insensible shell, or a cold behaviour with a tendency to avoid stimuli, will develop as a reactive formation (Figure 1.2).

The relationship—already analysed in the first quotations—between the physical contact and the mental contact between two ideas is verified once again in the analysis of taboo and in obsessional ceremonials. The displacement, so frequent in obsessional representations, which is trying to flee from the ideas leading to the

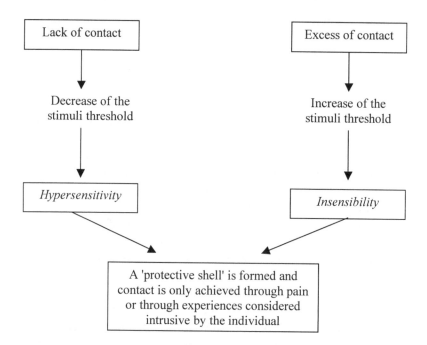

Figure 1.2. Contact, sensitivity and the threshold for stimuli

forbidden, is also produced with regard to the contact with objects. The contact with the object is taboo because it "makes contact" with the ideas related to that object.

In the work of Frazer (1922) quoted by Freud (1912–1913), the idea of the unclean, directly related to a sinful action or bodily state, is immediately associated with the forbidden contact. It is interesting to point out that if the prohibition is transgressed, the punishment is in the skin: ulcers and abscesses. Purification is reached with baths that clean the skin and through it the soul and the sin.

There is an association between the part of the other's body, which is attacked, and the part of the individual's own body, which will produce symptoms: if the individual cuts the hair of an enemy, he is forbidden to comb himself. And if his head itches, he will not be allowed to scratch himself with his hand (touch). After all, the body of the other and the individual's own body will be linked by a common signifier or significance. This kind of linking between the bodies is what makes itself manifest when someone establishes a primitive form of filial relationship by means of suffering similar lesions or diseases, or of suffering lesions in a similar location, to the ones suffered by the parents or those with whom a filial relationship is sought.

> The father of Ceferino, a patient with psoriasis, thought that sweat could cause his son diseases. In consequence and, "for his own good", the father used to check on him when he came back from work, and if he was sweating, would punish him brutally. In consequence, Ceferino spent his childhood hardly playing at all, because for a boy, playing means running, and running made him sweat. Sometimes he used to play and run and then try to dry his sweat and hide his activities from his father, but nevertheless, he always ended up being punished.
>
> Rolando is in the same group. He is a highly sensitive patient who is always in denial and who comes from a background where psychoanalysis is almost unheard of, something that allows him easily to hide his drive aspirations when he is among friends and family.
>
> Ceferino has had analysis for many years and cannot bear Rolando's denial, which is why he offers him "savage" interpretations through which he punishes, harasses and denounces

him, and attempts to uncover the feelings Rolando tries to hide. Rolando defends himself quite effectively session after session.

Once Rolando was late for a session, but despite all his excuses Ceferino was relentless. In the following session, Rolando complained about Ceferino for the first time, saying Ceferino had been so hard on him in the previous session that he had had a new outbreak of psoriasis.

I offered them the interpretation that Ceferino was repeating an infantile situation: he had taken Rolando as a projection of himself as a child and, by putting himself in the place of a father due to his extensive psychoanalytic experience, was interpreting him "for his own good" in order to help him. He was angry at Rolando's defence mechanisms because in defending himself, Rolando was hiding his wishes and his feelings in the same way that he, Ceferino, had done with the sweat.

Once the session was over, a dermatologist who takes part in the sessions as an observer examined Rolando. To our surprise, he did not have a new outbreak of psoriasis, but a huge inflammation owing to sudamina,[6] probably as a consequence of having suffered intense sweating during sleep. In this way Rolando, *who did not know anything about Ceferino's childhood history*, had mimicked even with his body the character which had been projected on him.

CONTACT, MOURNING AND THE MATERIALISATION OF PAIN

In the description of the taboo on the dead, all contact, even in a figurative sense, is conceived of as "material". This is related to the fact that in primitive thought, abstract matters have to be recognised as equivalent to concrete ones in order to be understood. This happens very frequently with psychic pain, which tends to be materialised in order to be conceived. The need to "materialise" pain is still very frequently seen in patients today, and injuries to the skin satisfy this need to materialise.

In the Bible, Job he rips his vestments as a sign of pain, which is interpreted by Fray Luis de León (1779) as proof shown by Job to God that he was not so deranged as to be unaware of the suffering caused by his skin wounds. This could well be the origin of the Jewish tradition of ripping the vestments in front of a dead relative, in the ceremony preceding the burial. In turn, the mourning process, which involves internalising the lost object, requires an absolute conception and differentiation between interior and exterior. If the interior and the exterior have not completed their development, instead of the "shadow of the object falling on the ego", what we see is "the shadow of the object *surrounding* the ego". This way of surrounding oneself with the lost object could be related to a body image which has developed only on the surface, without a dimension of depth, or at least with an interior which has not yet completed its construction.

The observances of some North-American tribes regarding the dead show how the shadow of the object is borne by the individuals, surrounding them instead of existing inside them. In the myths about death on which Freud comments, a symbolisation gradient of the lost object can be seen, one which progressively "materialises" itself, and always around the skin (Freud, 1912–1913 p. 53):

- The person in mourning is surrounded by a halo, a kind of "electricity" as it were, which corresponds to his or her status as taboo, and which is transmitted by contact, making it deadly.
- The person in mourning is surrounded by a shadow.
- He or she sleeps surrounded by thorn-bushes, which are laid all around his or her bed.
- He or she wears a breech-cloth made of dry bunch-grass.
- His or her own skin transmits, via bodily contact, the contact with the dead person.

Electricity, shadow, thorn-bushes, cloth and skin are covers (which become progressively material and closer to the individual's own body) which represent not only the spirit, but also the body of the dead person, and this relates more to the actual flesh the more primitive and scarce the capacity to symbolise its absence is. The state of taboo, in turn, transmits through contact the presence of the dead person, who punishes the living for wanting to seize what was once his. In addition to this, it also transmits the strict relationship which exists between contact and possession as well as between contact and temptation, that is to say desire.

The skin as a cortical layer: the functions of boundary, surface, protection and perception

In the previous sections, the relationships between the skin and contact and also the touching drive were emphasised. However, it was also mentioned that one of the paradoxes of the skin is that while it receives stimuli, it has a simultaneous function as a protective device or a kind of protective barrier against stimuli. On the other hand, the skin's close relationship to the phenomenon of perception also links it to conscience.

THE FUNCTION OF PROTECTION

Freud develops the idea of a protective device against excitements which exists in all living organisms. It is evident that this device is the skin, or at least the device depends on the adequate functioning of the skin. Freud says: "By its death, the outer layer has saved all the deeper ones from a similar fate" (1920, p. 27), which is actually the case with the tissue of the epidermis.

The development of the concept of a protective device comes from the idea, already developed in the *Project*, of a secondary function, the aim of which could be fleeing from stimuli (Freud, 1895, pp. 296–297). "Protection against stimuli is an almost more important function for the living organism than the reception of stimuli" (Freud, 1920, p. 27).

The reception of excitations would not be an aim in itself; rather, the intention would be to find out their direction and origin solely in order to protect itself. That is why only small samples of those external excitations are enough to fulfil that aim. The protective device against excitations is constructed thanks to the death of the external layer, which acts as a cover or membrane that stops excitations.

The study of the protective function is very important, because in clinical practice we see certain patients who could be understood in relation to the state of their protection devices. For example, the feeling of "being exposed", of anticipated pain, or of a wound that will not heal, generates a reaction which leads to the "building of a new protective layer as soon as possible", or "the closing of the wound", which in terms of character manifests itself as isolation or insensibility, sometimes even with paranoid reactions such as "bracing oneself in advance". Hypersensitivity causes external stimuli to be seen as excessively strong, and leads to the construction of an excessively protective shell (see Figure 1.2.).

THE SKIN AND CONSCIENCE. THE ROLE OF THE CORTICAL LAYER IN THE SYMBOLISATION OF TIME AND THE FUNCTION OF MEMORY

Unlike Kant, Freud considers that time and space are not two necessary preconditions of our thought. The psychoanalytic discovery of unconscious processes, which are a-temporal, could be proof of this: "(. . .) our abstract idea of time seems to be wholly derived from the method of working of the system Pcpt-Cs and to correspond to a perception on its own part of that method of working" (1920, p. 28). The "sensitive cortex", which can be put on a par with the conscious system (Cc), and which could be the organ destined for the reception of excitations coming from the external world, while at the same time it could be the organ of the "protective device against the external world", has the particularity of being located between the exterior and the interior. "The situation of the system between the outside and the inside and the difference between the conditions governing the reception of excitations in the two cases have a decisive effect on the functioning of the system and of the whole mental apparatus" (ibid., pp. 28–29).

This shows to what extent the construction of an interior and an exterior (that is to say, of space), as well as the construction of the notion of time, are related to the function of this external cortical layer and its respective functions: receiving stimuli, protecting from stimuli, positioning the cortical layer differently with respect to the internal and the external worlds, distinguishing between them, and orienting the behaviour (or the defence mechanisms) against those internal excitations which bring an excessive increase of unpleasure. "(. . .) a particular way is adopted of dealing with any internal excitations which produce too great an increase of unpleasure: there is a tendency to treat them as though they were acting, not from the inside, but from the outside, so that it may be possible to bring the shield against stimuli into operation as a means of defence against them. This is the origin of projection (. . .)" (ibid., p. 29).

In different passages of his work, starting from the *Project for a scientific psychology* and continuing up to his last works, Freud proposed the issue of the relationship between perception and memory. What was needed for perception was a receptive surface always ready to record stimuli, while a lasting record, something like a permanent trace of what had been written, was needed for memory. This could only be achieved by means of discrete systems dynamically connected to each other.

In *Beyond the Pleasure Principle*, Freud described two layers of our perceptive system: an external protection against stimuli, in charge of diminishing their magnitude, and the receptive surface. In "A note upon the mystic writing pad" (1925a) he imagines an explanatory model. His considerations regarding the model allow us to consider better the roles of the skin, contact and attachment in the development of the symbolisation capacity and of memory.

The mystic writing pad has three layers: a layer of celluloid, a slab of wax, and a waxed paper between the celluloid layer and the slab of wax. On the wax slab a permanent trace is kept of what has been written, and the layer of celluloid acts as the receptive surface which can be used again and again. As has been mentioned previously, in order to keep both faculties (perception and memory), the psychic apparatus distributes them into two different, albeit interconnected systems (in the example of the magic pad, by means of the waxed paper). This is one of the keys of the capacity for symbolisation: the establishment of a distance and at the same time a link between perception and memory. This link should be discontinuous so that the record of differences allows us to acquire qualitatively differentiated notions.

The development of the idea of time depends on the discontinuity of the perceptive system. In terms of everyday experience, this means that if we see someone every single day of the year and stay with that person throughout the day, it is hard for us to notice that she or he gets older or changes. In contrast, when we have not seen someone in a long time, meeting him or her again shocks us because it makes us see all of a sudden how much time has passed, both for the other person and for ourselves. This is one of the features of the traumatic effect caused by celebrations such as secondary school and university reunions. The discontinuity of the perceptive system is linked to the "loss of contact" between perception and memory: we recall our classmates because we have memories of them, but we do not perceive them because we have not seen them in a long time. This is an example of discontinuity of the perceptive system which makes us suddenly aware of the long time that has passed.

There is a mechanism Freud calls "attention" which also has a role in regulating perceptions and which, depending on its being available or not, will make us either permanently perceive something or not perceive it at all. The "attention" consists of a cathexis or investment available to the Ego in order to approach the external stimuli which impress the sensory organs: it allows the Ego to absorb those stimuli so that they become part of the neural net. When a discontinuity of the perceptive system does not occur, the development of the notion of time is hindered. Why would this happen?

- Because of a need for constant contact, as is seen in symbiotic patients.
- Because of the need to protect oneself against any kind of contact (which involves the disinvestment of the receptive system), as is seen in clinical practice with patients who surround themselves with a defensive shell.
- Because of a dissociation between a system and the other (which generates a lack of attention to certain things or a permanent trace in the inappropriate system, which restricts the capacity of new receptions), as is observed in clinical work with schizoid and dissociated patients.

Mention of skin diseases and their interpretation or articulation with psychic facts

- The Rat Man used to satisfy his sexual curiosity by watching his nanny while she treated the abscesses on her buttocks (Freud, 1909b).
- In the article "The Unconscious", when analysing "the organ speech", Freud establishes a relationship between the idea of castration and acne and blackheads, as well as the action of squeezing a blackhead or a pimple (Freud, 1915a, p. 199).
- Contact, when it comes from a powerful being, also has a healing power, in particular for skin diseases (scrofula) (Freud, 1912–1913, p. 42).

- The idea of impurity, directly related to a sinful action or a bodily state, is immediately related to the forbidden contact. If the prohibition is transgressed, the punishment is in the skin: ulcers and abscesses. Purification is also gained with baths (Freud, 1912–1913, pp. 39–40).

We believe that of these four mentions, the one linked to the organ speech is the most important. Freud tells the case of a patient who claimed he had deep holes in his face which were produced by pimples or blackheads. He used to squeeze them, and enjoyed seeing that something spurted out between his fingers. But then he would reproach himself for having caused a deep hole. Freud interpreted this action as a substitute for masturbation, and his worry about the hole as the fulfilment of the castration threat linked to the practice of masturbation.

In terms of a phallic fixation and of the castration complex, it is probable that Freud's interpretation was accurate, but the evidence with body dysmorphic disorder shows that there usually is a deep identity disorder which has been projected onto the aesthetic aspect. This is why Freud's diagnostic discussion shortly afterwards, establishing a difference between the symptom formation in this patient and the formation of hysterical symptoms, is so important. There is little analogy between the fact of squeezing out a blackhead and ejaculation, and there is even less between the infinite pores of the skin and the vagina. However, in the first case (blackhead and ejaculation) something "spurts out", and in the second case (pores and vagina) the cynical phrase "a hole is always a hole" can be applied. The similarity between the verbal expression, and not the analogy between the things expressed, is the decisive factor for the substitution, because there has been a predominance of working with words over what has to be done with things.

A patient who presented pustular psoriasis would not stop squeezing her pustules, feeling satisfied when she noticed that "matter" came out of her lesions. Inquiries about her childhood history revealed that she was very thin as a girl and that they used to call her "Tero" because her legs were very thin, like those of the bird,[7] and seemed to be just skin and bone. By establishing a link between her present behaviour with her childhood history, it was suggested to her that through her satisfaction on seeing that there was matter between her skin and her bones, she managed to gain a feeling of having an interior, which had been denied by the nickname they had given her and by the way people looked at her.

Finally, in *The Interpretation of Dreams*, Freud makes reference to a boil the size of an apple that appeared in the area of the scrotum. During the night he dreamt he was riding a horse without problem, as a way of denying the existence of the boil and of the pains in the perineum. In the interpretation of his dream, he linked the region of his body "chosen by the boil" (Freud, 1900a, p. 230) to the experience of having been replaced by another doctor in the treatment of a very intelligent patient with whom he believed he had developed great abilities.

Notes

1. Translator's note: All the quotations from Freud were taken from J. Strachey's Standard Edition.

2. Translator's note: Many of the expressions quoted here do not translate into English. When that is the case, a literal or similar expression in English is provided.

3. "Du bist Natur einen Tod schuldig" quoted from Shakespeare, according to Strachey (note by JN) (Freud, 1900a, p. 205).

4. "To be in someone else's shoes". See footnote 2 above.

5. "Pruritus" in the Spanish translation.

6. Sudamina is a dermatosis which affects the pores and can be caused by intense perspiration.

7. "Tero" is a typical bird in Argentina. Being called "Tero" could be similar to being told that she had legs like matchsticks.

CHAPTER TWO

Didier Anzieu's Ego-skin

The tactile sense as foundation

Didier Anzieu starts with two basic assumptions. The first is that *psychic life has sensitive qualities as a basis* because "every psychic function develops on the basis of a physical function the operation of which surpasses the mental area"[1] (Anzieu, 1987a, p. 107). The second is that "the tactile sense is the foundation, on condition that it is forbidden at the necessary time" (Anzieu, 1987a) (p. 152).

It is according to these basic assumptions that, in Anzieu's opinion, the psychic apparatus develops, taking as its starting point a basis provided by physical experiences of a biological nature in which the skin plays a fundamental role. These experiences, which are of both external and internal nature, will then be re-signified through the interaction with the agent who produces these stimuli (generally the mother) and later, on acquiring the symbolic capacity, will be represented again in an abstract form, becoming fantasies, symbols and thoughts.

By means of the physical stimuli, the skin can provide the psychic apparatus with the representations which constitute the Ego as well as its main functions. In this way, a construction of the self that Anzieu calls "Ego-skin" can be developed, one that carries out a series of fundamental functions in order to provide the Ego with the capacity for reception, perception, protection, cohesion, support, integration of sensations, identity and energy. Taking the Ego-skin

44

as a starting point, an Ego capable of thinking and of representing can be developed, an Ego that he calls the thinking-Ego.

The pathology of the thinking-Ego and of the Ego-skin shows us how the Ego can make use of physical perceptions, such as those of the skin, in order to communicate with others and to try to defend itself from either internal or external dangers. This Ego will be much more pathological and primitive the greater the number of failures it presents in its abstract functions and the greater its need for concrete perceptive experiences, which have not been symbolized or integrated with each other, in order to be able to maintain its existence.

Anzieu has a very precise clinical objective when he proposes that the analysis, in cases of difficult pathologies or narcissistic neurosis, or in borderline cases, must allow us to diagnose what the missing Ego function is and to see what kind of analytic work can be done in order to remedy that lack and to re-establish that function of the Ego. In order to explain the origin of failures in the structuring of the Ego, Anzieu turns to the theory of attachment and its relationship with psychopathology.

> [The patients] have had contradictory experiences, which were early and repeated, excessive attachments and abrupt and unforeseeable separations which have been violent to their physical Ego and/or their psychic Ego. Certain characteristics of their psychic functioning derive from this; they are not certain of what they feel; they are a lot more concerned about what they think are other people's desires and affects; they live within the "here and now" and communicate with others by way of narration, they do not have a spiritual disposition which can allow them, according to Bion's expression (1962), to learn from the experience of their own personal experiences, to represent that experience to themselves and to obtain from it a new perspective, as that idea continues to be disturbing for them. They find it difficult to separate themselves intellectually from that blurred experience, a mixture of themselves and the other, to abandon the tactile contact and re-structure their relationship with the world around sight[2] . . . They remain stuck to others in their social life, stuck to the sensations and emotions of their mental life: they fear penetration, either of sight or of genital intercourse. [1987a, p. 35]

The ego and skin diseases

For Anzieu, skin diseases maintain a very close relationship with the narcissistic failures and the structuring insufficiencies of the Ego. In the first place, there could be equivalence between the relationship the functions of the Ego have with thought, and the relationship the functions of the skin have with the body as a whole. Then there could be a second equivalence between the Ego and the skin, so that the failure in any of the functions of the Ego is accompanied by problems with the skin, or also with tattoos or inscriptions. Lastly, this equivalence would be so close that the more altered the Ego of the patient is, the deeper and more serious the skin disease he might suffer.

Anzieu wonders if skin diseases are produced by an excess or by a defect of contact with the mother during the first stages of life (1987a). Taking his experience with dermatological patients as a starting point, he claims that some skin diseases seem to be related to excessive stimulation and others with insufficient stimulation. He also wonders, basing himself on Spitz, if eczemas have the function of providing oneself with the stimuli one lacked as a child, or if they rather constitute a way of asking to be provided with them.

He comes to the conclusion that in all cases the main axis is the prohibition to touch. On the one hand, the excess of maternal care could be intrusive and dangerous, as it damages and transgresses the prohibition to touch which is necessary in order to allow the child to build an excitation screen and a psychic envelope of his own. On the other hand, the lack of maternal caresses and care could be considered equivalent to an excessive, violent and premature prohibition of sticking to someone else's body.

To this experience with dermatological patients was added the fact that Anzieu was analysing borderline and narcissistic patients who were uncertain about their own identity and who had many things in common with dermatological patients. From all this he deduced that "the seriousness of the alteration to the skin (which is measured by the growing resistance on the part of the sick person to chemotherapeutic and psychotherapeutic treatments) is related to the quantitative and qualitative importance of the failures of the Ego-skin" (1987a, p. 46).

He also approached the subject of pathomimia. Here he refers to the condition characterised by lesions to the skin which are self-inflicted and which try to imitate a disease with the intention of gaining a benefit, although in certain cases the only benefit would seem to be acquiring the status of a sick person. Other authors group these phenomena under the label of *dermatitis artefacta* or factitious disorders (see Chapter 9). According to Anzieu, in cases of pathomimia

> the physical symptom recrudesces, via the primary form of cutaneous "language", old frustrations with the exhibition of these patients' sufferings and renewed rage: the irritation of the skin becomes confused with mental irritation, by virtue of the somato-psychic undifferentiation to which these patients have remained fixed. [1987a, p. 45]
>
> The mutilations to the skin (. . .) are dramatic attempts to maintain the boundaries of the body and of the Ego, in order to re-establish the feeling of being intact and cohesive. [*ibid.*, p. 31]

Both in pathomimias and in many other epidermic diseases, the skin loses its function as a frontier, to acquire, predominantly, the function of a mirror of the soul.

The prohibition to touch

> The first prohibitions which the family applies to children when they gain access to the world of (locomotive) displacement and (infra-verbal and pre-linguistic) communication essentially refer to tactile contacts; with these exogenous, variable and multiple prohibitions as a basis, a prohibition that is of an internal nature is thus constituted . . . (Anzieu, 1987a, p. 149)

The prohibition to touch could be, in tactile terms, what castration, repression or the function of the law is in oedipal terms. The prohibition to touch is a double one, because it develops in two stages which refer to different kinds of contact.

> *The primary prohibition to touch opposes itself specifically to the attachment drive.* It is a prohibition of global contact, that is to say a prohibition of the attachment, fusion and confusion of bodies. It transfers to the psychic area what has operated in

biological birth. It imposes a separate existence on the living being who is in the process of becoming an individual. It is a prohibition that moves the individual away from the maternal bosom and favours a desire to return which can only be fantasised (this prohibition has not become constituted in the autistic individual, who psychically continues to live within the maternal bosom). The prohibition is implicitly shown to the child by the mother through the active form of a physical distancing: by putting him in his cradle she turns away from him, she turns him away from her by withdrawing the breast, by turning away her face that the child wishes to hold. In the cases where the mother does not carry out this act of prohibition, there is always someone in the environment who, in a verbal way this time, acts as a spokesperson for the prohibition. The father, the mother-in-law, the neighbour, the paediatrician all remind the mother of her duty to separate herself bodily from the baby in order to let him sleep, to not over-stimulate him, to prevent him from acquiring bad habits, so that he can learn to play on his own, so that he can walk instead of being carried. All this in order that he should grow up, in order to leave the environment and find a time and a space where he can live on his own. The corresponding threat of physical punishment is eventually fantasised as a "tearing off", leaving raw the surface of common skin between the baby and the mother (or her substitute, who can be the father). (. . .) Mythologies and religions have echoed this "tearing off".

The secondary prohibition to touch is applied to the mastery drive: not everything can be touched, seized or controlled. This is a selective prohibition of manual touch: not to touch the genitals and, in a more in general sense, the erotogenic zones and their products. Not should they touch people or objects in a way violent for them; they should only be touched limiting oneself to operating modalities of adaptation to the external world and to the pleasures it provides, which are kept by subjecting oneself only to the reality principle. The prohibition is formulated by verbal language or the language of gestures. The family and home environment opposes the child who is willing to touch with a "no", spoken as such or indicated with a movement of the head or of the hand. The implicit sense is as follows: you do not grab, you must ask first and accept the danger of rejection or of delay. This sense is explicit at the same time that the child acquires a sufficient mastery of language, a mastery to which precisely this prohibition leads: interesting objects are not pointed at with the finger, they are named. The threat of physical punishment, which corresponds to the secondary prohibition against touching, is eventually expressed by the family and social discourse in this manner: the hand that steals, or hits, or masturbates, will be tied or cut. [*ibid.*, p. 161]

This double prohibition is the one that could allow the passage from a bodily Ego to a psychic Ego connected with it. This passage could require the renunciation of the predominance of the pleasures of the skin and then of the hand, thus promoting and transforming the concrete tactile experience in basic representations, on the foundations of which intersensorial correspondence systems can be established. These basic representations, on a level which begins as figurative, maintain a symbolic reference to contact and tact, but can later reach a purely abstract level, separated from this reference (Anzieu, 1987a).

The former does not mean that the repressed tactile primary communications are destroyed (except in pathological cases), rather that they remain registered as a backdrop against which the intersensorial systems of correspondences are inscribed. They constitute a psychic space in which other sensory and motor spaces can couple, and they then provide an imaginary surface upon which to deposit the products of ulterior operations of thought. The Hegelian concept of *Aufhebung*[3] is particularly appropriate, in Anzieu's opinion, to describe the status of these eco-tactile traces which are at once denied, overcome and maintained (1987a). "This eco-tactile communication subsists as an originary semiotic source" (*ibid.*, p. 166).

Touching can have a sexual connotation, it can merely be a proof of existence, or it can be the means of constitution of the Ego-skin (Anzieu, 1987a). The prohibition to touch contributes to the establishment of a difference between orders of realities that remain confused within the primary tactile experience of the body (Anzieu, 1987a). These orders of realities could be expressed as follows:

- Your body is different from other bodies.
- Space is independent from the objects that inhabit it.

- Animate objects behave in a different way from inanimate ones.

Two structures of the tactile experience can be distinguished: contact via the hugging of a body, which covers a big surface of the skin and includes pressure, warmth or coldness, well-being or pain, kinaesthetic and vestibular sensations, a contact that involves the fantasy of a common skin; and manual touch, skin to skin contact considered to be childish, erogenous or brutal. Both prohibitions to touch aim separately at each of these structures.

Equally, the prohibition to touch corresponds to the two main drives: the aggressive drives ("do not touch inanimate objects that could break or be damaged; do not exercise an excessive force over the parts of other people's bodies") and the sexual drives ("do not insistently touch your body or the bodies of others in the zones sensitive to pleasure, because an arousal that you are not yet able to understand or satisfy would overwhelm you"). In both cases the prohibition to touch guards against the lack of moderation of sexual arousal and its consequence, the unleashing of the drive. Because of the prohibition to touch, sexuality and aggression are not structurally differentiated; rather, they are assimilated as an expression of drive violence in general. In conclusion, *the prohibition to touch refers to sexual drives and aggressive drives at the same time* (Anzieu, 1987a, p. 158).

The feeling of basic trust

Taking Montagu and Bowlby as his basis, Anzieu establishes a relationship between the contact with the maternal body and the attachment drive by means of grabbing, and the development of a feeling of basic trust that allows the baby to explore and classify objects from the external world. It is only by taking this basic trust as a starting point that the necessary separations from the mother can be attained.

> The baby acquires a power of endogenous control that oscillates between a feeling of confidence in his own activities and a euphoric feeling of unlimited omnipotence; if each step is controlled, the energy, far from dissipating itself due to the discharge in the action, is in fact heightened due to success [Anzieu

calls this phenomenon "libidinal recharge"]. . . this feeling of an internal strength is essential for the baby if he is to carry out the reorganisation of his sensory-motor and affective schemes, which are necessary for his maturation and his experiences. [Anzieu, 1987a, p. 68]

From this perspective, it is inferred that there could be a reciprocal interaction between the feeling of trust and the development of a symbolic capacity. Without this feeling of trust, the absence of objects cannot be tolerated; and without the notion of absence, the passage from the need for the concrete presence of objects to their nomination, something essential for the development of the symbolic capacity, cannot be produced. The symbolic capacity in turn improves the resources of the child by heightening his feeling of trust.

The notion of absence is intertwined with the capacity to produce, register and tolerate separations from the loved object. In Chapter 1, the Freudian example of the "mystic writing pad" is mentioned in order to establish a relationship between the acquisition of the notion of absence and the capacity to separate perception from memory. As the discontinuity of the perceptive system is intrinsically joined and connected to the permanent trace of what has been written, the notion of absence begins to be acquired and the concept of time starts to be constructed. These processes are hindered within symbiotic relationships in which separation from the loved object is not produced, and separations are traumatic. In contrast, when separations can be produced, registered and tolerated, the child can then manage without the concrete contact with loved things or loved people, and also without the use of the skin as a medium of emission of signals and an appeal to the gaze.

John Updike, an American writer who suffers from psoriasis, wrote a book of short stories called *Trust me. Short Stories* (1962), in the first chapter of which he writes about several situations in which a person who remains in the role of a child is compelled by another, in the role of a father, to do things for which he is not yet prepared: to throw himself into a swimming pool in order to learn to swim; to go to a ski slope for advanced skiers, etc. When the "child" dares to do these things, the "father" fails in his role of support: he cannot catch him in time in the water; he cannot offer him confidence to descend the slope. As a consequence, the "child" feels unprotected and angry with the adult, developing a great sense of insecurity. We could ask ourselves if the subject chosen by John Updike, which appears in the title of the book and is ironic in the first chapter, is not a reflection of the situation of affective distrust which has a latent effect on many people who suffer from psoriasis and which leads them to emit signals by means of the skin.

> Barbie, a patient with erythrodermic psoriasis (psoriasis that covers all the skin) and a great distrust of her mother, who was unable to understand her affective states, generally says, "today I'm bad with the skin" or "today I am OK with the skin" to make reference to her moods. These are reflected in her colour and scaling in such a way that other people usually say to her "you are fine" or "what is happening to you?" using her skin as a guide before she has said anything.

The conception of the Ego-skin

Anzieu insists time and again on describing the skin as an interface, that is to say as a surface constituted by an internal and an external face, which allows the distinction between the outside and the inside and at the same time provides an experience of container. With the term "Ego-skin" he refers to

> a figuration the child uses during the early phases of his develop-ment to represent himself as an Ego which contains psychic contents, taking his experience of body surface as a starting point. This corresponds to the period in which the psychic Ego becomes differentiated from the physical Ego in the operational aspect, but remains confused with it in the figurative aspect. [1987a, pp. 50–51]

It is a function of the mother to provide the child with an experience of envelope. This envelope, apart from providing warmth, food, caresses, softness and all sorts of care, must also emit signals and know how to interpret the signals emitted by the child. The provision related to his needs must also come with tenderness and love. What is more, as a result of adequate functioning of the prohibition to touch, it must allow the establishment of the necessary distance in order to avoid over-excitation and to foster progressive separations. If all this does not take place, the envelope that should foster not only the development of the excitation screen but also the feeling of boundary and well-being transforms itself into an envelope of excitation and suffering.

THE FANTASY OF A COMMON SKIN WITH THE MOTHER

The fantasy of a common skin with the mother underlies the entire process previously mentioned. The Ego-skin can have an internal and an external layer. The maternal environment can be the external layer and the surface of the baby's body can be the internal layer that emits signals (Figure 2.1).

Between the external layer and the internal layer a double feedback is produced, that is to say a feedback between the messages emitted by the child, represented in Figure 2.1 as black arrows going upwards towards the external layer, and the messages and replies of the maternal environment, represented by the grey arrows going downwards towards the internal layer or surface of the child's body. This double feedback works as an interface which is represented by the line of dots. The functioning of this interface is represented by means of a fantasy of a common skin between the mother and the child. The separation between the internal and the external layers must be gradual and progressive, as is shown in Figure 2.1, where the black line and the grey line become gradually separated.

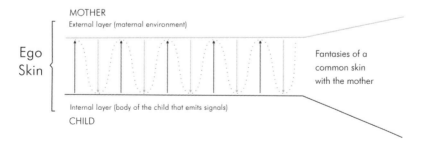

Figure 2.1 Diagram of the Ego-skin and the common skin between the child and the mother

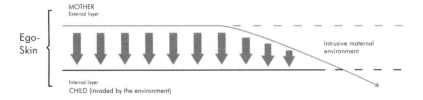

Figure 2.2 Intrusive maternal environment

If the external layer is too attached to the child's skin, he becomes stifled in his development and invaded by the environment (Figure 2.2).

If the external layer is too slack, the Ego of the child lacks consistency because the signals he emits, represented in Figure 2.3 by the black arrows going upwards, are not received or held by the external layer. It is as if they were allowed to go to waste.

The fantasy of a common skin is a necessary foundation of the Ego-skin. The problem is that when this common skin follows a narcissistic trend because an excess of excitation has predominated, the Ego-skin comes with secondary fantasies of a common skin which is reinforced and invulnerable, which in mythology and literature manifests itself as "shield skin", "glitter skin" or "shiny skin". For example, in Fisher's *The Knight in Rusty Armor*, the main character cannot take off his armour because he has become insensitive due to all his fighting, and his narcissism has become exacerbated though

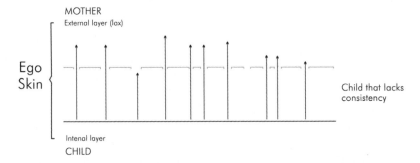

Figure 2.3 Ego skin with a slack external layer

boasting about his victories (see Figure 4.3, in relation to the Dundee case). In Italo Calvino's *Non-Existent Knight,* a medieval knight has a shining white, immaculate suit of armour, without a single chink; however, there is no one inside it because the individual who owns the armour only exists through it. Finally, in Perrault's *Donkey Skin,* a girl who has lost her mother tries on, as if they were a kind of "second skin", beautiful, shimmering dresses for which she asks her father and which she receives, but only on condition that she marry him (see David Rosenfeld's analysis of the short story in Chapter 3).

In reality, the need to recharge the narcissistic envelope in this way seems to be the defensive counterpart of a fantasy of raw skin: faced with a permanent danger of external or internal attacks, it becomes necessary to re-gild the shield of an Ego-skin barely certain of its functions of excitation screen and psychic container. Figure 2.5 shows a situation in which neither of the layers receives the other's stimuli, or each is pierced by them. As a consequence, what predominates is a fantasy of an envelope of suffering, and the common skin follows a masochistic trend: the Ego-skin will come with secondary fantasies of a torn and hurt common skin, which in mythology and literature is represented as bruised, flayed or fatal skin (Anzieu, 1987a). An example of fatal skin can be observed in Balzac's *The Wild Ass's Skin,* as will be explained later. Another example is that of Curzio Malaparte's *The Skin,* a work in which the skin is a symbol of the misery, suffering, shame and identity crisis of the Italian people after the Allied army's arrival in Naples.

If the separation between the internal and the external layers is abrupt due to death, abandonment or any other event that can bring

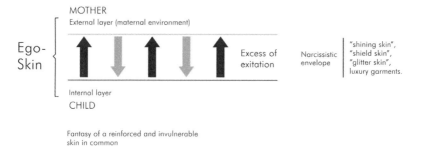

Figure 2.4 Ego-skin with an excess of excitation: narcissistic envelope

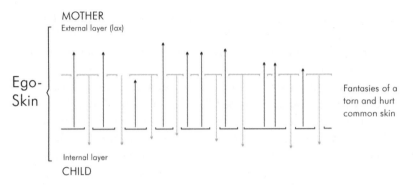

MOTHER
External layer (lax)

Ego-
Skin

Fantasies of a
torn and hurt
common skin

Internal layer
CHILD

Figure 2.5 Envelope of suffering

it about, fantasies of torn and hurt skin will also develop. In Figure 2.6 it can be seen that the two layers of the Ego-skin become separated much faster than in Figure 2.1.

If the internal layer is porous, full of holes or sieve-like; or if it is rigid and closed, then the subject, lacking the necessary feedback with the external layer, will only pay attention to it. *This is why patients suffering from these problems find it easier to speak of others—or of external problems—than about themselves.*

The normal evolution of the child and the development of his autonomy results in the disappearance of the common skin, causing resistance and pain. When the relationship between the mother and the child is that of a common skin in which the external layer and the internal layer are bonded together, the attempts at separation

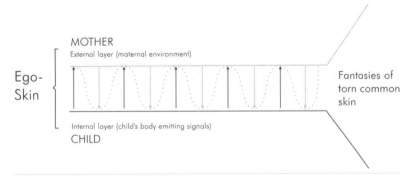

MOTHER
External layer (maternal environment)

Ego-
Skin

Fantasies of
torn common
skin

Internal layer (child's body emitting signals)
CHILD

Figure 2.6 Abrupt separation between the layers of the Ego-skin

are accompanied by fantasies of torn, robbed and bruised skin that emerge from the rupture of that common skin.

In Balzac's novel *The Wild Ass's Skin*, Rafael, the main character, has the noble title of a marquis but he has fallen from grace. Madly in love with Fedora, an idealised, aristocratic and cold woman, he finds himself rejected by her, without a cent, and willing to commit suicide by throwing himself into the Seine. Before doing so, he goes into an antique shop where he finds a talisman. It is the skin of a wild ass: a kind of ass to which certain magical powers are attributed. This skin assures whoever possesses it that all his wishes will come true, but with each wish that comes true not only will it shrink in size, but the days its possessor has to live will also diminish in the same proportion. With the terrible power of the talisman, Rafael starts making all his wishes come true, but he becomes increasingly unhappy because each time a wish is fulfilled the skin shrinks and he feels more and more sick. Despite trying to live without wishing for anything in order to extend his own life, he cannot avoid an encounter with Paulina, with whom he falls helplessly in love, and in whose arms he dies because he cannot stop wishing for her love.

In the fantasy of a common skin with the mother, where the external layer is stuck and does not properly receive messages from the internal layer, each attempt at separation made by the individual, represented here by the wishes of the main character, is experienced as the shrinking of the common skin which, since it does not un-stick, suffocates and kills him. The idea of a common skin which represents shared lives is clearly observed in the sentence engraved on the skin of the wild ass:

> If you possess me, you shall possess all, but your life will be mine. It is God's wish. Wish, and your wishes will come true. But regulate your wishes according to your life. It is here. On each of your wishes, I shall shrink like your days. Do you want me? Take me. God will listen. Amen! [Balzac, 1831]

THE SECOND SKIN

When the experience of envelope and of gradual separation fails, there is the development of a defensive variant that Esther Bick called *second skin*. Although the author herself referred either to the exaggerated development of innate activities and abilities or to the hypertrophy of a muscular mass, Anzieu extends the concept and proposes that the lack of an integrating dynamism of sensations, the projective identification that prevents certain mechanisms of feedback and multiple splitting, favour the development of a second skin. This could acquire different forms: autistic shell, masochistic envelope, belt of muscular rigidity or psychomotor agitation (Anzieu, 1987a).

THE NINE FUNCTIONS OF THE EGO-SKIN

The description of the functions of the Ego-skin emerges from the attempt to draw a parallel between the functions of the skin and the functions of the Ego (Anzieu, 1987a), which responds to a conception of "correspondence between the organic and the psychic". To begin with, the theory of the Ego-skin described three functions: protective barrier of the psyche, which would figuratively be a *sack*; filter of interchanges, which would figuratively be a *sieve*; and surface of inscription of the first traits or registers, which would figuratively be a *screen*. Later Anzieu developed a model illustrating nine functions of the Ego-skin, which will now be described.

SUPPORT

The Ego-skin has the function of maintaining the mind in the same way as the hands, the arms and the support of the mother have the function of holding the baby's body and the skeleton has the function of supporting and holding the body. In order for this function to be fulfilled, there must be a primary identification with a supporting object, which is interiorised and avoids the experience of void and internal inconsistency. This function is related to postural problems and its corresponding anxiety is that of void.

> Barbie, the patient with psoriasis to whom I referred previously, during periods in which her disease worsens, suffers from the appearance of cracks in her skin. Every time these cracks appear, with specific reference to the pain they cause her, she adopts a strange posture, hunched and semi-flexed, which makes it diffi- cult for her to walk or stand. Until now, none of the professionals who have examined her in these circumstances have been able

to explain or find a biological justification for the position of her body, which apparently does not have an antalgic function, but which shows without any doubt the failure in the function of support.

CONTAINER

The Ego-skin is the container of the mind as long as we consider it as a sack or a surface, generated by the care with which the mother provides the baby during the early stages of life (*handling*). In the formation of this sack or envelope as well as its containing function, we also witness the participation of the sonorous envelope, which complements the tactile one.

The lack of this containing function manifests itself as two forms of anxiety: firstly the anxiety of something internal which is diffuse, spread out and unreachable, which in general has the characteristics of the drive which cannot be pacified or identified, such as a nucleus without a surface. The calming of this kind of anxiety is attempted with an envelope of suffering, which is produced either by physical pain or by psychic anxiety. Secondly, the anxiety of having an interior that empties itself, the experience of having holes, the difficulty of retaining things: the *sieve Ego-skin*.

Barbie once referred to a dream in which she treads on a spider: it breaks into two pieces and a red gelatinous substance emerges from the inside. With this dream an anxiety related to the lack in the function of container manifests itself. However, it was the first dream in which an interior became clearly distinguished from an exterior. Years later, the appearance in a dream of a concrete bench, like those seen in some parks, was associated with the acquisition of solidity and consistency.

EXCITATION SCREEN

This is a function of the most superficial layer of epidermis which protects from physical stimuli and aggression. To do this, a structure with two layers (such as the one described by Freud in "The mystic writing pad") is necessary. The function of excitation screen is that of protection against stimuli.

Deficits in the excitation screen can be felt as "Pulp Ego", in the sense given by Tustin to autistic states, or as "Crustacean Ego". When the excitation screen does not work, a paranoid anxiety appears in the form of either persecution ("I am being robbed of my thoughts") or influence machine ("I am being made to think these thoughts"). What is essential is the feeling of being exposed or helpless, or in contrast, the idea of invulnerability. There are substitutes for excitation screen, such as the muscular second skin or the character shells.

In *The Non-Existent Knight* both the function of excitation screen and the feelings of being exposed or fragmented against which it protects are clearly presented. In the following examples, Agilulfo, the main character, oscillates between one state and the other when he feels exposed.

In each crack, the gusts of wind, the flying mosquitoes and the rays of the moon went through Agilulfo with all his shell. [Calvino, 1959]

Agilulfo was now backwards, with his back pressed against his breast, the arms crossed, protected, himself entirely, behind the shield. [*ibid.*]

INDIVIDUATION

In the same way as the membrane of the cells protects their individuality, and the granulation, colour, texture and odour of the skin present individual differences that characterise the individual, the Ego-skin has a function of individuation which consists of providing a sense of *being a unique being,* which depends on the strength of the feeling of its own boundaries, and on conceiving the self as a unity. A failure in the function of individuation could cause a feeling of strangeness and of the loss of separation from external reality.

INTERSENSORIALITY

This function is that of the "common sense". It is a function of integration and interconnection between the different feelings against an imaginary backdrop, which could be the surface of the skin. Its failure could cause feelings of physical fragmentation, due to the independent and anarchic functioning of the sense organs. The multiple splitting spreads built-up parts of the self within a space which is neither internal nor external, which must be later contained by a muscular rigidity, motor agitation or physical suffering.

In *The Non-Existent Knight*, a character called Gurdulú fails to acquire this function. For example, he cannot feel his own foot as part of his own Ego and he lets himself be pricked by a porcupine:

> Along the grass, a porcupine, which perhaps had been attracted by the smell, came close to the bowl and began to lick the last drops of soup. While it was doing this, it pushed its spikes against the naked soles of Gurdulú's feet. [. . .] Until the tramp opened his eyes: he looked around, without understanding where the feeling of pain that had woken him came from. He saw the naked foot, straight in the middle of the grass like a prickly pear's spade, and against it, the porcupine.
>
> "Oh, foot!" Gurdulú started to say, "Foot, hey, I'm talking to you! What are you doing planted there like a fool? Can't you see that this animal is pricking you? Oh, foot! Hey, stupid! Why can't you come over here? Can't you see he is hurting you? What a stupid foot! But how can you be so stupid? Foot! Will you please listen to me? Look how he lets himself be torn to pieces! Come here, you idiot! Do I have to tell you how? Pay attention: watch how I do it. Now I am going to teach you what you must do . . ."—and when he said this he bent his leg, dragging his foot towards himself and placing it away from the porcupine. "You see? It was so easy that as soon as I taught you how it was done, you could do it too. Stupid foot! Why did you stay there so long letting yourself be pricked?" [Calvino, 1959]

SUPPORT FOR SEXUAL EXCITATION

As with the baby, the skin is the object of the maternal libidinal charge, and the skin is the backdrop preparatory to genital pleasure. It can be considered as an erogenous envelope, a surface upon which the privileged erotogenic zones are situated, and the source of global sexual excitation.

The support function of sexual excitation has failures of its own: if the charge is more narcissistic than libidinal, the envelope loses its role as a source of reception and producer of erotogenicity at the service of genital sexuality, and becomes instead a shining envelope which provides an illusory invulnerability or immortality. If the erotogenic orifices are a source of pain rather than pleasure, the pain and the pleasure amalgamate, giving rise to perversions.

LIBIDINAL RECHARGE

This function refers to the role of the contact barrier as a means of distribution and organisation of libidinal energy. It is equivalent to the function of preconscious and unconscious processing of the charges between representations. When it fails, the corresponding anxieties are the explosion of the psychic apparatus due to over-charge, and the Nirvana anxiety, which is the anxiety of zero tension.

Anzieu's idea is that the baby is by no means just a passive receptor of the maternal stimuli. The baby's maturation and development depend on his interchanges with the maternal environment. The baby needs not only to receive care, but also to *emit signals* which can be understood and which are capable of releasing and sharpening the responses within the maternal environment. The aim of all this is to make this environment present when he needs it, through the development of signals.

When the baby acquires endogenous control, he starts to gain confidence in his activities and a feeling of omnipotence. The action, instead of functioning as a discharge, produces a *libidinal recharge* which anticipates the following stage, and has access to an internal strength which is indispensable for the reorganisation of his sensory-motor system and his maturation in order to face new experiences. This process of libidinal recharge is usually absent in those patients who tend to become chronically ill and lose faith in doctors, and even in medicine in general. What they need—the development of a feeling of confidence in regaining their health—is progressively lost.

INSCRIPTION OF TACTILE SENSORIAL TRACES

This function is related to the concept of the pictogram proposed by Piera Castoriadis-Aulagnier. It is the function of awareness of external reality and of the object in the skin by means of sensitivity—heat, cold, pain, touch and dermatoptic sensitivity (Anzieu, 1987a, p. 116)—as though there were an "originary preverbal writing, made of cutaneous traces".

The exercise of this function is related to social belonging (here this function is combined with the function of individuation) because "the belonging of an individual to a social group is marked by incisions, scarring, paintings, tattoos, makeup, hair styles. . ." and also by their dress, which is like a projection or a double of the skin (*ibid.*). In "The mystic writing pad" (Freud, 1925a), the inscription surface represented by the internal layer would correspond to this function of the Ego-skin, while the external sheet would correspond to the function of excitation screen (see Chapter 1).

The anxieties related to this function are, on the one hand, those of being marked in a stigmatising way, that is to say with defamatory and indelible marks which originate in the Superego and which "can signify a sentence of aesthetic mutilation" (Ulnik, 1987a). On the other hand, we also find the anxiety produced by the loss of the capacity to fixate traces and the disappearance of all the inscriptions.

TOXIC FUNCTION

This is a negative or a paradoxical function of the Ego-skin which tends to self-destruction. It is related to auto-immune reactions and to the lack of discrimination between the Ego and the not-Ego, between what is one's own and what is alien. According to Anzieu, this toxic function would play a part in skin diseases such as eczema and other allergies. The imaginary skin with which the Ego covers itself becomes a poisoned, suffocating, burning, separating tunic (1987a, p. 119). The first eight functions serve the attachment drive and the libido. The ninth function would not be libidinal but purely thanatic.

Following the orientation which proposes that the functions of the Ego-skin are homologous to those of the skin itself, we should take into account at least two more functions of the skin: the function of emission (for example, sweat and pheromones) and the function of production (of hair, nails, etc.).

Chart 2.1 Functions of the Ego-skin

Function	Description	Failure
Support	Support of the psyche Holding	Anxiety of void
Container	Containing function: contains the psyche Handling	Anxiety of something internal, diffuse "Sieve Ego-skin"
Excitation screen	Anti-stimuli protection	"Pulp Ego" "Crustacean Ego"
Individuation	Provides the feeling of being unique Considering oneself as a unity	Feeling of strangeness and loss of separation from external reality
Intersensoriality	"Common sense" Integration and inter- connection of the different sensations	Physical fragmentation
Support for sexual excitation	Erogenous envelope Source of global sexual excitation	Narcissistic charge: shining envelope Source of pain: perversions
Libidinal recharge	Distribution and organisation of libidinal energy	Explosion due to overcharge Nirvana: zero tension
Inscription of tactile sensory traces	Awareness of external reality and of the object in the skin Social belonging	Stigmas Disappearance of all inscriptions Loss of capacity to fixate traces
Toxic	Negative function, self-destructive Lack of discrimination between the Ego and the Not-Ego	Fantasy of poisoned tunic Eczema, allergies

Theoretical and clinical reflections taking
Didier Anzieu's contributions as a starting point

THE CONTAINER AND THE ENVELOPE WITHIN THE
THERAPEUTIC FUNCTION

Anzieu dedicates a paragraph to the *pack,* a healing technique for serious psychotic patients which derives from the physical enveloping of patients with damp cloths practised by French psychiatrists in the 19th century. This technique presents similarities to the African ritual of therapeutic shrouding, or the freezing bath of Tibetan monks. Anzieu relates that Woodbury added to the envelope of cloths the "envelope" of the group of therapists who closely surrounded the patient.

He reaches the conclusion that the Ego-skin also has a social support, which is based on "the presence of an environment which is united and attentive to the experience that the person in particular is going through". Likewise, the "physical envelope is one of the unconscious psychic organisers of the groups" (1987a). The *pack* can offer a double envelope, both thermal and tactile, which can work as a structuring "spare envelope", taking the place of the pathological envelopes and allowing the patient to abandon his defences at least temporarily. He establishes a difference between working with the psychic contents (as with neurotic patients) and working with the psychic container (as with borderline states). In the latter case the function is to remedy the failures and to re-establish the function of the container.

In Copahue, a thermal centre in the province of Neuquén in the Argentine Republic, patients are covered in hot volcanic mud, and they are later wrapped in nylon and towels, in a technique similar to that of the *pack.* Sacks of sand are placed under the back in order to retain the warmth. The situation created is the nearest thing possible to a regression to the maternal womb: the sacks of sand are equivalent to the lobes of the placenta, the mud is similar to the vernix, and the nylon and the blankets are like the foetal membranes (Figure 2.7).

Figure 2.7 Patient undergoing thermal mud treatment at the Copahue Thermal Bath, in Neuquén, Argentina (by courtesy of Dr Javier Ubogui)

THE ACQUISITION OF SYMBOLIC CAPACITIES

Anzieu describes four stages:

- The baby experiences his psychic substance as either liquid, which is accompanied by anxieties of emptying out, or as gaseous, which is accompanied by anxieties of explosion. There is no internal consistency because there is no function of support.
- The first thoughts of absence appear, which makes the lacks and frustrations tolerable. However, these thoughts still require the continuity of contact with the object, which functions as support and container. There is a conception of the internal and the external, but the space is bi-dimensional. "The meaning of the objects is experienced as inseparable from the sensual qualities that can be perceived on their surface" (Anzieu, quoting Meltzer, *Explorations on autism*, 1975).
- Access to tri-dimensionality and to projective identification. The internal space of the objects appears. Symbiosis persists.
- Passage from the narcissistic relationship to the object relationship. Acquisition of psychic time.

These "stages" on the way to symbolisation do not follow as exact a sequence as presented here. The lack of an organised feeling of cohesion of the body's boundaries is enough to prevent the emergence of a clear distinction between internal and external experiences, between the self and the representations of the object (Anzieu, 1987a). "The core of the experience of self and of personal identity is not completely differentiated from the dual unity of the mother-child relationship." (Anzieu, 1987a, p. 167)

Another important element to the acquisition of the symbolic capacity and of the capacity to differentiate the self from the environment is that provided by the *sonorous envelope*. Anzieu gives this name to the group of sound emissions and receptions between the child and his environment (in particular the mother) which help him acquire a capacity to signify and then to symbolise. Screams and babbling sounds would have a *pre-linguistic* meaning, while mimicry and gestures would have an *infra-linguistic* meaning. The signifiers must join themselves on the one hand with sounds, and on the other hand with meanings. Buccomotor co-ordination is essential for the first connection, and visuomotor co-ordination, related to gestures and mimicry, is required for the second connection. Although it is usually thought that mimicry and gestures pave the way for the managing of sounds, the truth is that for Anzieu there could be differences in structure between vocal communication and communication with gestures, which indicates that a more complex and abstract symbolisation structure is needed in order to overcome these differences.

Formal representations

Anzieu proposes the existence of formal representations, distinct from word-representations and thing-representations. The formal representations are the representations of line, of plane, of surface, of sphere, of the position of the body in space, of envelope, and of container. These representations are necessary in order to acquire the notions of:

Interior-exterior	
Right-left	which are representations of
Hard-soft	a tactile and kinaesthetic nature
Wrinkled or rough-smooth	
Splitting	
Inversion	which are mental operations
Symmetry	

> For the child [here he is referring to the baby] there is no diffe-
> rence between space and the objects that inhabit it. In conse-
> quence, when one moves an object, one moves at the same time
> the part of space in which the object is. And the child himself is
> an object that occupies part of space and can be pierced by
> another part. [1987b, p. 12]
>
> When an object is put into motion, it runs the risk of not
> stopping, and therefore generates in the child the anxiety of being
> pierced by the object [. . .] the child starts to scream when the
> object comes close to him. [*ibid.*, pp. 12–13]

The importance of the formal representations for clinical work is that
they would be particularly altered in narcissistic neurosis and
borderline states, and their alteration would lead to confusions
between the notions of inside and outside, and one's own and alien,
which would be a permanent source of conflict and anxiety. In order
to treat these patients it is necessary to help them build just these
kinds of representations which they lack. This frequently involves
working more on the container than on the content, which in turn
means not stressing the interpretation of fantasies, but rather
stressing the exercise of those psychic functions that are lacking or
in deficit by, for example, helping them to establish limits and
configure spaces, to discriminate between what is their own and what
is alien, to integrate "parts" of their personality, to acquire the notion
of process, and so on.

The theory of formal representations could also explain the
alteration in the concept of distance shown by patients in their
disruptive behaviour of abrupt detachment or abandonment of
relationships that were becoming close due to an affective approach.
It is as if the approach were experienced as an imminent danger of
fusion. Both this subject and that of the acquisition of different
symbolic capacities will be reintroduced in Chapters 4 and 6.

MASOCHISM

Anzieu attempts to explain the cases of perverse masochism and the
self-destructive behaviours of patients who inflict skin wounds upon
themselves. In order to do so, he proposes the model of "envelope
of suffering", which in his opinion has two characteristics:

- A failure in identification, which culminates in the search for marks of violence in order to appropriate one's own self. Thus, the marks and the pain become narcissistic emblems.
- The insufficiency of a common skin which can allow the confirmation of the signal emitted and received. This leads to survival as long as the individual continues to suffer.

In general, self-destructive behaviour is related to a significant other. The first experiences of pleasure and pain are linked to tactile contact, and this contact comes from the care of the mother. If she offered this care in an excessive, inappropriate or brutal way, that would be reflected in fantasies of a common skin which is constantly tearing and hurting itself.

> The fantasy (necessary for evolution towards a psychic autonomy) of having a skin of one's own remains fraught with guilt due to the previous fantasy that it is necessary to take it from someone else in order to have it for oneself, and that it is better still to let it be taken by someone else in order to provide him with pleasure, and finally to obtain it for oneself. [Anzieu, 1987, p. 122]

The body with loss of affect and identification remains subjected, beyond the pleasure principle, to the arbitrariness of the power of the other regarding it. The body of suffering has two characteristic traits: a *persecutory potentiality* (a concept proposed by Castoriadis-Aulagnier), due to which the subject needs a persecutory object, to which he attributes power and a death wish towards himself, in order to feel alive; and an *aptitude for acting* that involves the incarnation of suffering: torture, passion, sacrifice, the position of victim (Anzieu, 1987a, p. 255).

Self-destructive behaviour against the individual's own skin can be due to the wish to tear off content (internal object), an adhesive identification or a second skin, that is to say a container which is felt as a self-destructive envelope (Anzieu, 1987).

Tattoos sometimes show us in a concrete way the wish of some people to have adhered to their skin the image, the name, or directly the person whose absence they cannot bear. However, once this person is adhered and stamped in the tattoo, when there is a conflict with them or when that person disappears, the struggle, the tearing and the pain will be transferred to the skin. Guillot and Cruz, in a paper on prison tattoos, describe the case of a convict who tattooed on his arm the figure of his beloved partner, who had become pregnant shortly before he was sent to prison. When he discovered on leaving prison that the child was not his, he tried by all means possible to eliminate the "irritating cutaneous memory", thus scarring his skin (Guillot and Cruz, 1972; see Chapter 9).

THE OLFACTORY ENVELOPE

Commenting on the case of a patient with a strong smell of perspiration, Anzieu describes what he calls the olfactory envelope, in which the function of excitation screen (because the sweat protects against heat) is confused with the function of emotional signalling of secretions (1987, p. 197). The emission of smell and physical signals in general lends itself to *Entfremdung* ("alienation"), because its involuntary nature saves the patient from making efforts of thought and from feelings of guilt (*ibid.*, p. 198). The emission of smells has an erotic and seductive component along with an aggressive one, but as the smell emerges without the patient's intention, he does not take responsibility for it, as if it were a subject alien to his psyche. Besides, as the patient does not make reference to his smell, the therapist feels uncomfortable because talking about it makes him feel aggressive and insulting.

> In the case of Barbie, the idea that she involuntarily scales and that the smell is inevitable because it is produced by the creams she puts on serves as an excuse for her not taking the necessary care to avoid the effects it has on others. In this way she avoids making conscious her hatred of those others for being healthy or her yearning for revenge due to the lack of affection she suffered.

In these cases, the counter-transference resistances are firstly to consider that as the somatic is not articulated, it does not have communication value; and secondly, if the psychoanalyst feels rejection and even wishes to abandon the patient, the re-translation of these counter-transference feelings to the area of infantile history could cause him to fail to make conscious the aggression of which he is the object at the present time.

In situations such as these, in which the smell of the patient or his scales of epidermis affect the analyst, he should be able to disregard the affects that the situation can provoke in him (pity, disgust, anxiety, etc.), which would obstruct what he hears, while at the same time adding these objective facts (such as the scaling, for example) as analysis material despite the fact that the patient does not speak about them. Sometimes it becomes necessary to analyse the disregard of the patient as well as the effects of this disregard on the analyst, and this must be done without shame or taking the risk of hurting the patient's feelings, with the assumption that the analyst might otherwise be humouring the perverse aspects (I am referring to pregenital sexuality) hidden behind the somatic disease, which sometimes turns out to be the perfect alibi. *For Anzieu, the olfactory envelope is a variant of the sieve Ego-skin, because it is neither closed nor controllable and because it allows aggression to flow outwards* (1987, p. 197).

Notes

1. Translator's note: All the quotations by Anzieu have been translated from the Spanish version of the articles and papers which are listed in the References.

2. When he refers to re-structuring their relationship with the world around sight, this should not be understood as the predominance of the image over the concepts and abstractions of things, because that would only be the scopic version of the same thing. The author is alluding instead to "having access to a conceptual 'vision' of things and of psychic reality".

3. According to Hyppolite (1966, p. 860), the Hegelian concept of Aufhebung means to deny, to suppress and to maintain at the same time. We must bear in mind that Freud used to say that negation is a kind of Aufhebung (cancelling) of repression, but not an acceptance of the repressed material, because the essential part of repression—that of preventing the development of affect—still persists.

CHAPTER THREE

Contributions by other psychoanalysts and psychiatrists to the subject of skin and psychoanalysis

As has been seen in the work of Freud, allusions to the skin within psychoanalytic theory are manifold, and there are also several authors who have written about this subject within post-Freudian psychoanalysis. In addition, the skin is usually an "entrance door" for all those who become involved in psychosomatic problems, and when it is time to offer clinical examples, eczema (Schur, 1955; Pichon-Riviere, 1971), psoriasis (Korovsky, 1978), hives (McDougall, 1989) and other dermatoses are usually included. To mention all the authors would be an enormous task which is beyond the scope of this work. In consequence, I shall make reference to some authors whose ideas will be mentioned or discussed in the remaining chapters of this book, or to those authors who have developed subjects the intrinsic importance of which justifies their inclusion.

Roberto Fernández: the skin as an organ of expression

In "La piel como órgano de expresión" [The skin as an organ of expression] (1978), Roberto Fernández makes reference to Freud and to other psychoanalytical authors, and takes interesting contributions from biology in order to enrich his own theory. For example, he mentions Portmann, a scholar of nature, who emphasizes the purely ornamental value of certain forms of life beyond the mere functions of conservation, comparing the skin to clothes, where the protective effect is not everything; rather, it is accompanied by the striking trait of the model.

We could establish a relationship between Portmann's ideas and those of Garma, when he establishes a relationship between clothes and the skin. Garma claims that clothes originated in the idea of substituting the foetal membranes with animal furs. Then the furs were replaced with woven cloths, and later with different materials which acquired different shapes. He points out an evolution regarding the functions of clothes. From a primitive trait of "warm clothes", going through "modesty", the trait of "ornament" would be reached. The *protection* emphasised by Garma is of magical nature, and its end could be to fantastically preserve the cover of foetal vernix (Garma, 1961; Fernández, 1978).

In the constitution of living beings there would seem to be a difference between the external and the internal aspects. While in the internal what predominates is the functional importance determined by the need for a big active surface useful to metabolism, in the external many structures are formed, some of them symmetrical, which are aimed at perception, that is to say at influencing the sensory organs of others capable of registering them. Based on this, Fernández claims that all formal particularity or structural modification of the skin has something to do with the sensory organ of a living being capable of registering it. This is how its participation in social life can be conceived with multiple significations. The forms of appearance could serve the *self-representation*, and the alteration in the appearance could account for the variations within. Thus every living being could be "a form of life which [. . .] in many ways manifests its specific way of being by means of its figure and its behaviour" (Fernández, 1978; Portmann, 1968).

As has been mentioned in Chapter 1, the dam against the touching drive is revulsion. Quoting Chiozza, Fernández claims:

Horror and revulsion appear as reactions against the fear and hatred provoked by *what cannot be assimilated*. This can be expressed by means of nausea, hives, hypersensitivity or allergies, as both vomiting and scratching would look to "tear off from what is disgusting". This somatized fantasy of getting rid of a disgusting object ("full of scabs") involves the fantasy of getting rid of a maternal imago which covers, with a more harmful than protective effect. The object who cannot be assimilated could be an object in front of whom identification is prevented, with a consequent deficit in the subject's identity. This aspect, the identity disorder, will remain evidenced as a message in the dermatological disorder. [1978]

For Fernández there are two maternal functions which could be equivalent to the functions of the skin: *protection* and *acknowledgement*. Any child who lacks the provision of that protective function will feel hurt and "raw", so to speak, and every skin disease could express the traumatic loss of a narcissistic protective function.

The absence of the protective object who acknowledges the subject hinders the symbiosis which is useful for life, and remains registered as a longing for contact or for fusion. This can be expressed in different presentations, such as (in the somatic dimension) an altera-tion in the skin; or (as a character trait) a marked hypersensitivity or an extreme reactive hardness; or (as behaviour aspects) a tendency to adhere to relationships of an extreme affective dependency with expectations of acknowledgement (see Figure 3.1).

Regarding the function of acknowledgement, this could be related to what was previously said about the formal qualities of the external biological structures, which are directed towards an other who is capable of perceiving them. It could also be related to the deficits in

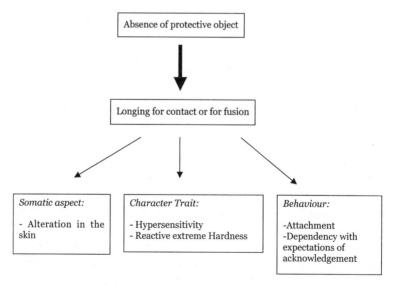

Figure 3.1 Consequences of the absence of a protective object

the subject's identity. Fernández proposes that the fact of not having internalised the function of acknowledgement could express itself in fantasies of rejection that could lead the subject to the experience of being a "stranger", of not being able to establish an adequate identity of belonging, and of feeling segregated.

The longing for an ideal presence which will at some time cover the subject will lead to the investment, in the fantasy, of the excremental products (faeces, urine) as narcissistic representations which, in a way similar to a double, at a certain time surrounded the subject by keeping contact with him. The corresponding symbolic derivatives will find expression in the fantasies of covering oneself with gold, surrounding oneself with valuable objects, and hyper-valuing clothes, ornaments, etc., as elements provided with magical properties of protection and value. Fernández comes to the con-clusion that in a subject who has a predisposition to this, every vital situation that involves putting his "self-protection" to the test (seeing how long he can cope with a certain situation) and facing a situation of change in his identity might be expressed by means of an alteration in the "screen" of interiority constituted by the skin (1978).

Esther Bick: the second skin

In her paper "The experience of the skin in early object relations", Bick proposed the term *second skin*, and related it to the functions of boundary, support, integration and formation of the internal and external spaces. Her discovery was so important that there is probably no author who has written about psychoanalysis and the skin who has not quoted her. She says: "In its most primitive form the parts of the personality are felt to have no binding force amongst themselves and must therefore be held together in a way that is experienced by them passively, by the skin functioning as a boundary" (1970, p. 484).

But this internal function—that of containing the parts of the Self—initially depends on the introjection of an external object, which must be experienced as capable of fulfilling that function. "Until the containing functions have been introjected, the concept of a space within the self cannot arise" (*ibid.*). If this object within an internal space does not appear, there will be confusions regarding identity. Further on, identification with that function of the object replaces the unintegrated state and gives rise to the fantasy of external and internal spaces.

Material will show how this containing object is experienced concretely as a skin. Faulty development of this primal skin function can be seen to result either from defects in the adequacy of the actual object or from fantasy attacks on it, which impair introjection. Disturbance in the primal skin function can lead to a development of a "second skin" formation, through which dependence on the object is replaced by a pseudo-independence, by the inappropriate use of certain mental functions—or perhaps innate talents—for the purpose of creating a substitute for the skin's container function (*ibid.*).

René A. Spitz: infantile eczema and maternal hostility masked as anxiety

In his book about the first year of life of the child (1965), Spitz related infantile eczema due to atopic dermatitis with "maternal hostility masked as anxiety". Throughout his researches, he discovered that children who suffered atopic dermatitis in the second part of the first year of life showed a higher level of (reflex) cutaneous excitability than other children (he looked at the cremasteric reflex and the grasping reflex, among others which were non-cutaneous).

The mothers of children with atopic dermatitis in the second six months of life showed certain curious particularities: they did not like to touch their child and always ended up persuading someone else to change, bath or give the bottle to him or her. The children remained deprived of cutaneous contact and the mothers displayed a hostility masked as anxiety (Spitz, 1965).

The children showed an increase in the cathexis or charge of cutaneous responses, as well as a delay both in learning and in social relationships. There appeared to be a delay in the eight months anxiety, which the author interprets as the child not managing to affectively distinguish the mother from a stranger, because the attitude of the mother has interfered with the object relationships and with the child's mechanisms of identification. The child faces affective signals which come from the mother and seem to correspond to a given situation, but which are in truth contrary to her feelings. The mother transmits something which is not consistent with her intimate attitude, nor does it correspond to her actions regarding the child (Spitz, 1965).

In his study, Spitz reflects upon the interesting findings of Pavlov's researches with dogs. A group of dogs was electrically stimulated in a given perimeter of the leg. It was expected that the animals would be able to distinguish between two different stimuli, but as the electrical stimulation points came progressively closer to each other, the animals developed an "experimental neurosis". Surprisingly, one of the dogs did not develop this experimental neurosis: in contrast, when discrimination between the two signals became impossible, the dog developed eczema in the perimeter of the electrical stimulation. When the experiment was over, the eczema disappeared.

Influenced by this Pavlovian experience, Spitz proposes to investigate, as a psychoanalyst, the remarkable fact that manifestations of a disease should appear in the same spot that has been denied the vital stimulation the child needs, and he supposes that the skin disease emerges as a response to conflicting signals. He finally wonders if the child's reaction might not have the nature of a demand directed at the mother in order to stimulate her to touch him or her more frequently. It could also represent a form of narcissistic withdrawal in the child, who could be providing him- or herself in the somatic sphere with the stimuli which the mother has denied.

Spitz believes that this dermatitis disappears after the first year of age because locomotion appears, and this makes children independent of the signals given by the mother. Children can do without the mother's contact, and replace it with contact with things or with other people which they can seek because they have passed from passivity to directed activity. This hypothesis put forward by Spitz shows once again the link that could exist between skin and movement, which had already been emphasised by Bick with her theory of the second muscular skin, and which had been suggested by Portmann when he emphasised that certain shapes drawn by some insects could only be seen when the design of the drawing was combined with the movement of the wings or with the position of repose.

Enrique Pichon-Rivière: itching and anxiety

In *La psiquiatría, una nueva problemática* [Psychiatry, a new problem], Pichon-Rivière included an article called "Psychosomatic aspects of

dermatology". In it he quotes a great number of authors, both dermatologists and psychoanalysts, who have an interest in psychosomatic
medicine. One of them, Menninger, points out that patients suffering
from skin diseases become a taboo for the other patients, and this is
motivated by the idea of contagion. Patients with mental problems
and those with skin problems could have more in common than is
apparent: they are both an object of rejection and misunderstanding,
and their sufferings are underestimated by those who have not
experienced them.

Another of the authors quoted is Ackerman (1939), who mentions
the case of a woman with neurodermatitis who, having prematurely
lost her mother, would ruin her skin and make herself odious for
others and for herself, becoming so ugly as to prevent the love of
her father and thus avoid remembering the crime the mother carried
out in fantasy (Pichon-Rivière, 1971).

In the article, the subject of itching plays an essential role. It is
considered a central symptom in dermatology, equivalent to anxiety
in the psychic aspect and to pain in the organic aspect. Itching is
interpreted as the result of displacement and as an extension of anal
itching, occasioned either by its repression or by difficulties in its
satisfaction. Considering the skin as an erotogenic zone and scratching as an action performed in search of erotogenic satisfaction,
itching is considered to be a form of masturbation, anal by nature,
with an intense repression of genital life.

After analysing itching, Pichon-Rivière focuses on eczema. First
he mentions researches and experiences in which remissions of
eczema were obtained by means of suggestion or hypnosis, and then
he approaches the clinical materials of patients with eczema from a
psychoanalytical viewpoint. He establishes a relationship between
the patient who covers himself with scabs and the infant's
helplessness and need for maternal protection (1971).

Max Schur: the organ action and the symbolic precursors in the skin

According to Schur, part of the fascination produced by the psychoanalytic study of dermatitis is that one can "see" certain responses;
the simultaneous observation of psychic and somatic phenomena
constitutes a unique experimental setting.

Schur carried out research on dermatological diseases by analysing a series of representative cases. Among these, a 22-year-old patient who was five months pregnant and who suffered from a generalised atopic eczema stands out. Her disease had started when she was one year old and had worsened until it covered her body by the time she was 141/2 years old. The last severe outbreak of her disease had coincided with her marriage. In his analysis of this patient, Schur considered the following phenomena relating to the skin: itching; scratching and other kinds of manipulation; outbreak of new lesions; and secondary elaboration of the lesions to the skin.

Schur proposes the term "physiological regression" which is produced when the Ego loses its capacity to think by using the secondary process, uses non-neutralised energy, and ends up in what he calls "re-somatization". In this kind of regression, preverbal stages previous to the constitution of the Ego are activated, in which the conscious experience remains limited to discharge phenomena which had been present genetically before the emergence of the affect of anxiety. These discharges could be "equivalents to anxiety".

According to Schur, itching could occur in situations linked to unconscious sources of danger, and patients suffering from dermatosis could feel that many aspects of their everyday life were sources of danger. As these patients live surrounded by this threat, they develop an attitude of vigilance and are always ready to feel anxiety. The somatic discharge of these states can be itching. Itching is frequently a night-time symptom which appears or increases before bedtime. Dermatologists usually explain this phenomenon by the change of temperature, but Schur's patient started to feel itching purely because it was bedtime, even if she was not already in bed.

In the same way that itching can be an equivalent to anxiety, it can also be an equivalent to hostile feelings. The fact that aggression becomes stratified can be discovered by means of analysis: while at one level it can represent self-punishment, at a more profound level it can mean a punishment aimed at an external object represented on the skin. One of Schur's patients spent most of his session complaining about a doctor who had subjected him to allergy tests. When these were finished, the patient claimed he had spent the whole night scratching himself. When he was asked why, he replied: "I had to show him what he had done to me" (1955, p. 137). This is a feeling of aggression towards the other deposited on the skin, but it also contains a projection linked to exhibitionism which is very common in patients with dermatosis: the entire world must see those terrible lesions. In the case of a woman who had been raped by her father, the scratching at night symbolically represented the elimination of her father's sperm from her skin.

Itching can also be related to libidinal drives. For people who have not undergone analysis, it is easier to establish a relationship between sexuality and the actions the patient performs in order to ease the itching than it is to understand the relationship that could exist between sexuality and itching proper. However, Freud says in his article "Repression" that when an external stimulus becomes internal because of the harmful effects it produces on an organ, the result is that from this organ a source of continuous excitation emerges that increases tension and acquires similarity to a drive.

> The gratification produced by scratching exceeds the mere elimination of the displeasure caused by itching, and in some cases it even comes to be the only, or the main way of sexual gratification. [. . .] The patient knows that what he is doing is bad for his skin: he feels guilty and humiliated because he cannot give up his behaviour. The battle against scratching acquires all the characteristics of a battle against masturbation. [Schur, 1955, p. 36]

As we can see, in the analysis of itching, its compulsive character, the masturbatory basis, the feelings of guilt and self-punishment and the mechanisms of punishing someone else by means of self-destruction are all emphasised. Itching and scratching can be dangerous obstacles when they are used to serve resistance.

Wishes to incorporate the object or to merge it with parts of the self can be manifested in attitudes aimed at the appendices of the skin, such as the hair and the nails. Schur refers to a case in which he could appreciate, *in statu nascendi*, the development of tricho-tillomania in a one-year-old child who had replaced the dummy with the pleasure of having his mother's hairs inside his mouth. This was later replaced by the action of pulling and sucking his own hair.

The case histories of patients with severe dermatosis show, according to Schur, that outbreaks or relapses of disease are generally related to a traumatic event or a particular conflictive situation. The problem is that obtaining the patient's history with an adequate level of profundity is very difficult, and this contributes to the scepticism of doctors who are more "organicist". However, in day-to-day analytical observation, the connections between the disease and the way of life become more convincing (Schur, 1955).

By making extensive use of the Freudian concept of *organ language,* Schur proposes the existence of a kind of defensive action that takes the primitive form of *organ action.* These kinds of defensive actions actually refer to what he himself calls precursors of thought, of affect, of drives, and of the defensive actions. He called these primitive actions and discharges "physiologic equivalents and precursors of defences" (*ibid.*).

When discussing the relationship between hysterical conversion and somatic symptoms in dermatosis, Schur points out the implicit vagueness and simplifications in certain studies of hysterical conversion which seek to explain everything on the basis of the influence the will can have over the striated muscles, unlike the influence the will has over the neurovegetative system.

For Schur, it does not seem fanciful to assume that in certain constellations in which a profound regression of the Ego is produced, the skin works as a transmitter of primitive symbols of thought, discourse and action. In these regressive states, the differentiation between the Self and the object can be vague, regression can be very deep, narcissistic and exhibitionistic tendencies can prevail, and the skin can be treated as a part of the self and simultaneously as part of the external object. In three cases of psoriasis treated by him, he claims to have found in the patients a great confusion regarding their own identity, a product of ambivalent identifications with the parents. Once the lesion has established itself, its morphological characteristics, its localisation and the secondary assessment that can be produced about it can influence or add elements to the identity confusion (1955).

Once the disease has begun, there are many factors which contribute to its chronic evolution and to its incurability. Among these factors we can consider metabolic, infectious, nutritional and immunological influences, as well as influences regarding the time of the year. These influences make doctors discredit the possible implication of psychological factors. Amid all this Schur asks himself:

can psychological factors be found which explain why a disease becomes chronic?

In many cases we can observe attitudes to the skin which are similar to those described by Freud in schizophrenic patients, although in these cases the patients are not schizophrenic. However, when the patients try to squeeze substance out of their skin, such as pus, blackheads, blood, serum, etc., this activity is symbolically overdetermined and has a clear compulsive and masturbatory characteristic. In these cases, characteristics identical to those of hypochondria are discovered, such as the narcissistic overvaluation of the symptom, or of the whole skin, for example. Exhibitionistic tendencies, the desire to punish someone or the subject himself, regression to the Ego and the prevalence of the primary process in the elaboration of the lesions and the manipulations all play a part as well. In general, these patients develop their manipulations in a dreamy state, disregarding the external world and with the mirror as the only representing object. Despite everything, the patients can manage to function in an excellent way in the rest of their lives, as if the pathological trait were encapsulated.

The question posed earlier could be answered by pointing out that the lesions per se can scarcely be significant and can have little or no relationship with a latent emotional situation. However, "once the symptom has established itself, it acts as a focal point of convergence for different pathological mechanisms" (Schur, 1955). Every somatic disease attracts narcissistic libido, and any response to an organic disease will involve a temporary or permanent regression which affects all the psychic structures. Whatever the cause that precipitates the dermatological disorder, the result will depend not only on the seriousness of the organic disease, but also on the level of mental health at the time when the disease started and during its evolution.

The function of the organic system which has been affected and its significance for the psychic apparatus play a very important role: a disease that causes itching will precipitate different responses from a disease that causes pain or disfigurement. Any dermatosis will tend to increase the narcissistic cathexes, and it will increase or rekindle conflicts surrounding exhibitionism.

It is difficult to establish a differentiation between the circumstances that precipitated the lesions and the circumstances that precipitate itching accesses. At the outbreak of the disease there would seem to be specific, or at least very clear circumstances which unleash the responses. But as the patients suffer from a state of floating anxiety and a constant vigilant and alert attitude (commonly called "tensional state"), they can respond to any situation with a new outbreak of disease, or indistinctly with accesses of itching. At this stage the connection with a primitive organ language or an "organ action", which was clear when the initial lesion was produced, is now lost. In this way, an economical factor which determines the appearance of new outbreaks of disease in the face of any non-specific change starts to predominate. However, the lesions lend themselves to secondary symbolic revisions, and only very careful analysis allows us to distinguish between primary symbolism and a secondary symbolic revision.

Specificity is variable: in some cases, a dermatosis can be precipitated by a multitude of causes because a constitutional disposition predominates. In other cases, a specific constellation of psychological characteristics is required for the disease to appear. In a high percentage of cases, the reconstruction carried out in analysis suggests that the organ election can be explained by the patient's vital life. Schur exemplifies these ideas by mentioning cases of alopecia areata in which the subject's own hair, or even the hair of the mother, was hyper-cathexed. In a case of eczema, the nickname the patient had had during his childhood was "Skinny". In another case, the patient had suffered trauma during the course of scarlet fever when he was four years old and had suffered burns on his skin when he was two. During his adolescence, his penis had chafed painfully after he masturbated, and the first lesion of his disease developed in the same spot. Finally, he mentions another case of eczema in which the patient had had nappy rash when she was one year old, and eczema had appeared immediately afterwards.

Regarding treatment, Schur proposes to help the patient—who uses his skin to think, feel and act—to learn to use the normal channels of expression. To do this, he considers that verbalisation, even if it is intellectual, helps to stop the regression of the Ego and the preverbal expression implicit in dermatological reactions (1955).

Gilda Foks: the skin and the functions of the Ego

Taking Chiozza's theory of specific fantasies as her basis, Foks and a group of collaborators try to find specific fantasies of the skin, thus arriving at conclusions similar to those of Didier Anzieu about the correlation between the functions of the skin and those of the Ego. In their work they emphasise Freud's references in *Beyond the Pleasure Principle* about the living vesicle and its cortical layer which receives stimuli and which is provided with a protective device against excitations. Just as the external layer protects the other layers with its own death, the skin could have in its corneal layer the representation of the dead protecting the living. They also emphasise the uses of language according to which, when there is an inability of the Ego to do something, we tend to say that the person cannot cope[1] (Foks et al., 1972). Based on the existence of fingerprints, these authors emphasise the relationship between skin and identity.

José María López Sánchez: studies on alopecia areata

López Sánchez has studied multiple pathologies from an original perspective, because he obtains his conclusions from psycho-biographical and psycho-diagnostic studies, during support psychotherapies with a psychodynamic orientation, and by means of psycho-drama as an exploratory technique. Regarding the skin, he has been particularly interested in alopecia areata, and he finds in these patients an alexithymic profile and an inhibition of aggression. He emphasises as prominent elements in the character of these patients the behaviours of submission and passivity, and in their narrative the existential assumption of the role of victim and a predominance of feelings of impotence, as well as fear of aggression and of punishment (1985, 2000).

In a paper on the same theme, other authors have alluded to that passivity, proposing that certain patients had the role of "dolls", fulfilling the function of a late transitional object for their mothers. The illusion that the hair will grow again transmits a fantasy of avoiding the consequences of castration, because what has been cut or has fallen out can re-appear just as it was before (Ulnik & Chopitea, 1991).

Noemí L. de Canteros: allergy and identity

The contribution of this author is centred on the study of allergies. According to Canteros, the hypersensitive reaction of the immune system is an exaggerated defence reaction of an identity which has not managed to reach an adequate individuation (1981). "The identity that feels threatened is an identity of a syncretic or symbiotic kind, an identity based on "we", and the hypersensitive reaction could be the expression of a wish for and fear of the object and of the situation which would require a change in this identity and a passage from the symbiotic state to individual identity." (*ibid.*)

In allergic patients it can be very difficult to differentiate cathexis of the object from identification, and the biological model of the relationship they maintain could be that of the host-parasite relationship (*ibid.*). Arrested in their development by an extreme dependence, these patients reject independent life. They tend to delegate to their symbiotic partners the tasks of adaptation, defence and competition, and as a consequence they keep themselves away from changes in the surrounding world, and have extraordinary difficulties in facing new situations. The prototype could be a fearful person who avoids situations of responsibility, expects to be always on familiar ground, and when a situation of change occurs, he or she reacts in a hypersensitive way (*ibid.*).

A great part of this author's experience is with asthmatic patients, but she refers more than once to atopic patients in general, and the alternation between asthma and eczema shown by some patients with these characteristics is well known.

Pierre Marty: the allergic object relation

In "The allergic object relation", Marty considers ideas which often coincide with those of Canteros, which are of a later date. For Marty, the primordial wish of the allergic patient is to get as close as possible to the object until he is confused with it. In order to achieve this, he makes two movements: the first is attracting the object, and the second is conditioning it.

The attraction of the object involves a confusion of the subject with the object as a consequence of the subject's difficulty with establishing its own boundaries. Marty offers the example of a woman who used to say that she loved being caressed, and that was why she loved cats. When Marty pointed out to her that in reality what she liked was to caress, because cats do not caress, and that it was she herself who carried out the action of caressing, she replied: "Yes, but cats rub against us and caress us when we caress them." Confusion in a common unity with the object makes the subject unable adequately to conceive a distance, and causes the production of massive projection or confusion of the subject with his environment.

Conditioning is a progressive inter-penetration that takes place all the time. Marty mentions the case of a patient with eczema who used to say: "What I want is for the boundaries with others to disappear, perhaps that is why I'm looking for physical contact. If I touch someone else's skin, I become mixed up with him" (1958). This is about making boundaries disappear through the work of projection and identification.

In Marty's theory, relationships can be established at different levels: at sensory, motor, phantasmatic, intellectual and other levels. An allergic reaction could be the manifestation of the establishment of a relationship at the humoral level. The disease can appear when regressive mechanisms which activate this humoral level are unleashed. This is what occurs in two typical sets of circumstances. The first is when an invested object reveals a characteristic of his own with which the allergic subject cannot identify. The second is when two equally invested objects manifest incompatibilities with each other. In consequence, the subject feels torn and incompatible with himself because he has become fused with both objects at the same time, and these do not get on together.

Regression can be interrupted by the irruption of allergy. If this does not take place, episodes of depersonalisation can occur. The relationship with the doctor or with the analyst can also interrupt regression, and can even prevent the allergy from appearing. The problem is that any proof of independence or of new qualities in the doctor could exceed the adaptability of the patient (Marty, 1958).

Perhaps taking Marty's claims as a starting point, we can explain the usual hypersensitivity of some patients who, owing either to some disagreeable detail, no matter how unimportant it might be, or to some small disagreement with the analyst, are capable of abandoning treatment, thus ruining everything that has been attained over the preceding years.

Mahmoud Sami-Ali: allergy, psychosis and spaces of reciprocal inclusions

In the same way as Canteros and Marty, and with many theoretical coincidences, this author refers to the skin mainly when he makes his contributions on allergy. To Sami-Ali, the world of allergy is constituted in such a way that the body and the world form an equivocal mass where "every relationship is the contact of a skin that touches another skin and where the active and the passive, to touch and to be touched are considered equivalent" (1991). In order to introduce a boundary, a difference, a polarity, it is necessary to create a distance precisely where it is difficult to do so. That can only happen if the allergic relationship with the world is displaced in terms of the tactile sense, giving way to a distancing created by the visual and the auditory senses.

Every allergy could be a questioning of what one is and what one is not (Sami-Ali, 1991). What can be at stake is personal identity in its most profound aspect, at the origins of subjectivity. The "bet" of the allergic patient would be to reduce everything to the identical, and his crisis could erupt when the other reveals himself in his otherness through "tearing himself off".

So far Sami-Ali's theory would not seem to be too different from that of Marty. Perhaps his contribution to this subject might be the relationship he establishes between allergy and psychosis, proposing that when the allergic patient is faced with a contradiction, due to the failure of the unique relationship, identical to himself, that he seeks, a no-escape situation might be created which marks the start of a psychotic elaboration (1991).

Psychosis could attack the very root of the contradiction, turning what is contradictory into the identical and giving way to the characteristic space of delirium, where the notion of "inside" is considered to be equal to the notion of "outside", and the part is regarded as equal to the whole. Sami-Ali called these kinds of spaces "spaces of reciprocal inclusions" (1979). They are those spaces in which the duplication of the same within the self is produced, as usually happens when a TV presenter speaks with a monitor behind him in which he himself is speaking with a monitor behind him, and so forth (Ulnik, 1993). With these considerations, Sami-Ali proposes a dialectic of substitution of psychosis and somatic disease which is extremely useful for clinical work.

Luis Chiozza, Susana Grispon and Elsa Lanfri: specific fantasies in psoriasis

These authors disagree with Anzieu in that for them the skin exists as an organ at the same time as the fantasy of the Ego-skin exists, rather than the Ego-skin deriving from the previous existence of the organ. Studying a case of psoriasis, they propose that through this disease the patient could express unconscious specific fantasies of "feeling raw"[2], so to speak, because of experiences of abandonment, humiliation and shame, and of "being scaled"[3] by the wish to have a protective shell amid the distrust caused by feeling cruelly hurt or criticised (Chiozza, 1991).

David Rosenfeld: skin disorders and the body image. Projective identification

Rosenfeld analyses a patient with eczema and studies Perrault's story *Donkey Skin*, in which a princess lost her mother; her father then wanted to marry her. She accepted on condition that he gave her a series of dresses, and finally she ordered a donkey to be sacrificed. This donkey was the source of the kingdom's wealth because it defecated gold. Once the donkey was killed, the princess covered herself in its skin and, with the help of a fairy, escaped without being recognised, until finally a prince took her as his wife and she was able to recover her own identity. In his analysis of the story, Rosenfeld refers to the relationship between the following: skin and identity, the importance of distances and the configuration of space, the role of projective identification and the pathological elaboration of grief.

Regarding projective identification, both the characters in the story and the patient analysed by Rosenfeld follow the same sequence: a) experiences of abandonment, suffering, loneliness and separation; b) development of an extreme need and feelings of lack, destruction, sadness, misery and melancholy; c) establishment of all those aspects within the other, thus establishing a *folie à deux* or parasite-host relationship; d) behaviours of helping the other in a grandiloquent way by offering help, becoming an ideal or intro-ducing themselves inside him; e) the interior of the other, where the Ego has entered, returns against the self in the form of aggressive, intrusive elements that prick, drill, penetrate, sting, fragment and hurt; the return of the other's interior is so aggressive because although the subject apparently helps the object, he has in fact attacked it in order to inoculate into him his own destroyed and denigrated aspects; and f) search for self-support when faced with the environment's lack of support.

Rosenfeld proposes that in the story there is a double pathological elaboration of grief: on the one hand the father who looks for a wife in his own daughter, and on the other hand the daughter who tries to make her father function as someone who can magically repair the skin of her mother for her by means of the dresses, with which she reconstructs the couple. We can see here that "the idealisation of the dress is an equivalent of the idealisation of the skin and the container of the body of the mother" (Rosenfeld, 1973). In the same way as was pointed out in the analysis of the theme of the skin and of touching in Freud's work (for example in *Totem and Taboo*), the dresses can represent the skin, and this in turn represents a person. And through the group of relationships with the dresses and with the skin, a group of relationships with an object, which can be either dead or alive, can be represented. The skin which represents the dead object is equivalent to carrying the image of an emptied out or destroyed figure upon the shoulders (*ibid.*).

Another aspect of the pathological elaboration of grief is accompanying the dead object in his destiny. The identification with him leads to a *massive disturbance of identity*. The importance of these claims lies in the following: "In many clinical cases we could observe the patients' attempt at tearing off parts of their skin as a way of getting rid of the persecuting object, which is destroyed and is characteristically introjected within the self" (*ibid.*).

Rosenfeld establishes a permanent relationship between skin and identity, and he describes in which way this connection was displayed in different pathologies. Schizoid patients can experience the skin as a sack containing disorganised internal organs which are piled up in an incoherent manner. When contact is established between two regions of the subject's own body, a precarious feeling of identity is sought, so the attacks to the skin and the production of wounds and flagellations attempt to re-establish that feeling, at least in a primitive way.

Regarding distances, Rosenfeld gives an introduction to Hall's proxemics and proposes that both the patients and the characters in the story have difficulty in regulating it. This is related to the fact that the boundary in terms of which distances are considered is the subject's own skin.

Dissociation and fragmentation both of the Ego and of the object favour the establishment of a double distance. In the story, the princess could establish a double distance with her mother, as she is represented both by the rotten skin of the donkey with which the princess covers herself and by the fairy who goes with her. The princess establishes an intimate distance with the skin and a great distance with the fairy. Freud's claim that "the shadow of the object falls over the Ego" is revived, as the absence of the object makes itself present around the skin in an encircling way.

Every time a patient is at the maximum distance, he tries to transform this into an intimate distance by wrapping himself with a fictitious skin that works as a shell and protects him from that abandoning-abandoned object, while at the same time it also represents this object. Other things can perform the function of shell: aggression against the self, as a way of self-support, or the muscular second skin, in the form of hyperactivity or muscular hyper-development.

Other authors

As we said earlier, to mention the contributions of all authors would be an enormous task which exceeds the limits of this chapter and of the book in general. In consequence, only those who are worth consulting due to their importance will be mentioned, taking into account that many of them are not psychoanalysts and that in some cases their work has eclectic characteristics or approaches the social, psychiatric and psycho-biological aspects, as well as the quality of life, of skin diseases. The contributions that stand out are those of Maximilian E. Obermayer, Theodore Nadelson, Herman Musaph, Enrique Sobrado et al., Mario Daian et al., Edgardo Korowsky, Emiliano Panconesi, John Koo, Peter and Caroline Koblenzer, Uwe Gieler, Iona H. Ginsburg, Andrew Finlay, Antonio Rodriguez Pichardo, François Poot, Robert and Claus Zachariae, John de Korte, Sylvie Consoli, Francisco Tausk, Francesc Grimalt, John Cotterill, Michael Musalek and Madhulika and Aditya Gupta. There is also a very interesting review (in French) of skin disorders from a psychoanalytical viewpoint in *Psychologie Médicale, XII/2* (1980).

Notes

1. Translator's note: There is an expression is Spanish which alludes to the fact that a person cannot cope, with direct reference to the skin. Translating the expression literally, it could be said that a certain person "has not enough skin to cope".

2. Translator's note: This is an expression is Spanish which cannot be translated, except literally as "to be with the skin torn", i.e. to feel devastated.

3. Translator's note: Another untranslatable expression in Spanish. The meaning is approximately the same as in note 2.

CHAPTER FOUR

The skin and the levels of symbolisation: from the Ego-skin to the thinking-Ego

As was pointed out in Chapter 2, Didier Anzieu claims that there is a system of basic traces or representations, the reference of which is tactile, concrete experience. With symbolic development, these representations will be the backdrop against which ulterior operations of thought are inscribed. As these tactile traces are denied and separated, though still maintained, the central idea is that they subsist in parallel with the representations mounted on them, thus configuring different levels of symbolisation. In this way, taking the Ego-skin as a starting point, an Ego capable of thinking and of representing can be formed, an Ego called the thinking-Ego (Anzieu, 1995).

With the understanding that different levels of symbolisation exist, the discussion as to whether a physical disease is from a psychoanalytical viewpoint a phenomenon, a symbol or a symptom could be settled at least in part, because it could be claimed that the disease is a form of symbolisation on a different level to that used in spoken language. In contrast, when the somatic is automatically excluded from the symbolic field, we limit ourselves to saying that where a word, a thought, an affect or a conflict should appear, what does in fact appear is the somatic, and in this case, all things considered, our only theoretical contribution would be establishing a relationship between two things by proposing a simple substitution. Then the theoretical development hides that substitution, seeming to explain in economic terms or by means of formulas and mathemes the way in which the somatic inserts itself into a system, which can be either economic or signifying, and which has been established *a priori*. In some cases the conclusion is not so different from that of the ordinary observer who, on seeing someone under a lot of stress, says: "Some day or other he will burst", confirming when he falls ill: "Well, what do you expect, bottling things up for so long? It had to come out one way or another." Without underestimating folk psychology, we nevertheless get the impression that this kind of interpretation, which is purely economic, is the product of simplification.

If we accept the fact that there are some levels of symbolisation which are more primitive than others, it becomes necessary to explain the characteristics and, if possible, the genesis of symbolisation. In section 2.6.2, following Anzieu, evolutionary stages in the acquisition of symbolic capacities were described, and reference was also made to the existence of formal representations. In the following section, Anzieu's ideas regarding five levels of symbolisation which function with different logics will be summarised.

Five levels of symbolisation and their consequences in clinical work with somatic patients

Anzieu (1995), taking as a basis the works of Claude Lévi-Strauss on myths and the growing complexity of the problems they treat, proposes five levels of symbolisation. Each level corresponds to a different logic. These five levels will be described with reference to clinical situations in which they are brought to bear:

- Logic of sensible qualities
- Logic of time and space
- Relationship logic
- Logic of time and movement
- Abstract logic

LOGIC OF SENSIBLE QUALITIES

This is based on the oppositions between sensible qualities:

- raw and cooked
- fresh and stale
- dry and wet

- rough and smooth
- hard and soft
- hot and cold
- light and dark

This logic could correspond to the rising thought and resources of the following complements:

- Binary opposition
- Term to term correspondence
- Constancy of the object

BINARY OPPOSITION

This is the organisation of the tactile qualities as a backdrop against which other sensible qualities emerge as figures (for example, the expression to "contact" someone on the telephone). Instead of binary opposition, it should perhaps be called "equivalence of sensations and transposition of sensible qualities".

By this mechanism something can appear as a backdrop to the appearance or worsening of a disease or a somatic symptom. For example, when an offence is experienced as a wound and a bleeding wound appears on the skin, or when a person bears a problem, a burden, or responsibility for the care of someone else and experiences discomfort on his back such as dorsal or lumbar arthrosis or perhaps a lesion (Figure 4.1.).

In the epicrisis of Elizabeth R's case history, Freud develops this subject and discusses the origin of this transposition of sensible qualities. At times he seems to suggest that words are what have an influence on the body, marking it and mortifying it until it is transformed or complies with them (somatic compliance). At other times he seems to suggest that the systematic repetition of the same feelings in the same spot of the body actually generates the fact that the speech acts make reference to them.

Both in hysterical conversion and in somatic disease there is the same process of transposition, by virtue of which it could be considered that in hysteria the transposition is generated from language to the body while in the somatic disease we move from the physical sensations and modifications towards language. Freud

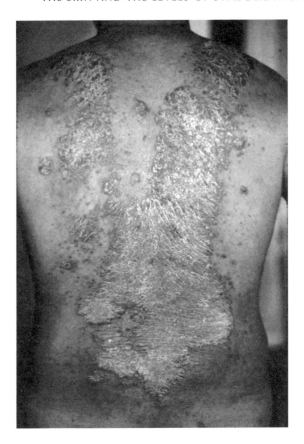

Figure 4.1 This patient, a long-distance driver, presents extended psoriasis plaques on his back. Although rubbing against the back of the seat can cause a chronic and reiterated trauma which, due to the Koebner phenomenon,[1] justifies its location, it is significant to point out that the patient said he felt responsibility for the passengers he was carrying, as well as their gaze, on his back. (By courtesy of Dr Javier Ubogui)

comes to the conclusion that both somatic sensations and speech acts extract their material from the same source, because in phylogeny the expression of the emotions by means of somatic reactions corresponded to functions which were originally adequate and full of meaning (Freud, 1883–1895). The point is that through this transposition of sensible qualities, the psychic and the somatic find each other and exercise a "reciprocal influence" (*Gemeinsamkeit*) on each other (Freud, 1905a).

TERM TO TERM CORRESPONDENCE

This establishes correspondences between pairs of opposite terms which are appropriate to one sensory organ and the oppositions appropriate to another sensory organ, as Rimbaud[2] does, for example, when speaking of the colour of the vowels (Anzieu, 1995). In patients with skin diseases this correspondence can be appreciated when they speak of a hole that progressively fills up when referring to a plaque of alopecia in which hairs start to appear, or when they speak of a "stain" that "turns on" or "turns off" when referring to a lesion of psoriasis that becomes inflamed or gets better. Here the luminal opposites turned on and turned off, typical of sight, correspond with the tactile opposites inflamed (hot) and not inflamed (cold).

CONSTANCY OF THE OBJECT

This incorporates into the same object (initially the mother) the different categories of sensations which are then recognised as emerging from her and not from different people. The perception of the unity of the object makes possible the acquisition of its constancy; it is the first consensus, in an etymological sense, between sensations (Anzieu, 1995).

   This subject is essential because in fragmented personalities, or in those who feel the danger of fragmentation when faced with the different aspects of splitting that they must maintain, it is usual for the function of union of sensations to be altered. This is the case with patients who become fragmented because they suffer from a sudden alternation of attachment and detachment, or have various different people involved in their upbringing. When they experience different people providing them with contradictory sensations, or the same person displaying incompatible emotions and modes of behaviour towards them, or having the same feeling directed towards two or more people between whom they are forced to choose, the most usual consequence is fragmentation. Faced with a lack of union of sensations and with the inability of the psyche to work through and integrate them, unification is achieved by means of the disease. As patients feel that their disorder accompanies them and will never leave them, they obtain from it the feelings of constancy and companionship that they lacked with significant people. This becomes evident in discourse, when they say that the disease "will never abandon them" or that it "has moved in permanently". Sometimes the disease is not what provides the feeling of unity; rather, it facilitates a feeling of fragmentation, lending itself as the receiver of this feeling. Instead of experiencing the madness of their feelings of fragmentation and depersonalisation, the patients project onto their lesions the different "parts" into which they feel themselves divided. According to the location of the disease, they will be liable to say: "this part is more rebellious"; "the problem is in my hands"; "I'm OK from here to here, but from here onwards I'm not well"; etc. And in this way, mediated by the look of others, they will be able to achieve a feeling of unity. What remains broken, cracked, fissured and divided into parts is the skin (there for all to see) and not the subject himself. The disease provides him with such strong sensations that they overshadow the rest, and it also awakens sensations in the environment (the look, horror, anxiety), thus facilitating projection. In turn, the visibility of the disease seeks to make the feeling of suffering indisputable: faced with the usual lack of understanding on the part of the other of the subject's own needs, he attempts an appeal to the other's visual perception (as in the dream taken up by Freud in Chapter 7 of *The Interpretation of Dreams:* "Father, don't you see I'm burning?") in order to make him react, and thus obtain consensus and acknowledgement (see Chapter 12).

LOGIC OF TIME AND SPACE

The logic of the sensible qualities makes way for a logic of forms:

- Empty and full
- Container and content
- Internal and external

This has to do with what Anzieu calls formal representations or transformation representations. They are so called because they are related not only to opposition and constancy but also to forms exposed to changes which can produce them or destroy them. For example, full and empty are two poles subject to a change which can make polarity disappear (when filling or emptying introduces the categories of half full or half empty in an evolution of "filling" or "emptying").

> A patient who was very dependent on his wife had separated from her; something he could not bear. Despite being separated, they used to meet to have sex, and he could not refuse because his job depended on her, since she was the one who had obtained it for him using political influences. The manifestations of psoriasis were a lot more intense on one half of his body than on the other, and in some parts, for example the glans, the division line was clearly visible, to the point that the limit between the sick skin and the healthy skin was a straight line which seemed to cut his sexual organs into two. The patient used to say, without con-sciously associating it with his lesions, that half of him was still with his wife and longing for her, and that he needed to be caressed by her but at the same time he felt resentful towards her because she had kept half of their home. Seeing his resistance to the corticoid treatment, the dermatologist prescribed a thermal bath with mud and algae. He was extremely satisfied with the use of the bath tub and the algae baths, because the water that surrounded his whole body and the action of the mucilage contained in the algae, which made his entire skin softer, provided him with a feeling of physical integration which he lacked. The disease started to change, though initially it did not disappear; rather, its location changed and lesions started to appear on his legs, where he had not had any lesions before. With the intention of making scientific and rational use of the placebo effect (Ulnik & Ubogui, 1998b), it was explained to him that the disease was now migrating towards his feet and that this could mean it was about to disappear. Very pleased with that explanation, the patient continued with his treatment, and the disease did indeed go into almost complete remission. In this way the patient, who lacked the ability to symbolise a process (such as that of "separat-ing" from his wife), incorporated this symbolic notion through what was happening on his body. This was achieved by means of an alternative medical treatment (the algae baths) which functioned as an envelope, thus facilitating the integration of the

parts of his body. His fears, awakened by the changes in his body, were resolved through recourse to a cure myth that incorporated the notion of process, because he imagined that his disease was indeed "disappearing". At the beginning of his analysis his discourse was full of expressions that indicated symbiosis, fragmentation and indiscrimination. For example: "She is 46, I am 54. *That's 100 years between us.*" "She has a project and thinks she will carry on with it, *but there are things that belong to both of us. . .* Watch it! The psoriasis is mine!" "*On the one hand,* I feel better. *On the other* it is spreading."

By the end of his treatment, his discourse had changed remarkably: "I've already got a bed, a fridge, a bookcase. *I am re-making myself.* I believe I am getting more satisfied with what's coming." "I am worried, but not anxious. I am more comfortable at work because I've worked to get where I am. The work I am doing is work I have been asked to do, I do it and I get recognition for it." "I have got rid of 'with everyone and for everyone'. I am re-building things: yesterday I met my children and we spent time talking about family things." "I used to complain about her turning me out of the house. Now I think it was her right to do it, it was her own place, not our place. Now I've got my own place and I protect it."

RELATIONSHIP LOGIC

Instead of opposing the terms themselves, this logic opposes the different ways in which these terms oppose each other. For example, similar-different: two terms can oppose each other due to their difference, their colour, their degree of a certain quality. That is to say this incorporates a third element according to which the opposition of the terms is developed.

Taking the acquisition of this capacity to discriminate as a starting point, the logic ceases to be binary, because two terms can be different in multiple attributes and similar in others. When a patient uses this capacity to assess his own state, he no longer uses the polarity "in a rash"-"not in a rash", and starts to notice differences in the state of his lesions. This allows him to realise that he is better even though he still has the same lesions. In this way he can say: "I am getting better, because although the lesions are still there, they are less pronounced, less red or look like the ones I had in the summer after my holidays, which bothered me less."

LOGIC OF TIME AND MOVEMENT

This introduces a thought which is not based exclusively on spatial representations, but also on the transformations that need time and lead to the introduction of a logic of movement. This kind of thought incorporates the notion of process or of becoming. The fact of first planning an action and then developing it in order to dispose of the object allows the subject to be aware of the notion of the *duration* of a time that goes by. The child learns from experience that objects which are far away from him require a longer time to reach: thus he begins to establish a relationship between space and time. Ultimately, the experience of a temporality capable of conceiving changes starts to emerge.

The acquisition of this capacity in patients boosts their feeling of trust and favours the continuity of treatments, because they come to understand that healing is a process: one which occurs progressively as they actively do certain things, and moreover, one for which they must cover a path. Likewise, it discourages the idealisation of alternative healers who promise magical solutions from one day to the next.

ABSTRACT LOGIC

This characterises logical thought, with conceptualisation and reasoning. Anzieu says that this kind of thought has two forms, one iconic and the other abstract, which he respectively relates to metaphor and metonymy. Although this kind of thought is not altogether explained in Anzieu's chart, it could be claimed that it is the most evolved, and that it constitutes the final stage in a sequence of progressive acquisitions which are connected with each other but can also work independently or in parallel.

Affects, the body and words

Piera Castoriadis-Aulagnier, using the concept of originary, defines a method of representation by means of a discourse that we experience as "word-thing-action". This activity of representation uses a pictogram that ignores the "image of word" and has as its exclusive material the "image of physical thing". She proposes a mode of psychic activity which is foreclosed from what is knowable but is nevertheless always in action, in a definitive way and for every subject: a type of psychic activity which constitutes a representative backdrop persisting in parallel to other more evolved kinds of psychic production (1988). In the same way as Ulnik (2000) and Zukerfeld (1992, 1999), Castoriadis-Aulagnier advances the co-existence of modes of functioning—both more primitive and more evolved—in the same subject, and even at the same time.

As for Anzieu, for Castoriadis-Aulagnier the psyche takes elements from the model of the functioning of the body and metabolises them into a completely heterogeneous material. *It is this process of metabolisation that is altered in psychosomatics.* Referring to primary violence, Castoriadis-Aulagnier says:

> The maternal word spills out a flow which carries and creates meaning and is ahead of the capacity of the *infans* to recognise its signification and to take it up on his own (. . .) the *infans* (. . .) lacks the possibility of making the significance of the statement his own (. . .) what has been 'heard' will inevitably be metabolised into a homogeneous material regarding the pictographic structure. [1988]

In fact, what goes on in psychosomatics is that a signification, a command, a message, an affect or a sensation undergoes a re-transcription to a material which is homogeneous with a structure (that for Castoriadis-Aulagnier would be the pictographic structure) and is heterogeneous with relation to the original characteristics of the said material, signifier, affect or sensation.

The problem arises in the process of metabolisation. This is sometimes regressive, such as a word or signification that is re-translated into a physical sensation ("I feel hurt by what you have said" appears as a bleeding lesion on the skin), and at other times it is like a rumination or a vicious circle, in which the signification covers a path which is initially processed regressively and then becomes progressive. An example would be when anxiety is re-translated into itching, and the itching is then processed through the mechanisms typical of the unconscious and begins to condense an enormous series of sensations and meanings, or suffers a process of fixation. In conclusion: affects and somatic sensations are treated as if they were words. In the work of Freud there are concepts which are useful in understanding the connection produced between physical innervations and words: the concepts of "judgement" and "primary judgement" in the *Project of psychology*, and the concept of "organ language" in the article "The Unconscious" are the most illustrative.

The mechanism of projection performs a fundamental role in the relationship that is established between the objects of the external world, the body, affects and words. Generally speaking, in the beginning there could be a syncretic fusion of thoughts, words, the body and the objects from the external world. The mechanism of projection could act as a pivot or hinge in the genesis of that syncretism; for example, when the Ego projects itself and becomes confused with the objects of the external world, or when the Ego introjects external perceptions that will have an influence upon the functioning of the body. This same mechanism of projection could act afterwards in the dissolution of that syncretic fusion of words, thoughts and things, because the gradual and discriminated projection of what has been previously introjected and confused could enable the construction and acceptance of reality.

The relationship between the body, words and things is exploited by the Shamans in their healing practices, and through them they obtain what Lévi-Strauss called "symbolic efficacy". "The symbolic efficacy could consist precisely of this inductive propriety that certain formally homologous structures could have with regard to each other; structures which are capable of constituting themselves with different materials at different levels of the living being: organic processes, unconscious psyche, reflexive thought" (Lévi-Strauss, 1958b).

Words, objects and the skin in film and in literature

The variety of levels referred to above can also be appreciated in film, painting, literature and other art forms. This may be the reason why Lévi-Strauss says that the poetic metaphor provides a familiar example of the inducing procedure that homologous structures themselves have. Although for him the use of the poetic metaphor does not allow us to exceed psyche, for Rimbaud the metaphor can be useful for changing the world.

With regard to art, Gombrich explains that in an Aztec sculpture of the god of rain, the mouth, which is a part of the body, is represented by serpents, which in turn embodied the strength of lightning. In tropical areas where the god was worshipped, rain was a matter of life or death, and the images not only related to magic and religion but were also the first form of writing. The sacred serpent in ancient Mexico would eventually evolve until it constituted a sign to express lightning, and in this way perhaps avert a storm (Gombrich, 1950). So an equivalence was established between lightning, serpents, lips and satisfaction of hunger by means of the harvest.

Another example of the inter-relation between levels can be seen in the film *Silkwood*. The main character (Meryl Streep) works at a nuclear power station in which radioactive plutonium is used. When her boyfriend leaves her and she is left alone, she becomes contaminated (we are led to believe that someone has put plutonium into her clothes) and then contaminates her own home, thus forcing the authorities at the station to subject her to a special bath in which her entire skin is cleaned with abrasives and blasted with water at high pressure. They then proceed to remove all the furniture from her home (the whole interior) and scrape the walls in order to eliminate the paint, which is also likely to be contaminated. Here the external scene expresses the internal scene: the paint of her home is scraped in the same way as her skin is scraped; she loses the internal contents of her home in the same way that she loses the love of her boyfriend. The scene of emptiness and desolation is both external and internal, and her home remains as neglected as she is herself. In turn, the internal contamination and the suspicion that her clothes were deliberately contaminated is a symbol of the way in which absence is experienced as the presence of something bad. We can see other similar examples in John Updike's novel *The Centaur* (1963).

Poets, through the use of metaphors, would appear to have smoothed the path between things and words. On the other hand, the images which are typical of one particular perceptive field are mixed in prose with those of others without that altering the coherence of the group, which, on the contrary, is remarkably embellished and enriched. However, the same permeability can also describe the path covered by the unconscious in order to produce effects in homologous systems.

Considering the fact that Updike himself suffers from psoriasis and is worried about what his skin looks and feels like, it is fascinating to see how his personal concern, which he reveals in the autobiographical book *Self Consciousness* (1989), is projected into this novel, first onto the skin of his characters and then onto the surface of things.

> The main and greater part of the garage was approached on an asphalt ramp as rough, streaked, gouged, flecked, and bubbled as a hardened volcanic flow. [Updike, 1963]

The author develops beautiful metaphors in order to describe affective states. In some the metaphoric function is intact and the distance between the terms being compared is evident.

> As the string of a helium balloon slips from a child's absent-minded fingers, so fear set Caldwell's mind floating free. [*ibid.*]

The key to comparison is in the expression, "as", which reveals the distance implicit within it. In contrast, when he says "fenders like corpses of turtles, bristling engines like disembodied hearts" (*ibid.*), although the comparison is conscious, which is evidenced by the word "like", what is not conscious is that "disembodied" and "corpses of turtles" are images that stem from Updike's own body, with scabs which are like shells and scales and strips of skin torn from his body, as he himself narrates in his book (see "At war with the skin" in *Self Consciousness*, 1989). The path between the body and things as well as that between things and the body is covered again and again:

> (. . .) for it seemed the cutters were biting not into a metal shaft but into a protruding nerve of his anatomy. [1963]

It is also remarkable the way faces, clothes, the hands, the floor, leaves, in brief, all the objects and parts of people's bodies are blemished in Updike's narrative. They would seem to be everywhere as a fan-shaped projection of the physical blemishes that distress both the real Updike and the one projected on to Peter, a young man with psoriasis who is one of the main characters in the novel.

As we were saying previously, words are things, but in Updike's work things are also words. In the following paragraph, Peter's father is trying to move his car, which is bogged down in the middle of the snow.

> The wheel slips. Several times as he drapes the cumbersome jacket of links around the tire, the tire lazily turns and shucks its coat of mail like a girl undressing. (. . .) In the underworld beneath the car the muted stink of rubber and the parched smells of rust and gas and grease seem breathed syllables of menace. [*ibid.*]

In *The Centaur* there is a process of fusion at its highest expression between the things of the world, the body and words. It is all a preamble to the moment at which Peter, the young and shy main character, is to show his psoriasis to Penny, with whom he is in love and from whom he fears rejection. First there are physical descriptions: Mark, a friend of Peter's, has a reddened face and a "body as slippery as an amphibian's". From Mark's body the story passes to the body of the group: a multitude, a crowd of bodies squashed together about to leave the school, where it is hot, for the exterior, where it is snowing. In the passage from the interior to the exterior a false linking is produced through a bridge word, which in this case is the word "crowd". The author, talking about the people going out of the school, exclaims "What a crowd!", and then, as if continuing with the idea:

> What a crowd of tiny flakes sputters downward in the sallow realm of the light above the entrance door! Atoms and atoms and atoms and atoms. (. . .) The snow seems only to exist where light strikes it. (. . .) The town of white roofs seems a colony of deserted temples; they feather together with distance and go gray, melt. Shale Hill is invisible. [1963]

We should keep in mind the situation, namely that Peter, who has psoriasis, is in love with Penny. As he fears that she will reject him on discovering his psoriasis, he decides to "confess" his disease, but not with words but by displaying himself. What should develop in the field of language has transferred to the field of the gaze. And in the story the transposition of sensible qualities is developed: the crowd obviously formed by people suddenly becomes, in the passage from the interior to the exterior, a flurry of snowflakes which are compared to atoms. It is as if the author had projected first onto his characters and then onto the landscape the feeling of disintegration of existence experienced by a patient when all his subjective values are reduced to nothing as he faces another who will judge and reject him due to his outward appearance. When the patient shows himself, he anticipates what is to come: the passage from existence for what one *is* to existence for what is *seen*, like the snow, which seems "only to exist where light strikes it" (*ibid.*).

Finally, the anticipation of rejection, abandonment and loneliness is transferred to the town: "Shale Hill is invisible". What happens to the town is what happens to the Ego-body of Updike and his representative in the novel, Peter. Immediately afterwards, the personalisation of things takes place, and a series of sentimental scenes is displayed:

> The streetlights strung along the pike make a forestage of brightness where the snowfall, compressed and expanded by the faintest of winds, like an actor postures—pausing, plunging. Upward countercurrents suspend snow, which then with the haste of love flies downward to gravity's embrace;[3] the alternations of density conjure an impression of striding legs stretching upward into infinity. The storm walks. The storm walks but does not move on. [*ibid.*]

Things are introjected into the body—still an indefinite body—of a universal subject that is the storm itself. The environment and the subject are one, not unlike what happens to the Truman character (Jim Carrey) in the film *The Truman Show*, in the scene when it is only raining on him.

> Those who remain inside the school are ignorant of the weather, and yet like fish taken up by a swifter ocean current they sense some change. The atmosphere in the auditorium accelerates. Things are not merely seen but burst into vision. [*ibid.*]

The problem is that after the alternation between things and people, both get lost: all that remains is the environment and the omnipresent look. The same process that occurs in the people at school and in the snowy environment would seem to occur in the fantasy of Peter: while brooding about how to show his skin to Penny, who "looks at him with eyes whose green seems newly minted", he turns his red back on the crowd.

> Secret knowledge of his spots obsesses him; should he tell her? Would it, by making her share the shame, wed them inextricably; make her, by bondage of pity, his slave? Can he, so young, afford a slave? On fire with such cruel calculations, he turns his red back on the crowd shoving and sluggishly interweaving around the soft-drink bin. When an iron hand seizes his arm above the elbow and brutally squeezes (. . .) [*ibid.*]

In the same way as we observe these phenomena in art's different expressions, when a patient experiences an affective state, he might also experience the psychic pain or the terms of a psychic conflict as concrete things. This leads both to the "physical expression" of conflicts and to the projection of physical ideas and sensations on to concrete objects of external reality. In these cases it is usual for the disease to worsen or to perpetuate itself because it is lending "somatic compliance" to an unconscious idea or to an affect that cannot be developed.

In the treatments, symptoms, complaints, devices, etc. that the patient associates with his disease, attempts are made to define the boundaries of the body or to acquire symbolisation categories that can allow access to a higher level. For example, the use of dressings, plaques, creams or mud, apart from satisfying fixations of the drive (mud as excrement with which the subject is allowed to smear himself), allows the patients to play with the categories of open-closed, hard-soft, etc, which would otherwise not be clearly established. A scabby and impenetrable lesion can bring some relief to a patient's experience of having an open body, and can permit him the acquisition of the opened-closed category. Likewise, anxiety regarding the orifices of the body can determine a patient's pathological behaviour concerning the location of his disease: for example, the appearance of itching and the manipulations of scratching and self-infliction in the places where the skin enters the body and becomes a mucous membrane or simply stays out of sight (ears, genitals, etc.).

The personalisation of the lesions or of the disease, as well as the disease being chronic or incurable, will foster in the patient the acquisition of an object which has the quality he longs for: *constancy*. In this way he will not have to face the notion of absence. The disease also provides sensitive polarities of differing levels of complexity which will be useful in emerging from confusing or ambiguous experiences in which differences cannot be characterised.

Dundee was a schizoid patient whom the other patients in the psychotherapy group used to call "Crocodile Dundee" because he always wore a brimmed hat and safari or camping clothes, despite the fact that he lived in the middle of the city of Buenos Aires. Dundee explained his mode of dress by claiming: "I reside where I don't live," which meant that although he lived in the centre of Buenos Aires, he resided in the Argentine south, among lakes and mountains, which was where he wanted to live and where he could picture himself living. Clinically he was not psychotic. His performance at work and at university was acceptable; besides, he was conscious of the fact that he lived in Buenos Aires and not in the south.

As a consequence of his dissociation, he experienced enormous difficulty in feeling. When the psoriasis began, it extended until it had covered his entire body with thick scabs. In spite of his condition, he continued to spend his holidays in the south, where he would go climbing in the mountains and liked to stay in the middle of an uninhabited area in a hut (*tapera*: a word used to refer to huts that have been abandoned by gauchos or by Indians). When he decided to seek medical help, his condition was so serious that any movement, even the slightest movement made with his body, caused him pain or opened up cracks in the folds of his skin. In this way Dundee provided himself with qualities of sensitivity that he could not perceive otherwise.

He was prescribed a treatment with methotrexate, as well as individual and group psychotherapy. When he began to improve, he gave me Robert Fisher's book *The Knight in Rusty Armor*, which is about a man who had a suit of armour he could not take off, which was related to his loss of sensitivity. Feeling sad because he could lose his son and his wife, he started to cry, and the tears caused the armour to rust, disintegrate and fall to pieces in the same way as Dundee's scales of epidermis (Figures 4.2, 4.3 and 4.4).

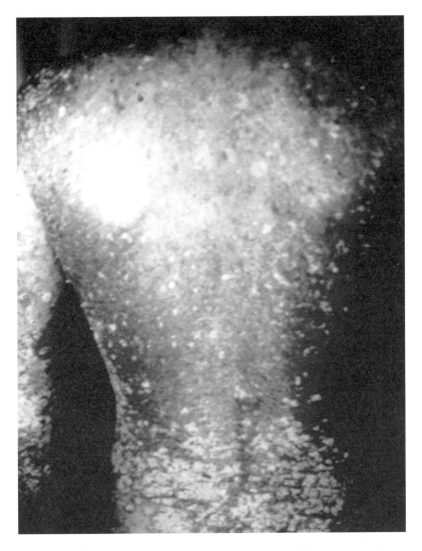

Figure 4.2 Dundee (back) when he started treatment (by courtesy of Dr Javier Ubogui)

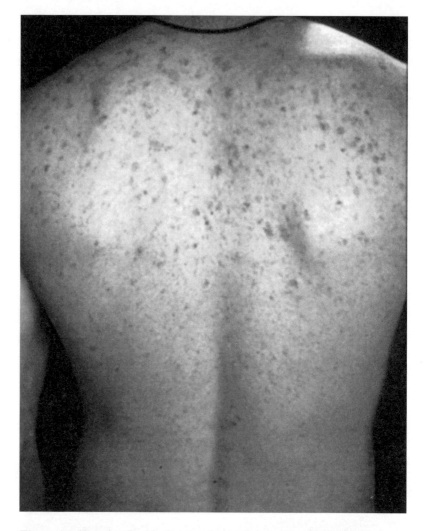

Figure 4.3 Dundee (back) after treatment (by courtesy of Dr Javier Ubogui)

The experience of treating Dundee made me recall the analysis of autistic children mentioned by Frances Tustin. According to Tustin, in order to be born psychologically, the child must carry out primary integrations of his sensations, to be able later to recognise his mother as external to himself, and progressively recognise the external

Figure 4.4 Cover of the book that Dundee gave me: The Knight in Rusty Armor

world and its boundaries (Tustin, 1981). One of the first integrations that must be carried out is that between hard and soft sensations. When there is a dichotomy between a soft Me and a hard Not-Me, the soft Me is excessively vulnerable (*ibid.*). This leads the child (and the patient with a skin disease) to carry with him something hard, or to develop obsessive defences in order to protect himself from the experience of an excessive vulnerability: "[. . .] these children are concerned with having an "extra piece" in their bodies. This piece must always be hard." (*ibid.*) For that reason many psychotic children take hard toys to bed instead of soft ones. The example of the crab which protects itself by getting into the hard shell of another creature shows the need for intrusive identification. In the case of patients such as Dundee, the extra hard piece that protects against the sensation of softness is not an external object; instead it is literally "carried" in the form of hardness, scabs, and swelling of the skin.

Just as in autistic children behaviour is linked to, and regulated by, the functioning of the parts, rhythms and organs of the body, which are experienced as fixated, inanimate and mechanical objects with their own laws (Tustin, 1981), in some chronic patients life remains regulated by and linked to the functioning of their somatic disease. The difference is that in these cases the idea that it is something mechanical and inanimate is modified. Perhaps Tustin describes it in this way because the psychotic children she saw liked to take hard objects to bed, or were interested in the mechanical functioning of things. In the patients I am referring to, it is an object that feels alive, namely the disease, although it is mechanical and capricious regarding its "mood" to evolve. These patients usually say that their lives are regulated by psoriasis, as if this was a capricious and out-of-control monster which has ended up controlling their lives. What is nevertheless clear is that it is a regulation that "lacks the necessary adequacy and flexibility to deal with human situations and with people" (Tustin, 1981).

Notes

1. The Koebner phenomenon is when any trauma on the prone skin of a person suffering from psoriasis will produce a lesion of psoriasis on the traumatized spot.

2. Arthur Rimbaud was a French poet of the 19th century whose work was characterized, among other things, by establishing a symbolistic analogy between nature and subjective moods.

3. Please notice the need for embrace.

CHAPTER FIVE

"It works for me": symbolic efficacy and the placebo effect

The remedy and the disease

In 2000 the National Psoriasis Foundation (NPF) in the USA published a book containing a selection of comments sent by its members between 1991 and 1999 to a column called "It works for me" in the Foundation's bulletin. The surprising fact about these comments is that the patients testify to having obtained favourable results by using the most varied and peculiar range of household products, and original combinations of elements intended for cleaning, for veterinarian use or for cosmetic use, as well as lubricating products, and so on, that they used for the treatment of their psoriasis.

In an earlier paper (Ulnik & Ubogui, 1998b, p. 117) we stated that the placebo effect can be defined as the difference between the action expected from a drug or healing procedure according to its physical or pharmacological effects, and the action that actually occurs. With this definition we make clear that any pharmacological substance or any physical procedure—even the most powerful—can have a placebo effect which is added to the expected action.

The "It works for me" column is one of the most eloquent documents on the extraordinary power of the placebo effect on psoriasis. As an original testimony, it is study material that can be understood in the light of the conclusions mentioned in Chapter 4 on the levels of symbolisation and the encounter between the psychic and the somatic levels. However, in order to provide a more complete approach, I will now mention certain ideas from Lévi-Strauss's book

Structural Anthropology which explain some of the intervening mechanisms in non-traditional cures of certain diseases.

In "The sorcerer and his magic" and "The effectiveness of symbols", Lévi-Strauss helps us consider why patients can find these kinds of practices effective. The relationship that primitive people have with the witch doctor is reproduced in the relationship that modern people have with the doctor, but it can also be reproduced regarding the "remedy". We will use the word "remedy" because the elements used by the patients are not always medication or drugs, but are instead considered by them as forms of treatment used to remedy the problem. In this way, we could paraphrase Lévi-Strauss (1958a) and say that the efficacy of a "remedy" depends on three factors:

- The person who provides it believes in the efficacy of the element that has been provided.
- The sick person believes in the power of what he or she is being provided with.
- The trust and the strength of collective opinion form a kind of gravitational field in the heart of which "treatment" is organised.

In the case of "It works for me", the doctor and the sick person are one and the same, and the publication of the bulletin seeks to provide the favourable intervention of collective opinion represented by members of the NPF. At first glance, patients are suggesting that others follow their example, but unconsciously their intention is to make a singular practice public and to obtain consensus in order to legitimise it.

The condition of the disease is a state of dismantled experiences and sensations which are hard to control. In the face of this, the existence of a system formed by a coherent theory of cure is like an oasis in the dessert. The system, any system, is always less anxiety-provoking than disorder and the lack of all systems.

> [. . .] the value of the system will no longer be based on real cures which benefit isolated individuals; rather, it will base itself on the feeling of security provided to the group by the founding myth of

the cure and within the popular system according to which, on this basis, its universe will be reconstructed. [Lévi-Strauss, 1958a][1]

For example, Lévi-Strauss presents the system of the Koshimo Shamans:

> Every disease is a man: boils and swellings, itching and scabs, spots and coughing, and consumption and scrofula; and also this: constriction of the vesicle and stomach pains. . . As soon as we have succeeded in capturing the soul of a disease, which is a man, the disease, which is a man, then dies; its body disappears within our interior. [*ibid.*]

The shamanistic complex is organised around two poles: one is formed by the intimate experience of the Shaman and the other by collective consensus. This consensus is more important than success, because the essential problem would instead revolve around the existing relationship between remedy and healing. It could be added that another important factor is the relationship between remedy and disease, because although the disease might not get better, it does interact with the remedy both in its physical evolution and in its symbolic significance. This interaction leads to what Lévi-Strauss calls "abreaction of the disorder" (*ibid.*).

Collective conscience and symbolic efficacy

In "The effectiveness of symbols", Lévi-Strauss proposes that the Shaman's song and his manipulations constitute a "psychological manipulation" of the sick organ (Lévi-Strauss, 1958b). The expression "psychological manipulation" suggests an essential idea: *the psychological aspect can act over the physical aspect by means of "manipulation"*. In witchcraft, the "hands" that carry out this manipulation are the operations, spells, songs, actions and objects of the Shaman, and all of them are included within a weave or myth that constitutes a system in which the organs and the disease are also included. In "It works for me" the same manipulation takes place; the difference is that in this case there is no Shaman, but a group or collective conscience, which is constituted by the members of the NPF. As an example of this, please consider the following comments:

Estar and mineral oil for dry skin
Please *advise psoriasis sufferers that Estar* [OTC tar product] *is a wonderful product.*[2] My legs were in a horrible state, and they are now clearing up. The psoriasis on my arms cleared completely. I also use a lot of plain mineral oil to combat drying of the skin. [NPF, 2000, p. 16]

Jergens moisturizer
As a loyal NPF, I must tell of my success.[3] I have been on methotrexate with great satisfaction, but my knees and elbows still gave me problems. After seeing Jergens Advanced Therapy Lotion advertising—"It heals from the inside out"—I decided to try it. I have been using it over three months with great results. [*ibid.*, p. 17]

In the second example it can be observed that the patient feels he is putting his loyalty at stake by means of his testimony. In addition, thanks to the remedy, he acquires the sensation of discriminated internal and external spaces, as well as the sensation of a direction of cure: "from the inside out".

Coming back to "The effectiveness of symbols", Lévi-Strauss shows how the myth and the action constructed and carried out by the Shaman both try to abolish in the spirit of the sick person the distinction that separates the mythical, physical and physiological universes, the external world and the internal world, thus tracing a kind of affective geography (Lévi-Strauss, 1958b).

In the same way as the shamanistic cure consists of making thinkable a situation given initially in affective terms and making acceptable for the spirit the pains that the body refuses to tolerate, the "methods" of these members of the NPF try to transmit, through the concrete elements of everyday life (soaps, oils, food, milks, minerals, etc), a "physical manipulation" of affective and psychological disorders which have been projected and "placed", so to speak, on the skin. At the same time, and without being aware of it, the patients carry out a "psychological manipulation" of their physical lesions. The sequence could be as follows: the soaps, oil, milk, lubricants, etc. bring a physical action which is conscious, and they have a psychological meaning which is often unconscious: of softness, maternal presence, caresses, cleaning of guilt and sins, etc.

Through their physical action they act upon cracks, dryness, wounds and scaling of the skin, and through their psychological action they produce a soothing, integrating, unifying or containing and limiting effect on the unconscious experiences of fragmentation, lack of love or dilution of identity which are "placed" and hidden within the cracks of the skin (see Figure 5.1).

The relationship between a corticoid and a lesion is external to the sick person's spirit, whereas the relationship between a bath and his disease is internal to his spirit because the patient feels dirty and unclean due to his disease. See the following example:

Household bath oil
Two teaspoons of olive oil and a large glass of milk added to the bath water is an old remedy called "Sulzberger's household bath oil", according to a dermatology medical textbook. It can make the skin soft (benefit) and the bathtub slippery (risk). [NPF, 2000, p. 2]

Thanks to the representations prevailing in the sick person's conscience, the "remedy" has a real effect which is halfway between the organic world and the psychic world. Its ingestion, application or provision turns out to be a concrete operation that goes through

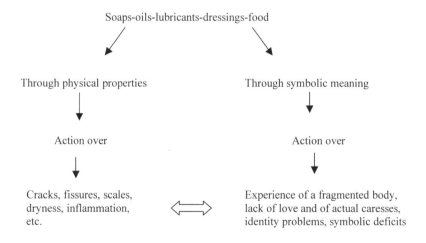

Figure 5.1 Physical properties and their symbolic meaning

the screen of consciousness without encountering any obstacles in order to provide a direct message to the unconscious. This operation is not only carried out by means of words, although it certainly is carried out by means of symbols, "that is to say, significant equivalents of meaning, which belong to an order of reality different from the latter" (Lévi-Strauss, 1958b). In the last example, adding milk to the bath provides a maternal component to the action of having a bath. The allusion to what is slippery, even if it is a real characteristic of the bath oil, nevertheless refers, perhaps, to the insecurity with which the patient was held during childhood.

The homologous structures

In the unconscious psychic aspect the myth of the Shaman has a structure which is analogous to the one desired at the level of the body, and "the symbolic efficacy could consist precisely of this inductive propriety that certain structures could have which are formally homologous to each other and which are capable of constituting themselves, with different materials at different levels of the living being, in organic processes, unconscious psyche and reflexive thought" (Lévi-Strauss, 1958b). In the following examples we can see the spontaneous attempt made by patients with psoriasis to apply "remedies" using well-known elements of their everyday life which have analogous structures to the affected functions or parts of their bodies.

WD-40 helps my arthritis pain temporarily. [NPF, 2000, p. 11]

WD-40 is a lubricant used for any mechanical device when its hinges and gears are noisy or stuck. Every person suffering from arthritis knows that articulations are like the gears and hinges of the body, and that pain is added to the subjective sensation of lack of lubricant or "grease" which is necessary for the articulation to move easily. It is evident that the WD-40 applied topically cannot have an antalgic or lubricant effect on the articulation. However, it provided relief to this patient due to the association between the affected part of the body and the function of the element applied.

Use Crazy Glue to seal cuts that don't heal. [ibid.]

Crazy Glue is a kind of glue, and apart from proving useful to this patient in order to join the edges of a cut in the skin, it also proposes the idea of sticking together and uniting parts, an idea which is necessary in order to alleviate the internal sensations of a fragmented body.

It could be claimed that we are talking about a real, visible and tangible disease, which causes a magnitude of suffering that only the sufferers themselves can account for. In view of the reality of the disease, referring to psychological components both of the signs and symptoms of the disease and of the remedies used to treat it would seem to be a denial of the disease. However, we could say, along with Lévi-Strauss that ". . . the traumatic power of a given situation cannot result from its intrinsic characteristics but instead from the capacity certain events—which emerge in an appropriate psychological, historical, and social context—have of inducing an affective crystallisation that takes place in the mould of a pre-existent structure" (Lévi-Strauss, 1958b).

We will now analyse some examples of patients' testimonies taken from "The best of It works for me".

Keywords and the signifier as "remedy"

Sometimes certain words used by the sick person turn out to be the key to understanding what is at stake:

Shampoo soak
Neutrogena T/Gel shampoo brought so much improvement to the scalp and hands of one NPF member that she added two capfuls to her nightly bath. "I find my psoriasis much improved, no more itching, and with a *healthy glow. My dermatologist is very pleased.*[4] The most amazing part is that I could never use tar products before. I hope they never discontinue T/Gel shampoo!" [NPF, 2000, p. 4]

This patient is oriented towards the scopic desire of the other, and that is why she does things emphasising the acquisition of a "healthy glow". The dermatologist who is pleased embodies the other at whom her actions are directed. She has probably had experiences either of abandonment or of attachment followed by detachment:

relationships and pleasurable attitudes alternating abruptly with sudden interruptions. That might be the reason why she emphasises the wish that the product which does her good may never be discontinued. She has included this product in her evening bath, turning it into an element of her environment with which she wraps herself every evening, feeling "immersed" in it.

The following example shows how the name of the "remedy" has a value of signifier that satisfies one of the patient's needs (in this case the need to be kissed) which is hidden under the idea of moisturising:

Olive oil moisturizer and tar
My regular moisturizer, which I have used for eight years, is called Kiss My Face, purchased from the health store. It has olive oil, aloe vera, plus other good ingredients, and I apply this after my oil bath. It's all time-consuming but works. [*ibid.*, 2000, p. 26]

In other cases, a connecting thread of meaning is observed between the medium in which the element chosen as "remedy" is usually used and the organ or part of the body to which it is applied. In the following example there is an evident association between the udders of the cows and the patient's own breasts.

Bag balm
I recently tried "Bag balm" ointment on my psoriasis at the recommendation of my husband, who heard it mentioned on a radio show as being an excellent treatment. For those of you who don't know what this is (as I didn't), it is an antiseptic ointment used *on cows' udders* to prevent chapping, abrasions, windburn and sunburn. Apparently it has been around for years and can be purchased in a farm and tractor store (for those of you who live in rural communities). (. . .) I have also used it *underneath my breasts*.[5] [*ibid.*, p. 28]

Another similar example is that of a woman who puts on anthralin (a substance which stains) with disposable gloves "like those used in restaurants". Then she puts on washing-up liquid to clean off the anthralin. The association between restaurants and the washing-up liquid submerges an alien element (the anthralin) within a well-known universe (the kitchen).

Identity problems

The methods used can "resolve" identity problems such as the feeling of having a double personality, sexual identity difficulties, or depersonalisation and fantasies of becoming someone else.

Example of double personality

Shaved head
When I did PUVA, it was necessary for me to shave my head so that the light could get to the scalp. I have never regretted shaving my head. I keep my hair as short as possible because it is so easy to medicate, oil and shampoo the scalp. My wig is such a lifesaver. I can wash my head and in a few minutes it's dry. Put on the wig and I'm ready to go. [*ibid.*, p. 12]

We can see that the manoeuvre of shaving the head is something coherent and sensible, as the patient is receiving phototherapy treatment. However, the interpretations of her behaviour do not attempt to question the usefulness of what patients do; rather, they attempt to reveal their unconscious meaning. For example, it is understandable that the patient shaves her head and wears a wig, but her insistence on the fact that she has never regretted doing it and that she considers her wig to be a lifesaver is quite striking. The way in which she prepares to go out with the wig suggests an identity "outwards" which is dissociated from the "inwards" identity of her home.

Permission to be a child and to play

A day at the beach
Playing in the ocean—nothing beats two days at the beach in the sun and salt water for clearing away scales. [*ibid.*, p. 10]

Metamorphosis

Coconut oil conditioner
I have been using Palmer's Coconut Oil Formula. It has a pleasant smell. I have no scales and my scalp is clean. You don't need coverings, etc. Just apply it—keep it on a day or two—don't

put too much on. Then wash your hair. *It took one week to see my transformation.*[6] [*ibid.*, p. 12]

PROJECTIVE IDENTIFICATION AND REVERSAL INTO THE OPPOSITE:

Inner strength

Here's something that works for me. Whenever I start feeling really blue about having psoriasis, I find someone, generally a stranger, who has perfect, unblemished skin. Then I just observe them for a while. They never notice their skin, or touch it, or think about it. They take it with a grain of salt, never realizing things could be quite different. It reminds me of the good old days when my skin was similar. I become more serene just knowing I'm a wiser, stronger person because of living with psoriasis. I feel a silent sense of security knowing I faced a difficult situation and found the strength to persevere. [*ibid.*, p. 34]

Observing someone without psoriasis reminds her of herself without psoriasis when she was younger. She watches him for a while and manages to continue to be herself, but at the same time to be equal to someone else. Then she takes over the narcissistic feeling of the other, but nevertheless maintains her own awareness of suffering from psoriasis. With both identities she manages to control her depression and re-establish her lost narcissism.

PHYSICAL FRAGMENTATION

Mineral oil

I like to moisturize *my scalp and the rest of me*[7] at the same time. Add one or two tablespoons of mineral oil to a bathtub full of hot water. Then soak for about 20 minutes, keeping your scalp under water as much as possible. [*ibid.*, p. 25]

This testimony shows how useful the bath is for providing an experience of unity to anyone who feels divided into parts. Please notice that the patient manages to feel he is "one" thanks to the chronological simultaneity of the moisturising of his "parts": the scalp and the rest of himself.

Shaving and MG217
I've had psoriasis on my legs since 1981 following a skiing accident and a skin graft. I've tried most everything and have had excellent medical care, but the past three months have been a miracle for me. My legs have almost cleared following this routine. I use an electric razor on my legs every other day, and after my daily shower I apply MG217 with Jojoba. [*ibid.*, p. 23]

The patient tries to eliminate something related to the graft: with the shaver he displaces onto the hairs (which can be eliminated) the feeling of strangeness that comes from the graft accounting for his wound (something which cannot be eliminated).

SEXUAL IDENTITY AND ENVELOPE-CONTAINER

Occlusion for legs
I work in a professional field where suits, dresses and skirts are required, no pants allowed. Having moderate psoriasis on my knees and lower legs creates a problem. Recently, I have been diligently putting an ointment at night followed by Saran Wrap [Author's note: Saran Wrap is a piece of plastic for wrapping food]. This has helped me reduce the thickness. Then I apply the makeup to my psoriasis so that it blends to my natural leg colour (or as close as possible). Then I put on two pairs of nylons. I cut the waistband on the first pair to reduce pressure. I then feel comfortable going out into the business world. [*ibid.*, p. 20]

This is a woman who has to cope with the business world. In that world she cannot wear trousers—thus pointing towards sexual differences—and she dislikes this because she surely feels that in such an environment she has to "wear the pants" just like men do. Her feeling of lack of support in that environment is replaced by a series of artificial envelopes: Saran Wrap, makeup, two pairs of nylons. In the end she does not wear trousers, but it is as if she did, because the trousers are in fact replaced by all the envelopes she puts on her legs.

Construction of a boundary and dialectics of contact with others

Water repellent cream

For my feet and hands, my pharmacist recommended Kerodex 71 (a barrier cream), a non-greasy, invisible, water-repellent cream, which enables me to swim and do water exercises without excess peeling. I apply two applications on my hands and feet before going into the pool. For bathing, I apply one application. I have had such good results that I want to share this with others. [*ibid.*, p. 16]

While she emphasises the need for a barrier and a repellent, she simultaneously expresses the wish to share this information with everyone, and to mix with others in the water. It is precisely because of this fusional desire to share things with everyone that she later has to reinforce the function of barrier-boundary that repels and is waterproof.

The meaning of diets and nutrition

Because of its importance, the subject of diets might almost deserve a whole chapter. It has not been demonstrated that there exists a diet which cures psoriasis, but in truth, the contrary has not been demonstrated either. What is clear is that there is no single diet which is equally useful for all patients, and that testimonies of successful results come from completely different diets.

In "It works for me" we can read testimonies of successful results obtained through the implementation of diets which either prescribe or forbid one or more of the following elements: sour food, alcohol, almonds, apple juice, bacon, bananas, barley, lentils, meat in general, red meat, dark rice, butter, tinned food, cheese, chocolate, citrus fruits, liver oil, dairy products, coffee, corn, aubergines, all kinds of fibre, fish oil, folic acid, fried food, Gotu Kola, green peppers, honey, ice-cream, Metamucil, salmon, selenium, potatoes, yoghurt, vitamins, zinc supplements, etc. The variety is so great and so irrational that the phenomenon deserves a psychological approach.

In the organism there exist two forms of activity which constantly oscillate between each other: one of them can be called "incorporation within oneself" and the other "ejection from oneself". The first activity—incorporation within oneself—involves a process of metabolising or transforming what has been incorporated, in order for it to become homogeneous with the interior or with what belongs to the individual. The second activity—ejection from oneself—involves a process of expulsion that ends with the denial, the oblivion, the disavowal or the projection of the existence of what has been ejected. Breathing and eating are two key examples: incorporation within oneself could be comparable to the action of inhaling or eating, while ejection from oneself could be comparable to exhaling, spitting, vomiting or defecating.

As both the visual aspect and the tactile and painful sensations that psoriasis can produce are disagreeable, the patient wants to eject the disease from himself. The first way of doing so is by thinking "This isn't mine, it has nothing to do with me, it comes from outside." If it comes from outside, it must come from something toxic, something external which is bad for the patient and which has been put into him. The most elementary and easy representation of this is food. "If I'm like this it's because of something I've eaten: something in my diet, which of course isn't part of me. If I stop incorporating it, it won't be inside me any more (because it doesn't come from me but from the outside) and I'll get better."

On the other hand, watching the skin that is opened up, torn or cracked causes the certainty we normally experience about the external boundary of the body, and its function of protective barrier against stimuli, to weaken. This barrier has to do with the skin functions of permeability and non-permeability, integrity, protection against pain, regulating temperature, general sensitivity, capacity to cause pleasure and pain, etc. With an undefined or altered awareness of boundaries, preoccupation with conservation of the internal world and avoidance of the external world considerably increases. In consequence, it is hardly surprising that apprehensions regarding food—a paradigm of "the external world" which is incorporated and the residues of which are eliminated—should appear.

Thus the prescription of diets, in particular for patients whose sensation of physical boundaries is more altered, is almost religiously accepted. The word "religiously" was not chosen by chance, as the process of eliminating from the interior what is considered to be toxic or dirty, and of avoiding what is potentially toxic or is categorised as unclean in the external world, is assimilated by the patients to a process of purification which is very similar to those of certain religious customs and ceremonials.

Just as diets prescribe what should not be eaten, thus contributing to the feeling of detoxification and purification, they also prescribe what should be eaten: generally foods with "natural" characteristics, which are considered to be pure. They sometimes satisfy the fantasy of providing an element which patients feel they lack.

In addition, the disease is something that evolves in a way the will cannot control and that pertains to the body. Diets generate the illusion of exercising mastery over the body by means of what is ingested and expelled. The control that cannot be exercised over the evolution of the disease is displaced towards control over food. Many doctors, and particularly alternative healers, use the resource of the diet to exercise control over their patients and to be present every day of their lives through the action of eating. Let us look at some examples:

Natural foods
Cut out sugar, dairy, red meat, acidic foods; eat only natural, whole foods. [NPF, 2000, p. 10]
   I found out that dairy products and pork cause my psoriasis to flare. [*ibid.*, p. 12]

Radical diet
I am happy to report that I have made some radical, but easy, shifts in my diet in the last month and my psoriasis virtually disappeared. I have been eating more fresh vegetables and subsequently less meats and canned foods. But mostly I think it is the addition of many more grains to my diet [a long description of cereals and food for each of the meals follows]. [*ibid.*, p. 36]

Final reflections on the placebo effect

Psoriasis, like so many chronic diseases, awakens in the patient the following questions: Why me? What I have I done to deserve this? What has caused this disease? Alternative healers provide answers which attempt to make the sufferer's situation thinkable in terms which accord with his imaginary world (Lévi-Strauss, 1958a). The more the theory they propose coincides with the beliefs patients have about the functioning of their own bodies, the greater the "symbolic efficacy" (Lévi-Strauss, 1958b) of treatment and the stronger its placebo effect. When healers use substances which have a pharmacological action, placebo effect is added to the action of these substances: placebo effect is the result of all the actions and explanations with which they accompany the actual taking of the substances.

Psoriasis is not only a skin disease. It is also a kind of suffering which is usually accompanied by beliefs that depend on the unconscious psyche, the family history and the social environment of each patient. The beliefs held by the patient about the way in which his body functions and the pathogenesis of his disease have an influence upon the acceptance or rejection of treatments, which is an essential factor in the cure of the disease and in the production of the placebo effect.

Although the actions of many healers are to be condemned, it should nevertheless be admitted that they use the same placebo effect that the doctor uses: less ethically, but sometimes more effectively. The doctor usually accepts the strength of placebo in studies of double blind clinical trials, but in everyday clinical work, in which he defines placebo as an inactive substance, the connotation of non-authenticity plays down one of the essential ingredients of therapeutic power: conviction.

Placebo effect in a wider sense is an aggregated benefit which can depend not only on the conviction with which the doctor handles it and on the patient's faith in the doctor, but also on the symbolic efficacy that a therapeutic procedure has within the imaginary and unconscious world of the patient. Placebo effect can be handled ethically and with a rational approach. Psoriasis is a disease which often presents a need to choose between many possible treatments, and working in interdisciplinary teams is useful in determine which of those treatments might have a greater placebo effect on each particular patient.

Notes

1. Translator's note: all the quotations taken from Lévi-Strauss's book have been translated into English from the Spanish version of *Structural Anthropology*.
2. My emphasis.

3. My emphasis.
4. My emphasis.
5. My emphasis
6. My emphasis.
7. My emphasis.

CHAPTER SIX

Reflections on attachment

My own interest in the theory of attachment stems from my clinical experience with psoriasis patients. Plaque Psoriasis is a chronic inflammatory scaly skin condition. The inflamed skin acquires a red colour (erythema) while the cells reproduce, migrating from the basal layer to the surface with a speed that does not allow them the necessary time to mature and form a cohesive layer, thus generating the permanent development of thick dry scales which can barely adhere to the surface and have a silvery appearance. Patients usually have outbreaks of the disease after key significant episodes, among which separations—due to divorce, migration or the death of loved ones—occupy a very important place.

In keeping with the aspect of separations, it has been observed that patients can show an extraordinary dependence on the therapist, or in contrast, a tendency to become detached, to want to get away or suddenly "disappear" from treatment at the first opportunity that presents itself, which could be anything from a holiday to a long weekend or a change in the schedule. In the same way, they may come back to treatment after a while as if nothing has happened, displaying a trusting and friendly attitude and without accounting for or making any reference to their absence, even if it has been quite lengthy.

Another very common characteristic is that of establishing symbiotic relationships in which separation is inconceivable. This kind of relationship can develop with their partners, parents, siblings, or any other significant person from whom they cannot become differentiated.

It would seem that "in the same way as the germinal cells of the skin need adherence to the mesenchyma in order to be able to grow and differentiate from it as they start to distance themselves from it, so we human beings also need attachment to objects in order to be able to grow up and mature. What is more, we too become differentiated as we are gradually able to separate ourselves from them. If we break away at a time that is not appropriate, or if we cannot separate within an adequate time, it is certain that we will not succeed in developing well and differentiating successfully from the aspects of our self and our life that have to do with the skin" (Ulnik, 1987b, p. 194). In this paper it is stated that the aspects of our life that have to do with the skin are:

- A balance between the capacity to protect ourselves from external stimuli on the one hand, and the permeability to assimilate them to the benefit of growth and maturation on the other.
- The capacity to establish a frontier or boundary between the internal and the external, and to establish a difference between what belongs to us and what is alien to us.
- The ability to articulate verbally expressed feelings with loving caresses and the corresponding change of the colour, softness, temperature and humidity of the skin.
- The ability to represent our identity outwards.
- Self-assurance, which is related to the sensations of support and enveloping.
- The capacity to discriminate between different kinds of "contact": social graces, acting in a "tactful" way, political contact, affectionate contact, sexual contact, and so on. [*ibid.*, p. 196]

The existence of the diseased skin itself and the sensations produced by it; the reactions of society at the sight of the patient's diseased skin; something previous to the outbreak of disease, for example a pathology of attachment which is later aggravated by the presence of the diseased skin—all of these factors can lead to the skin having an influence upon the attachment behaviour and the proxemic system[1] of patients suffering from psoriasis, while at the same time the effects of that behaviour and the proxemic differences with others could also have an influence upon the condition of the skin.

The hypothesis put forward in "Observations on psoriasis" (Ulnik, 1986) was that patients presented a pathology of attachment, and for this reason I shall now develop this concept and its clinical consequences, and also give an introduction to proxemics, which will then be related to affective distance and skin diseases.

Theory of attachment

The considerations that follow have mostly been obtained from the work of John Bowlby and from the contributions made to this area by Marrone, Fonagy and Main. The theory of attachment was developed by John Bowlby, and it brings to the fore the human need to form close affective relationships which manifest themselves in behaviours of proximity, distancing and contact with the carer, as well as in affective reactions in the face of separation.

> What I call attachment theory is a way of conceiving of the propensity shown by human beings to establish solid affective bonds with other people, and of explaining the manifold emotional disorders and personality alterations—including here anxiety, anger, depression and emotional withdrawal—occasioned by the involuntary separation from, and loss of, loved ones. As a theory, it deals with the same phenomena that until now had been treated as need for dependence or object-relations, or symbiosis and individuation. [Bowlby, 1986, p. 154]
>
> In brief, attachment behaviour is conceived of as a pattern of behaviour that consists in an individual acquiring or keeping proximity towards another differentiated person and preferably individual and who is usually considered to be stronger and/or wiser. [*ibid.*, p. 157]

The experience of security is the aim of the attachment system, which works as a regulator of the emotional experience. The *infans* will search for the physical proximity of the carer in the hope of being comforted and of recovering homeostasis. Separation anxiety is an inevitable response when the figure to whom one is attached is inexplicably absent.

A child who has had a reasonably safe maternal relationship and who has not been previously separated from his mother will show a predictable sequence of behaviour when he is exposed to a situation in which he is forced to separate from her, such as, for example, going to nursery school or during hospitalisation. This sequence can be divided into three phases: the phase of protest, the phase of despair and the phase of turning away or detachment.

In the beginning, the child cries and pleads with his mother to return, and hopes that this pleading will be successful. This is the phase of protest, which can persist through many days. He then calms down, although it is clear to a more trained eye that he is still longing for her return. When he has lost hope he moves on to the phase of despair. Finally a very important change takes place. The child seems to forget about his mother, and when she comes back to fetch him he seems to be uninterested, or may even appear not to know her. This is the third phase, that of detachment. During each of these phases, the child has tantrums and episodes of destructive behaviour, which are frequently violent.

The behaviour of the child on his return home depends on the phase reached during the period of separation. He is usually considered to be apathetic; he neither asks for anything nor reacts to anything. When this state eases, the intense ambivalence of feelings towards his mother becomes manifest. He does not want to separate from her, even for an instant, and if separation occurs, he shows great anxiety and anger. When separations have been repeated or too prolonged, the child stabilises in the last phase, that of detachment, and may never recover the love he used to feel for his parents (Bowlby, 1986).

The essential point in Bowlby's thesis is that there exists an intense causal relationship between the individual's experiences of attachment to his parents and his subsequent capacity to establish affective links, and that certain variations in that capacity, which manifest themselves in marriage problems and conflicts with the children as well as in neurotic symptoms and personality disorders, can be attributed to certain variations in the way the parents performed their respective roles. The main variable which has attracted attention is the extent to which the parents of the child firstly provide him with a secure basis, and secondly encourage him to explore, taking this as a starting point. What is also essential is the extent to which the parents acknowledge and respect the desire of their child.

One of the most common sources of anger on the part of the child is the frustration of his desire for love and care. His anxiety generally reflects uncertainty about whether he will be able to count on his parents. The function of anger seems to consist of providing vigour to the tremendous efforts he has made both to recover the lost person and to dissuade her from leaving again, which are typical of the first phase of mourning. It is only when all his efforts to recover the lost person are futile that the person is capable of admitting defeat and making his way in a world which accepts that the loved one is lost forever.

The parents' respect for the wish of their child to explore and gradually widen his relationship both with other children and with other adults is as important as their respect for the child's attachment desires. The typical patterns of pathogenic parental actions are as follows:

- One of the parents does not respond to the behaviour of the child, the objective of which is to be looked after or to be actively rejected.
- Discontinuities in parental assistance, including periods spent in hospital or at another institution.
- Persistent threats on the part of parents who do not love their children, by means of which they control their children.
- One of the parents threatens to abandon the family. These threats are used either as a method of imposing discipline on the child, or as a way of coercing their partner.
- One of the parents threatens to abandon or even kill their partner, or threatens to commit suicide.
- The parents induce a feeling of guilt in the child by saying that his behaviour is or will be responsible for the disease or the death of either of his parents.

Any of these experiences can lead the child or the adult to live with constant anxiety—unless he can detach from the figure to whom he is attached—and in consequence to have a low threshold for showing attachment behaviour. This state is better defined as *anxiety attachment* (Bowlby, 1986).

An opposite pattern to anxiety attachment is an attitude of "hardness" when faced with any situation. These individuals tend to collapse and present psychosomatic symptoms or depression when subjected to overwhelming stress, in the face of which they can no longer keep up their attitude. Many of these people have suffered experiences similar to those who develop anxiety attachment, but have reacted in a different way, namely by inhibiting the feeling of attachment and its corresponding behaviour, and by rejecting (even with contempt) any desire for close relationships with anyone who might provide them with love and care. They are deeply distrustful within their intimate relationships in order to avoid the pain of being rejected. Within other kinds of relationship they are distrustful in order to avoid being subjected to the obligation of becoming someone else's carer. In Italo Calvino's *Non-Existent Knight*, Agilulfo, the main character, has the personality of a hard and insensitive type and shows detachment from people and things, but every now and then he devotes himself to providing care. In truth, this is a knight who does not exist, because he has become an empty suit of armour due to his constantly having to defend himself (Calvino, 1959).

There are two patterns of behaviour related to attachment: the behaviour of exploration, which opposes itself to attachment, and the behaviour of providing care, which complements attachment. In general, the action of providing care compulsively, as a way of masking the need for attachment, implicitly involves latent resentment.

Attachment as drive and its relationship with the skin

As was mentioned in the chapters concerning the skin in the works of Freud and Didier Anzieu, attachment can be considered as drive, and, as such it is intimately connected with what Moll called "contrectation drive", which is the impulse to be in epidermic contact with another person.

Attachment behaviour does not necessarily involve epidermic contact, but starts from it as a reference point, since it is from the distance between the skins of two persons that the notion of proximity emerges (although later, by extension, we can talk about affective or ideological proximity with someone who is physically far away). In the same way as watching is a surrogate for touching, the notion of proximity can later be modified with the contribution of what Hall calls "visual space", which is connected with the subordination of the world of tact to the visual world, as well as with the contribution of the olfactory and the coenaesthesic functions (Hall, 1966, pp. 79, 84). Although a person could imagine him- or herself ". . . surrounded by a series of fields that are widened and reduced" (Hall, 1966, p. 141), there is no doubt that the participation of the skin in the construction and dynamism of those fields is essential.

The source of the attachment drive could be the skin, since we must remember that its value as an erotogenic zone depends on several factors, including the instinct of contrectation, the constitutional disposition to the pleasure of epidermic contact, and the experience of close contact with the body of the mother. The ideas already developed with regard to contact as a superior unity—which, although it can refer to the idea of physical contact, physical proximity or contiguity, also alludes to the idea of similarity or psychic analogy (see figure 1.1—reinforce the relationship between skin and attachment. Although their meaning is not altogether clear, there are studies which demonstrate that those individuals who reply to questions on attachment with scorn show an increased conductivity in their skin (Dossier & Kobak, 1992, quoted by Marrone, 2001, p. 68).

The dam against the attachment drive would seem to be the affective state that we usually call coldness or affective distance, which often manifests itself as physical distance and which, if it is considered as behaviour, is called detachment.

What Anzieu called the "prohibition to touch" performs an essential function in the regulation of the attachment drive. Although he refers to physical contact, as previously pointed out, touching an object can function as a means of seizing it, because the touching drive is intimately linked to the mastery drive. The prohibition to touch can function in the sense of avoiding the tendency to global contact which leads to the fusion and confusion of bodies, but it can also have a regulatory function over the desire for mastery that leads the child to want to seize at everything. In either of these ways, the prohibition to touch could function as a regulator of the attachment drive.

Attachment and its clinical implications within the doctor-patient relationship

The considerations that follow are the result of more than ten years of interdisciplinary work with dermatologists in the field of psycho-dermatology; however, they can be extended to the doctor-patient relationship in any medical field.

PATTERNS OF BEHAVIOUR IN THE DOCTOR-PATIENT RELATIONSHIP

If we take the patterns of behaviour that emerge from research on attachment as a basis, we can categorise patterns of behaviour in the doctor-patient relationship which are very common in dermatology and which can certainly be applied to other medical fields.

We must remember that according to Marrone, "a child who has enjoyed a secure attachment is happier, easier to look after and less problematic than an anxious child. In contrast, an anxious and ambivalent child will show a tendency to cling to his attachment figure and will be emotionally more demanding. An avoidant child will be prone to being distant. The behaviour of insecure children provokes negative responses in both their parents, and with this a vicious circle is developed." (Marrone, 2001, p. 87)

The doctor-patient relationship in a certain way reproduces the relationship between the child and his parents. For this reason we will describe for each kind of attachment a particular kind of relationship with the doctor. Following the ideas of Mary Ainsworth (1969, 1985 and 1978), Fonagy (1999) describes the following patterns of behaviour:

- Secure children
- Anxious/avoidant children
- Anxious/resistant children
- Disorganised/disoriented children

SECURE CHILDREN

- They quickly explore the environment in the presence of their carers.
- They become anxious when facing a stranger and they avoid it.
- They feel upset by the brief absences of their carers.
- They seek to establish contact with their carer when she comes back and feel reassured by her.

In these cases the carer was able to re-establish the child's disorganising experiences or emotional responses.

IN THE DOCTOR-PATIENT RELATIONSHIP

Patients who experience a secure attachment are relieved when they go to the doctor, and consult him with a feeling of trust. They are worried if the doctor is away or on holiday, and dislike being seen by another doctor, feeling reassured when their doctor comes back. They might investigate their disease on the Internet or with acquaintances, and it is likely that they will read the medication's directions for use. However, they do all this because they feel they can count on their doctor and can consult him about what they have found out. Thus if the medication's directions for use or any information on the Internet does not coincide with what their doctor has told them, they dare to ask, but they accept the doctor's explanation with confidence the and follow his instructions.

The main characteristic of these patients is their trust in their doctor, which in turn leads them to have confidence in themselves as well as in their capacity to heal or get better.

ANXIOUS/AVOIDANT CHILDREN

- They feel less anxious about separation.
- They do not prefer the carer to a stranger.
- They do not seek proximity after separation.
- They are children who over-regulate.

The carer has not re-stabilised the children's emotional response, and might have been excessively stimulating or intrusive. The child over-regulates, which means that he increases the stimulus threshold necessary to activate his attachment system. In consequence, he appears to be indifferent towards the carer's absence. These children can be described by their parents as good or sociable children, because they are willing to be in anyone's arms and can be left with the nanny or with relatives without complaining.

IN THE DOCTOR-PATIENT RELATIONSHIP

Patients of this kind seem to be indifferent towards their doctor, as if the doctor-patient relationship were non-existent. This is the kind of patient who will consult any doctor from the medical plan list as long as he lives nearby. It is a matter of indifference whether he is seen by one doctor or another, as he does not truly give himself to any doctor. He might not be aware of the seriousness of his disease or of the state he is in. What is more, he does not attend follow-up consultations. He might bring to the consultation medication he has already begun taking, creams (or containers) which were prescribed by other doctors, though he cannot recall who prescribed what. He cannot properly differentiate the doctor from the paramedic, the alternative practitioner or the healer. In some cases he may be considered a "good patient" since he does not complain, he causes no bother and he asks no questions.

The main characteristic of these patients is not being aware either of the other or of their own condition as a consequence of over-regulation.

ANXIOUS/RESISTANT CHILDREN

- They do not explore or play much.
- They feel disturbed by separation.
- They have difficulty in recovering, displaying agitation, tension and constant crying. They become uncomfortable.
- The presence of the carer fails to calm them down or reassure them.
- They do not manage to obtain relief from the presence of the carer.
- They under-regulate.

The child under-regulates: *he increases his expression of discomfort in an attempt to awaken the expected response on the part of the carer.* The child has a low threshold for threatening conditions and becomes anxious for contact with the carer, but feels frustrated even when this contact is available.

IN THE DOCTOR-PATIENT RELATIONSHIP

These kinds of patients usually provoke rejection or authoritarian responses in the doctor. The reason is that they come to the consultation to complain about being ill-treated by the doctor himself or by other professionals, or to complain about the side-effects of the medication the doctor himself prescribed, but at the same time they never miss a consultation and insist on asking for appointments time and again. The doctor will even believe that they do these things in order to bother him, and will usually enquire, somewhat inquisitively, whether they have followed all the instructions correctly, and then often get angry if they haven't. If the doctor feels the need to respond to every demand with an offer, then an unnecessary prescription will follow, the final result being the prescription of several medications, or referral to another doctor, which unconsciously means rejection. The doctor feels that nothing can please the patient because while he seems to be looking for an answer, when he finally obtains one he is still not satisfied. The patient does not follow the doctor's instructions, but then complains about the lack of results. The doctor may then become authoritarian as a result of anger, as he feels questioned or attacked. The patient questions this authority by throwing his failure back in his face in an attempt to "soften" him and obtain the understanding and the affection he lacks but doesn't know how to ask for, though what he really obtains is the opposite effect.

The main characteristic of these patients is a demand, in the form of complaint or reproach, which is impossible to satisfy. It is important to clarify that anxious or insecure attachment during childhood is a risk factor in psychopathology, but is not necessarily psychopathological in itself.

DISORGANISED/DISORIENTED CHILDREN

- Their behaviour is not directed towards any particular purpose.
- They try to escape even in the presence of the carer.
- They have the capacity to explain the behaviour of the carer in mental terms, but this capacity does not play a central and effective role in self-organisation.
- As they are generally victims of abuse, in order to defend themselves they develop proximity at the mental level with the abuser in order to be able to anticipate danger. However, this proximity is unbearable, and is paradoxically accompanied

by a search for physical attachment with the same abuser, since despite being victims of abuse, they depend on and love the abuser. This is where disorganisation stems from.

- They resort to an adaptive fractioning of the reflective capacity, meaning that they are able to reflect upon and understand certain types of behaviour in others within certain contexts to which they have to adapt, yet they manage to do this only at the expense of splitting and dissociating certain affective states.

The carer has been a source of reassurance and fear, and attachment is a source of conflict. The three-year-old child bases his prediction on his own representation of reality and not on the mental state of the other. In contrast, these patients are sharp "readers" of the carer's mind but poor "readers" of their own states (Fonagy, 1999, p. 10). Their mental capacity, born from over-adjustment, is out of step with their own organisation and affective states. The child depends on abusive, intrusive or sick parents, and feels the need for them at the same time as he suffers from their treatment of him.

IN THE DOCTOR-PATIENT RELATIONSHIP

The patient shows incomprehensible patterns of behaviour: he becomes disorganised with regard to the taking of medication and the keeping of appointments. He can behave irregularly in the demonstration of affect and trust, showing no characteristic pattern that makes him predictable. His attitude is baffling: he shows an acute understanding of certain directions, but his behaviour does not correspond to the intelligence he shows, and he sometimes seems not to understand elementary things.

He can feel he is a "patient" of some doctor or healer who has not only failed to cure him but has hurt him or deceived him. Although he is aware of this, he is able to mention the doctor's name, thus demonstrating his adherence to this so-called "doctor".

Sometimes one is left with the impression of a "multiple personality", which is a product of his dissociative behaviour. The same may happen with the evolution of his disease, which does not usually respond to predictable parameters. Thus, the day after an extraordinary improvement, an extremely serious relapse can occur, disappointing both his doctor and his family.

He may start an unjustified dispute, which should be tempered by the success and dedication previously obtained. When this happens, he seems to be ungrateful. He may miss his appointments and make his doctor reschedule, only to miss the rescheduled appointments, thus showing his ambivalence. He can detect the emotional state of the doctor and can even "manipulate" it, causing anxiety, impotence, anger or tenderness in him. He can love, fear and hate the doctor at the same time. His clinical history may become disorganised.

The main characteristic of these patients is the incongruity of their behaviour, emotional reactions and response to treatment.

SECURE ATTACHMENT, NARRATIVE COHERENCE AND THE REFLECTIVE FUNCTION WITHIN THE DOCTOR-PATIENT RELATIONSHIP

NARRATIVE COHERENCE

Taking the analysis of the patient's replies to the Adult Attachment Interview (AAI) as a starting point, its authors have tried to assess the way in which a person organises his thoughts and verbal language regarding attachment, that is to say its narrative coherence. This coherence involves the capacity to make clear connections between past events, their results, and thoughts and feelings related to those events (Marrone, 2001, p. 114).

Every doctor has the experience daily of facing patients who manifest contradictions, make irrational connections between phrases, confuse prescriptions, treatments, doctors, advice, television ads, and so on. Taking into consideration the pace of modern life added to institutions' demand for high performance from doctors, those individuals who are prone to telling interminable stories with irrelevant details quickly become insufferable. Questioning is an essential part of any medical record, and the attitude of some modern doctors who base their diagnosis only on images and lab tests, thus trying to avoid dialogue and thorough questioning of patients, is highly questionable. However, it is also true that many patients appear incapable of sticking to the point, seem to confuse the chronology of their diseases and even of their life in general, are imprecise in the localisation of their suffering, make inappropriate comments, use inappropriate jargon and simply cause confusion with their "metaphors".

Part of this confusion is due to the fact that, as Umberto Eco (1973) says, the patient is suffering discomfort and has to use words to describe it, words which act as signs of this discomfort but are not the discomfort itself. Apart from this, it is highly probable that the doctor has never felt "the same" discomfort. Consequently, the words the patient chooses are "in the place of" his discomfort, and if the patient has symbolic difficulties and cannot coherently choose and relate his own words, the sign or signs used can end up being confusing or wrong.

> One of the important discoveries made by Main and his colla-borators is that the degree of coherence with which a person speaks indicates his capacity to access the information related to his relationship history, and to keep this information organised in a reflective way. This faculty is in turn related to the security of attachment. [Marrone, 2001, p. 115]

According to Marrone, a cooperative attitude with the other during dialogue could depend on the same factors.

Is a safe attachment so important for the development of coherence? What is the relationship between the one and the other? There are probably many key elements in this relationship. On the one hand, the security to separate and explore allows the subject to be the architect of his own history. And although he might have been told many parts of his own history, it is probable that he will make it more his own the more integrated it is with his feelings as well as with the "pieces" of history he keeps and needs to integrate. On the other hand, the authorisation and acceptance of his own feelings allows him to bind and integrate the painful and even shameful aspects of his life by developing resilience (Zukerfeld, 1999) in the face of the adverse aspects of his life. And lastly, the fact of feeling protected and contained, in addition to the feeling of having counted on someone during bad times and having been considered as the bearer of original thought, allows this thought to develop complexity free from the hindrance produced by certain dissociative defence mechanisms in the availability and connectivity of memories and psychic associations.

REFLECTIVE FUNCTION

Regarding the doctor, coherence is important; but even more important is the *reflective function*. This concept was developed by Peter Fonagy, who states that the acknowledgement, evaluation and interpretation of mental states in the other are crucial for the development of the capacity to reflect upon interpersonal situations. Based on these ideas, and taking the responses to the AAI as a starting point, Fonagy and others created a scale according to which individuals with a high degree of this reflective function show a capacity to:

- Acknowledge that both the individual and the other have their own mental states, with characteristics that can be made explicit.
- Accept that an individual can acknowledge the mental states of the other, but also admit the limitations of such a perception, at the same time taking into account that the perception of the other's mental state also depends on the individual's own mental state.
- Acknowledge that the other can experience feelings different from those he openly shows, and that in consequence interaction should be considered from different perspectives.
- Accept that the individual can be seen by others differently from the way he sees himself or would like to see himself.
- Realise that the individual can use defence mechanisms against anxiety or painful emotions.
- Make significant historical and intergenerational connections, as well as taking into account the family group dynamics (Marrone, 2001, pp. 122–123).

Those doctors who possess the reflective function will be able to renounce the apostolic function, described by Balint as the idea that all patients should be converted to the faith of the doctor (which involves suggesting activities and restrictions based exclusively on the doctor's own value judgements). They will be able to accept their own limitations, their tiredness, their moments of ignorance, and everything that can modify their own mental state. They will understand that the patient's feelings and interactions with the doctor and with others depend on the patient's own childhood and family history, and thus be able to accept and understand the tacit or manifest intervention of members of the patient's family in the evolution and treatment of the disease. They will be able to tolerate the fact that the patient might not see them with the pleasure, love and esteem they might expect; or that they might see reflected in the patient's "mirror" an image of themselves of which they were not aware (Fonagy, 1999; Marrone, 2001, pp. 122–123).

PATHOLOGY OF ATTACHMENT IN THE DOCTOR-PATIENT RELATIONSHIP

Based on his supervisions with Bowlby and on his own clinical experience, Marrone describes a series of pathogenic communications on the part of parents or carers which make an essential contribution to the development of insecurity and to the pathology of attachment. These are:

- Rejection of the child's petition to be supported and understood
- Denial of the child's perception of certain family events
- Guilt-inducing communications
- Invalidation of the child's subjective experience
- Threats
- Non-constructive criticism
- Shame-inducing communications
- Intrusive attitudes and "mind-reading"
- Double-bind
- Paradoxical comments
- Discouraging comments
- Comments which question the child's good intentions, or which deny the child's right to have opinions of his own
- Self-referred comments
- Replies which denote disinterest
- Exaggerated responses to the child's anxieties
- The communications of parents in conflict who try to ally themselves with the child against the other parent
- Unfavourable comparisons

According to Marrone, possible reasons for a father or a mother to communicate with their child in these ways are:

- The parents might project their own feelings of guilt, shame or negative discrimination onto the child.
- The parents might identify with their own parents, who treated them in such a way when they were children themselves. That is to say they are treating the child in the same way as they themselves were treated.
- The child might not have been wanted by one or both parents.
- The child might be a scapegoat, as a result of an unfortunate family situation being attributed to him.
- One of the parents might wish to exercise strict control over the child and discourage him from exploring the world due to their own insecurity, which leads them to cling to the child.
- In a reconstructed family, a child from a previous marriage could be rejected by the stepmother or -father.
- The child might take after another person (generally one of the grandparents) towards whom the father or the mother feels great animosity.
- The parents might have wanted the child to be the other sex.
- The child might be treated as an extension of the father or the mother, in order to satisfy his or her own narcissism or need for accomplishment, fame or success. If the child does not meet this need, he or she will be attacked.
- Intolerance of the child's anxieties and painful emotions on the part of the parents (2001, p. 96).

An almost identical repetition of the foregoing can occur within the doctor-patient relationship.

THE DOCTOR MIGHT PROJECT ONTO THE PATIENT HIS OWN FEELINGS OF EXPERIENCING REJECTION, OR OF GUILT OR SHAME.

For example, it is common for an individual to choose to study medicine, and on qualification to choose a speciality related to an illness suffered by one of his loved ones which he could not cure or repair. By devoting his life to the treatment of patients with the same illness as his loved one, he tries to alleviate his feelings of guilt, or to search for answers to something that made him feel impotent and racked by doubts. However, if the patient worsens or does not recover, the doctor might project his own feelings onto him and accuse him of not wanting to get better. Sometimes the doctor feels ashamed of or rejected by the illness from which either he himself, or one of his family members, is suffering (something which frequently happens in dermatology and psychiatry), and so he obtains relief by depositing on the patient the role of a sick person who is suffering from a shameful condition.

THE DOCTOR IDENTIFIES WITH OTHER DOCTORS OR TEACHERS WHO TREATED HIM IN THIS WAY.

From the very beginning of his medical studies, the doctor can suffer humiliations, excessive demands or mistreatment from some of his teachers who, on the basis of their own prestige, exercise inconsiderate power and authority over their students and resident doctors. The doctor may then identify with these figures and, without even being aware of it, abuse his own role of authority and power that the patient lends him.

THE PATIENT MIGHT BE "UNWANTED".

This happens when the doctor is obliged to see a patient who has been referred to him, either when he has some distant familial ties with the patient, or for institutional reasons. The level of severity of the disease also has an influence: some doctors prefer to see patients without complications, while others consider mundane those cases which do not stimulate them to think, or which do not challenge their knowledge. Lastly, the sub-speciality developed by the doctor makes him feel a keener interest in some patients than in others who are outside his field of interest and knowledge.

THE PATIENT MIGHT BE A "SCAPEGOAT".

The patient can be the scapegoat for a conflictive situation with Social Security, or with the medical insurance scheme, which will not pay the doctor's fee, or alternatively with the professional who referred him. The doctor's particular personal situation can also cause him to vent his feelings on the patient, whose occupation, gender or civil status may be similar to that of someone with whom the doctor is in conflict.

THE DOCTOR MIGHT WANT TO KEEP STRICT CONTROL OVER THE PATIENT.

When the doctor feels the need to keep strict control over the people on whom he exercises influence or the people he loves, he may discourage the patient from exploring other possibilities (natural medications, the Internet, family advice). This can also happen if the doctor is insecure and feels questioned by the patient's enquiries. The doctor (and the patient) may be unaware of this situation of control in which the prescription of certain diets, or routines involving actions which may have to be repeated several times a day, can lead to the memory of the doctor being constantly present in the life of the patient. In this way the doctor plays the role of a judge or supervisor who will be angry at any transgression and to whom the patient has to justify himself on each new consultation.

THE PATIENT MIGHT COME TO THE CONSULTATION STILL FOLLOWING PRIOR TREATMENT AND THE STYLE OF ANOTHER DOCTOR OR ANOTHER INSTITUTION.

The doctor might reject a patient who continues to feel admiration and respect for the previous doctor who referred him for his present treatment (for example, a patient may change doctors because he is unable to afford the doctor's private fee, turning to his present doctor because he is available on Social Security). This situation becomes pressing when the patient judges one modus operandi against another, or when he continually mentions his previous doctor or institution, making comparisons with those he is currently attending.

THE PATIENT IS TREATED LIKE A NARCISSISTIC EXTENSION OF THE DOCTOR.

If the doctor is insecure or narcissistic and feels the need to succeed in order to justify his position, or if he is writing a scientific paper and expects certain results in order to defend his thesis in favour of a certain technique or treatment, he may attack a patient who does not respond satisfactorily to his efforts.

THE DOCTOR MIGHT SHOW INTOLERANCE OF THE PATIENT'S ANXIETIES AND PAINFUL FEELINGS.

This attitude is usually seen when the doctor has a sub-speciality within the hospital, where he sees patients of a lower social status (who tend to complain less, are more long-suffering, and are better able to bear misfortune and pain) and where he treats extremely serious conditions every day. Then, when he sees patients of a higher social status with less severe conditions in his private consulting room, he cannot understand their fears and apprehensions and finds them exaggerated.

GROVES SYNDROME

Twenty years ago, a psychiatrist from Boston called James E. Groves described the characteristics of the "hateful" patient. Emilio Suárez Martín, a dermatologist from Madrid recently published an editorial in the magazine *Piel* (Skin) in which he analysed the types of patient described by Groves and described the way they present themselves in dermatology, grouping them into three types and giving them the new names of The Bore (Type I), The Smart Alec (Type II), and The Liar (Type III).

Suárez Martín's article will be examined with the help of elements from attachment theory and from psychoanalysis, in order to analyse the behaviour of these patients from this perspective. It is not my intention to establish a new classification, or to recognise Groves' types as equivalent to the psychopathological disorders seen in psychiatry handbooks, but instead to describe mechanisms and explain behaviours using different models proposed by psychoanalytical authors.

Type I (The Bore) is the patient who takes possession of the doctor's consulting room and time. He is incapable of coming to the point, he may often arrive with a piece of paper (as an aide memoire) so as to leave nothing out, and he does not hesitate to telephone the doctor at inappropriate times, either during holidays or at weekends (Suárez Martín, 1998, p. 63).

These patients could be considered as suffering from a pathology of attachment, showing a tendency to "stick themselves" to the doctor. In actual fact, it is probably a variety of anxious attachment which is neither avoidant nor resistant. From a psychopathological perspective they are similar to obsessional neurotics; however, they differ in that their central mechanism is probably projective identification or adhesive identification. What the doctor experiences as "sticky" or "heavy" in the case of projective identification is the patient's intrusive attempt to project dissociated aspects of his own in order that he might control them once they have been deposited in the doctor. In contrast, what he experiences in the case of mimetic adhesive identification is the patient's attempt to establish a whole unity with the doctor by means of primitive mechanisms of imitation, in a two-dimensional space without boundaries and without notion of time (see Chapter 1, where Meltzer and Liberman are quoted). The patient is not so much "installing himself" in the consulting room as in fact seeking to install himself "within" the doctor, or to cling to him (see Chapter 3, where reference is made to allergic patients described by Canteros, Marty and Sami-Ali).

The Type II patient (The Smart Alec, Groves's entitled demander) is the one who asks for help, but simultaneously discredits the doctor, questioning his prescriptions, debasing his advice and "lecturing", or showing off his knowledge of his own disease and all the existing treatments, which are always ineffective for him. His knowledge can be based on the fact that he has been a patient for a long time, or that he has worked at a surgery dealing with this speciality (it does not matter if he was a switchboard operator, an orderly or a porter). He usually mentions strange and barely scientific references, which are also hard to find. He claims he has a lot of experience and has seen it all before: no therapy ever works for him (Suárez Martín, 1998, p. 64).

This kind of patient fits better with the description of resistant anxious attachment. It is probably a narcissistic variant in which the patient finds it hard to bear not only the difference separating him from the doctor, but also his need to receive the doctor's help. He generally responds well when the doctor puts himself on his level and agrees to a role interchange, as if he were dealing with a child, and to "discuss as equals" each suggestion, thus accepting the position of impotence or equality in which the patient puts him.

Projective identification continues to be the mechanism at work here, and what lies behind this behaviour is an extreme fragility of the Ego and an identity disorder similar to the one presented by Woody Allen in the film *Zelig*, in which the main character merges, even physically, with each of the people with whom he interacts.

Hugo Bleichmar's classification of the different kinds of masochism is also useful in understanding this condition. The "entitled demander" could be classified together with the group of patients who display *masochism as an undercover form of sadism*: those who use their disease to induce feelings of guilt in the doctor or frustrate his wishes; or those with sadistic-paranoid masochism: those who imagine or provoke unfair treatment in order to feel superior or to be able to get back at someone without feeling guilty (Bleichmar, 1997, pp. 90–93).

Lastly, in Suárez Martín's text Type III (The Liar) condenses Groves's Types III (manipulative help-rejecters) and IV (self destructive deniers). These kinds of patients are the ones who self-inflict lesions and then deny having done it, or who do not follow the doctor's prescriptions and complain, are manipulative and reject our help. To love someone who is ill and does not allow him- or herself to be helped is one of the most painful things we can experience. It is very probable that these patients take to these extreme patterns of behaviour because they have learned from their relatives that if they agree to be helped and improved, no one will subsequently pay any attention to them. It is as if identity and love were centred on the fact of being ill. In the chart proposed by Bleichmar, these patients respond to another two different types of masochism: "masochism to inspire pity and thus obtain love from the other, who is pained by the suffering, and traumatic masochism, in which the patient self-inflicts a graduated suffering for fear that it might occur suddenly and beyond his control" (Bleichmar, 1997, pp. 83–85).

Attachment, distance and proximity: their relationship to the skin and the Ego functions

Attachment can be related to a discipline called proxemics, developed by the anthropologist Edward T. Hall, which measures the spatial configurations of human beings in terms of distance. Taking into account that in general terms attachment behaviour is the search for proximity to beings considered to be protective, the configurations of distance and rejection (in which the skin plays a very important part) play an essential role and are explored in many of the questions that attachment tests suggest asking patients. In this way, both in the questions of the Adult Attachment Interview (AAI), and in the studies of Bartholomew and Horowitz quoted by Marrone, what is sought are correlations between the individual's internal operative models, self-esteem, regulation of distance regarding attachment figures in adult life, and strategies for maintaining proximity.

This proximity is considered not as physical but as affective distance. However, the use of terms such as "to feel close to", "a close person", and the emphasis put on the experiences of separation clearly show that there is a basis or eco-system of physical experiences (such as tactile experiences of separation, nearness and proximity) which acts as a substrate upon which the affective experiences of feeling close or far from someone are mounted. These affective distances are no longer tactile as they have undergone the modifications imprinted by language and culture: nowadays it is no longer necessary to touch someone in order to feel close to them.

Proxemics (Hall, 1987)

The objective of Hall's investigations is to analyse the use people make of space—the space they maintain between themselves and others—by means of the distance and the space they construct around themselves at home and at work. Hall's aim is to deepen knowledge in particular of the complex connections produced between people's natural tendencies and the cultural influences to which they are subjected. People receive and emit these influences by means of forms of communication which are simultaneously produced at very different levels. We are all familiar with the verbal level, yet in Hall's studies the emphasis is placed on the idea that the use people make of space and distance between themselves and others configures a level of signs which are transmitted in a non-verbal way and which condition their relationships and conflicts with others.

To the extent that language is an essential element in the formation of thought, people are captives of the language they speak, and this in turn modifies the perception they have of the world around them. To Hall, these principles, which are based on the works of Whorf, are applicable to the whole of human behaviour, in such a way that people from different cultures could inhabit different sensory worlds. This could explain the fact that they have at their disposal different proxemic systems which involve a different use of space and a different regulation of distance from others. *Proxemics is a kind of non-linguistic communication established through signs which are constituted by means of spatial configurations of distance, such as the distance between a person and his or her interlocutor.*

Hall distinguishes eight types of distance between two speakers and he groups these into four types he calls intimate, personal, social and public distance. In order to classify distance into these four types, Hall based his research on observations of both animals and people. Territorial behaviour, which involves the use of the senses in order to distinguish a space or distance between oneself and another, is typical of both animals and people. It also involves the use of behaviours which establish and protect space. The specific distance chosen for each situation depends not only on the particular relationship established each time by the individuals involved in that situation, but the way they feel and what they do. Following Hediger, Hall adopted the concepts of personal distance and social distance.

- Personal distance: "personal distance is the term given by Hediger to the normal space that non-contact animals maintain between themselves and others" (Hall, 1987, p. 22), as if it were an invisible blister surrounding the organism which separates one individual from another.
- Social distance: Social distance is that which a social animal needs in order to be in contact with its group. It is like a hidden bond that links each individual to its group and varies in different situations: for example, it is reduced when the individual feels threatened (*ibid.*, p. 23).

While personal distance is the distance between two individuals, social distance is the distance which exists between an individual and the group to which he or she belongs. Finally, based on the behaviour shown by birds and monkeys, Hall also adopted the concept of intimate distance, which is related both to sexuality and to struggle. In contrast, the idea of public distance developed through consideration of western people, who are transformed into public people or can have "public relations" (*ibid.*, p. 155). Hall conceives of people as having boundaries that go beyond their body and are dynamic for each relational situation, as if they were "surrounded by a series of invisible but measurable bubbles" (*ibid.*, p. 158) which extend or contract their boundaries and their space according to each case.

In his work *The Silent Language* (1951), Hall made an initial classification which he later corrected and improved in his book *The Hidden Dimension* (1966). In this work he identifies eight types of significant distance between two speakers, which are as follows:

Intimate distance, close phase

This is the distance of the act of love or erotic contact, and also of wrestling, protection and confrontation. Physical contact or the great possibility of a physical relationship predominates. The muscles and the skin are in contact; the arms embrace. The perception of the physical traits of the other is deformed and the tactile and olfactory sensations predominate.

Intimate distance, far phase (15–45 cm)

The head, legs and pelvis do not easily come into contact, but the hands can reach and hold the extremities. The other person's warmth and breath can be noticed. Words are spoken by means of an audible murmur—a whisper—and something confidential is transmitted. Among middle class, adult North Americans the use of intimate distance in public is not considered acceptable. This distance can also be that of groups of passengers on public transport during the rush hour.

Personal distance, close phase (45–75 cm)

The sensation of proximity is derived in part from the existing possibilities of what each of the participants can do to the other with their limbs, i.e. at this distance one person can hold or detain the other. "A wife can be within the circle of the personal area near her husband with impunity. If another woman does so, however, it is a very different matter" (Hall, 1987, p. 147). If they are indoors, people speak in a low voice, whereas if they are outdoors they speak in a loud voice. What is transmitted can be confidential. This distance is considered to be acceptable in everyday relationships between two spouses, but is not acceptable between two businessmen.

PERSONAL DISTANCE, FAR PHASE (75–120 CM)

To say that someone is "at an arm's length" is a way of expressing the far phase of personal distance, which extends from a point situated immediately outside the area of a person's easy contact up to a point where two people can touch their fingers if they both extend their arms. This is the limit of physical domain in a proper sense. Beyond this limit, it is not easy for a person to "lay a hand on" someone else. Matters concerning two interested parties as well as those concerning personal relationships are treated at this distance. Physical warmth is not perceptible and the voice level is moderate. Within the scheme of *The Silent Language* it was considered a neutral distance, at which people speak in a low voice and may transmit a personal matter. The line that separates the far phase of personal distance and the close phase of social distance is known as the "limit of domination". Nobody touches or expects to touch another person unless a special effort is made. The voice level is adequate to make oneself heard from a distance of 6 metres.

SOCIAL DISTANCE, CLOSE PHASE (1.2–2 METRES)

At this distance impersonal matters are treated and at the close phase there is naturally more involvement than at the far phase. People working together tend to use this close social distance, which is also a distance very often used by people taking part in an improvised or informal social meeting. Within the classification of *The Silent Language* it was also considered to be a neutral distance, at which people raise their voices and transmit non-personal matters.

SOCIAL DISTANCE, FAR PHASE (2–3.5 METRES)

This is the distance adopted when someone says to the other "stand up so that I get a better look at you", wanting to be able to scan the whole body easily. It is typical of commercial and social discourse and is formal in character, for example a bureaucrat receiving a visitor, separated by the width of the tables. The voice level is quite high and it can easily be heard from a nearby room if the door is open.

> This is the distance that can be used in order to isolate or separate people from one another. For example, it allows them to continue with their work in the presence of another person without that person seeming to be impolite. Office receptionists are particularly vulnerable, because most bosses demand from them a double service: to reply when something is asked of them, to be polite with visitors while at the same time continuing to type. If the receptionist is less than three metres from another person, even if it is a stranger, she will feel sufficiently involved so as to feel virtually compelled to have a conversation. If the distance is greater, however, she can continue freely with her work without the need to speak. In the same way, husbands who come back from work usually sit to rest or to read the paper at three or more metres from their wives since at that distance a couple can start a brief conversation and interrupt it at will. [Hall, 1987, p. 151]

In *The Silent Language* what was termed social distance was also defined as the distance at which people speak volubly and emphasise their voices, and it is also characterised by the transmission of public information which is destined to be heard by people other than those at whom it is aimed.

Public distance, close phase (3.5–7.5 metres)

At 3.5 metres an agile individual can act in an avoiding or defensive way if threatened. Distance can be a vestigial, albeit subliminal, form of escape reaction. The voice is high, though not at top volume, and the speaker adopts a formal style. In *The Silent Language* this was considered a distance at which people speak in a loud voice and transmit something to a group, and was exemplified with the figure of a speaker at a formal dinner.

Public distance, far phase (7.5–9 metres)

This is the distance automatically maintained in front of public figures, such as the president. The usual public distance is not limited purely to public figures, as anyone can make use of it on public occasions. The voice and gestures should be amplified or exaggerated, since a good part of the message is transmitted with gestures and the position of the body. The person as a whole becomes diminished, as though in a scene or framed. In *The Silent Language* this was considered to be a distance beyond the limits, at which people speak in a loud voice, and greetings and goodbyes are performed at a distance; or that which corresponds to the public figure who is inaccessible to an individual in particular.

THE CONCEPT OF AFFECTIVE DISTANCE

The concept of distance put forward by Hall is a measurable concept which is applied to Euclidean space. When we speak of distance in psychoanalysis, we refer to a more abstract idea, not so easily measurable, which allows us to say that a patient puts affective distance or that he establishes a double distance between himself and the object. This abstraction of the idea of distance reaches its extreme during the mourning process, when we say that the absent object is experienced "as a presence that surrounds the whole Self" (Rosenfeld, 1973) because "the shadow of the object falls upon the Ego" (Freud, 1917).

This concept of distance, both physical and psychic, is a theoretical construction arbitrarily developed in order to establish an order within the real space that is beyond our capacity to perceive or even understand. Is there any relationship between the "classic" concept of distance—or the one conceptualised by physics—and the term "distance" that we use in psychoanalysis? Our relationship with the body might reveal the point at which these two concepts come into contact, and to achieve this, the concept of "body image", as developed by Paul Schilder, will be instructive.

When we establish a distance from the other, the body becomes a possible point of reference, and in addition, the skin plays a privileged role because it is the body's external boundary. Thus, at primary school, when children are told not to stand too close together, they respond by stretching their arm out to a point at which where they can scarcely touch their classmate's back. Distance, then, can be described as that which must necessarily be maintained so that bodies cannot come into contact with one another if individuals keep their place. For a couple, however, distance might be what is necessary in order for them not to kiss, while for soldiers, distance is marked by the reach of their weapons.

In consequence, the idea of distance will vary according to the conception each person has of his or her own body, and according to the context in which each is placed: if someone believes he is wearing a "shell", he may not find it necessary to be at such a distance from his enemy; if someone feels he is too dependent, he may need to be too close to everyone; if there is a symbiotic relationship, distance might not exist, or in contrast, it might pose a threat of disintegration.

According to Hall, Hediger termed the interpersonal space that an animal needs in order to feel safe before it escapes "flight distance". Hall goes on to apply this concept to people and mentions a certain type of schizophrenics who speak about what happens within their flight distance as if it were happening literally *within themselves*, because their boundaries are beyond their bodies. From this observation he reaches the conclusion that people's self-esteem is intimately related to the establishment of their own precise boundaries. The skin fulfils a very important role in the establishment of the individual's own boundaries, and when these fade or are attacked, a dermatological disease or a self-inflicted pattern of behaviour can be the means of re-establishing the lost boundaries, or of constituting precarious boundaries where none had previously been established.

RELATIONSHIP BETWEEN DISTANCE AND SYMBOLISATION OF SPACE

Liberman claims that in the initial stages of psychic development, there are no differentiated symbols which would allow the individual to discriminate between the mental representations of the internal object and the object itself, whether an object of love or an inanimate material object. Nor are the parts and the whole well-differentiated. The notion of "absent object" is an evolutionary acquisition, a mental precondition for the creation of differentiated symbols (Liberman et al., 1982, p. 351, note 19).

> Taking the emergence of the symbolic capacity as a starting point, both realities, the internal and the external, will emerge as inter-

related worlds as well as being differentiated by means of specific temporal-spatial dimensions; *the qualities of closeness, distance and spatial and temporal mobility of the object will be subjected, in external reality, to the order of topographic space and chronological time, while in the psychic reality, they will derive from the vicissitudes of emotional evolution.*[2] [Liberman et al., 1982, pp. 354–355]

The construction of space is a representation-symbol which is inscribed during a process involving successive stages of differentiation: this involves the correlative construction of a space external to the Self in addition to an internal, physical and mental space. This process reaches completion in adolescence, and the mature symbolic representation of space enables individuals to place both themselves and the others within the area of interpersonal relationships. It fulfils the function of an internal map which guides them through the variations of known spaces and allows them to get their bearings in new spaces.

The baby's first space is a *space of the mouth*. A space existing only in the present, it is recovered according to the baby's needs, through the real or hallucinated presence of the object, and it can be lost as a result of the experience of frustration. It is a space of fusion and unity which is recreated every time the union with the internal object—in the constitution of which the response of the real object is essential—is re-established.

Almost simultaneously with the organisation of the space of the mouth, other spaces related to the different sensory ambits are constituted. There will be a *tactile space*, an *aural space* and a *visual space*, which are initially not co-ordinated with each other. From these first sensory spaces, the baby starts to conceive of the existence of a space alien to himself. This is an *immediate proximal space* which is the space close to the surface of his body. Thus are the first notions of boundary and discrimination between Me and Not-Me established. Through its three functions—container, boundary and contact—the skin is of essential importance as the primary arena of interchange in that it enables development of the notions both of differentiation and of union. At the same time as it marks a limit, it also maintains an absence of discrimination from the other and plays a part in the successive moments of union and separation which are necessary in evolution. The area of physical contact is where the boundary comes into existence and the baby will cover the objects he needs if they are in that area. The immediate proximal space is not only a space, i.e. a place of objects and separation relationships, but a non-space, a place of fusion that tends to dilute (Liberman et al., 1982, p. 408).

Within this space, which is mainly explored through the sense of touch, the capacity to bind and organise by means of visual perception starts to develop. By means of the privilege of vision, the space becomes configured as a scene in which objects appear and disappear, and perception from a distance makes the notions of presence and absence relative. The development of hearing allows the baby access to the experience of the presence of an unseen object, which is announced via the voice behind the baby's back, thus extending the visual space of 180° to 360° (*ibid.*, p. 409).

With crawling comes a vision of space, which becomes structured as a *space of action* (*ibid.*, p. 410), giving rise to successive processes of discrimination based on experiences of real comparison: this will allow the baby to differentiate objects from the primitive meanings he initially attributed to them. This stage is completed when the child can walk upright. This new perspective allows him to organise space according to the new notions of up, down, right, left, backwards and forwards. The progressive displacements will allow him to integrate tri-dimensionality. He will understand that objects in space are not only a surface, but also have volume and weight. An important moment is the acquisition of the notion of perspective, linked to that of reversibility. To achieve this, the presence of the mother is essential as a guiding object, allowing the baby to come closer and withdraw without the fear of remaining lost in external space (*ibid.*, pp. 410–411).

According to Liberman, those patients he calls psychosomatic (Liberman et al., 1982, p. 412) have had the passage from one evolutionary spatial conception to the other successively hindered, which gave rise to pseudo-development. The conception of space in these patients has therefore not attained the correlates that accompany the construction of the visual, spatial image, which would enable the retention of representations which are neither lost nor diluted, as happens with the sensations arising from the proximal dimension. There might be no notion of a stable space, that is to say no notion of the existence of objects when they are not present in the near space. In these patients, then, there is a contradiction: they have constructed a visual representation, but it maintains the qualities inherent in the conception of proximal space or in the space of action. It can be diluted at times of anxiety; it is structured and de-structured according to different activities. In order to keep it organised, they depend on the direct visual presence of the object seen from the same perspective. They cannot differentiate abstract representation from immediate sensory data.

The authors describe two models of this distorted organisation of space. In the first, space is a scene that constantly draws the person forward. In consequence, it is a "space of action" following a fixed trajectory, as if they were walking through a "tunnel"—similar to the gangway for boarding a plane, or that used by football players when going onto the football field—which prevents them from being aware of what is "beyond". It forms an exoskeleton which becomes equivalent to always holding on to their mother's hand. They can have access to new spaces without feeling anxiety, as the Self repeats the same attitude. The different spaces are organised as if they were one and the same scene. In addition, the difference between life at home, at work and at leisure is erased. This kind of organisation is exemplified by those patients who calculate a certain time and route in order to reach the analyst's office and who, when coming from another place, arrive late as they are incapable of correlating time and space, because they always maintain a fixed routine (Liberman et al., 1982, p. 416).

In the second model, a static conception of space predominates. This is an unchanging space in which different objects lack relief or the qualitative sensory details that would enable the person to distinguish them according to the emotional experiences they awaken. These people inhabit, by means of schizoid techniques, a self-created proximal space of their own, which allows them to move from one place to another within a non-space, as if it were a "crystal bubble" that isolates them from real space. Vision takes on the function of keeping this vital space under control, a space they then try to turn into a static space. The self-created proximal space also functions as an exoskeleton; however, in this case it is equivalent to going about the world not holding on to the mother, but rather *within* a mother who supports them while at the same time isolating them from any experience of contact. A patient may tell his analyst: "Your office is nearby," even if in fact he lives far away. Then, if the analyst goes on to ask him how that is so, the patient might reply: "It is near my mother's house." When this type of organisation fails, anxieties tend to revolve around ideas of dispersal or disappearing "as if they had vanished from the face of the earth", or those of "suffering sudden impact with objects in motion, being run over or falling" (Liberman et al., 1982, p. 418).

FUNCTIONS OF THE EGO, EGO-SKIN AND CONSTRUCTION OF SPACE STARTING FROM THE CONCEPT OF AFFECTIVE DISTANCE

The considerations proposed by Liberman and others are related to those of Anzieu and Tustin, and can be applied clinically to patients with skin diseases. As was mentioned earlier, patients present different patterns of behaviour: a disruptive pattern of sudden detachment in which they abandon relationships which are on the verge of becoming close (a product of affective closeness); or a "stickiness" that makes them unable to tolerate separations; or a successive alternation between these two movements: coming closer and drifting apart without ever cohering. The explanation for such behaviour could be related to difficulties in the exercise of the Ego functions which have to do with the construction of space, the concept of the boundary and their relationship to the skin.

According to Anzieu, very young children have not yet mastered the mature form of those functions, which is why for a baby there is no difference between space and the objects that inhabit it. In consequence, when one moves an object, one moves at the same time the part of space in which the object is. Since the child is also an object that occupies part of space and can be pierced by another part, when an object is put into motion, the risk that it will not stop generates in the child the anxiety that he will be pierced by the object, and the child starts to scream when the object comes close to him (Anzieu, 1987b).

We must bear in mind that for Anzieu the skin performs the same functions from a physical perspective as those pertaining to the Ego when seen from a psychological perspective, and that certain patients with narcissistic or borderline pathologies, who present failures in the Ego functions, also tend to suffer from skin diseases. For Anzieu "there is a relationship between (. . .) the extent to which the Ego is altered and the extent of the skin disease" (Anzieu, 1987b).

For Tustin, who takes the problem of psychotic children in order to explain failures in the processes of symbolisation that a normal child must develop, one of the mechanisms through which these failures are manifested is intrusive identification. These patients live through other people in a pathological and excessive way, like a crab which protects itself by entering the carapace of another creature.

Anzieu's and Tustin's work on early development, autistic cores and the role of the skin in the body image and constitution of the Ego alludes to both the sieve-like Ego and the shell-like Ego as clinical manifestations of failures in the symbolisation of the body and of the skin as a boundary. They also consider the former to be a consequence of the use of adhesive and mimetic projective identification. Likewise, works that follow the theory of attachment also refer to the dialectics of movement—coming closer and moving further apart—implemented by the child in order to regulate his distance from the other on whom he depends and whom he frequently takes as a reference point.

The concept of distance as defined by physics states quite simply that distance is the interval that separates two points in space. However, according to the dictionary, distance can also be the difference between one thing and the other: *there is a great distance between an honest man and a thief.* With this definition we can see how physical distance can come to represent a discrimination or separation of a moral nature. The concept of "distance" used in psychoanalysis, however, is even wider, because the object's qualities of closeness, distance and temporal and spatial mobility will be subjected not only to the order of topographical space and chronological time but also to "psychic reality, which *derives from the vicissitudes of emotional development*" (Liberman et al., 1982, pp. 354–355). This idea, added to the consideration of affectivity within a model that takes into account both the intra-psychic and the inter-subjective aspects, enables us to put forward the term *affective distance* as the result of the two kinds of distance: physical and emotional. It could be deduced from this that the idea of affective distance is useful in assessing not only the body image of a subject (in particular, his own idea of physical boundary, which is related to the skin), but the kind of object relations established according to this parameter.

AFFECTIVE DISTANCE AND SKIN DISEASES: INFERENCES FROM ATTACHMENT AND PROXEMIC BEHAVIOUR

In my experience with patients suffering from skin diseases, I have noticed that the patient's need to feel loved or protected or his need for attachment to others manifest themselves as a difficulty in differentiating the affective distance he keeps from others in different kinds of relationships. To the extent that skin diseases generate feelings of rejection both in others and in the patient himself, it is likely that differences will appear in attachment and proxemic behaviour compared to the rest of the population. These differences have important clinical consequences, because they determine patterns of behaviour that do not respond to the expectations of others regarding the affective distance which is appropriate to the particular kind of relationship established. This causes frequent conflicts that make the patient feel more rejected and isolated. For example, if he confuses the personal area with the social area, for instance by looking for love and contact at work, he can get too close to others, thus creating the wrong impression and being rejected. If he confuses these areas in the opposite sense, for example being cold and distancing himself from his friends for fear that his friendship and love will not be reciprocated or that he will be rejected in some way, others might never feel he is close enough to trust him either with their confidences or with their love. Some patients might never reach an intimate area and might thus be deprived of the erotic contact and caresses their skin longs for. Consequently, as many of the authors quoted in this book say, the patient may feel segregated and ostracized like a stranger, and the longing for contact could express itself as an alteration in the skin. Furthermore, the patient could develop "hard" character traits, or he could be covered by a second skin. Indeed, manifestations of the disease might develop in the very same organ which is deprived of the vital stimulation it needs.

Notes

1. The concept of proxemics is explained in section 6.5.
2. My italics.

CHAPTER SEVEN

The case of Mr Quirón

In the previous chapter the concepts of attachment, proxemics and affective distance were connected, and were then related to the subjective construction of space. In the following case material the implications of these concepts will be shown.

Introduction

Quirón is an intelligent, cultured 47-year-old man who works as a biologist at a prestigious pharmaceutical company. A widower with two children, he is the youngest of four siblings, and was raised partly by his mother, partly by a maid whose name is Apacible,[1] and also by his elder sister. He became ill with psoriasis when he was 18, and he has consulted me because his disease is greatly extended and he has not found any lasting positive response with previous treatments. This is his first experience of psychoanalytical psychotherapy. The son of elderly parents, he became used to playing alone and to receiving the attention given to an only child, although this attention was divided between the three women.

As an adult, his relationship with women is conflictive: feeling passionate towards them, he easily establishes relationships with them due to his good looks, his culture and his social position. However, he fears that once he falls in love with a woman, she will smother him, wanting to attach herself to him and depriving him of his personal space and independence. At the same time, he cannot bear not to have a woman devote her attention exclusively to him, and he feels uncomfortable if a woman neglects him to look after children from a previous marriage or a relative. He dedicated a great part of his life to his wife, who had become depressed and started to deteriorate long before she died, thus affecting his sexual life as well as the couple's social life. All his efforts to help her and change the negative direction of her life were in vain. He was left with the feeling that he loved someone who would not let herself be mended.

He finally found the love he was looking for in Luisa, a Colombian woman who makes him feel happiness and love, but from whom he has to separate periodically, either because she has visited Argentina or because he has visited Colombia and they have to return to their respective homes. This distance, which becomes periodically smaller and bigger, has stabilised the relationship. Every time he feels suffocated, pressured or uncomfortable, her return to her country of origin turns out to be a solution, and from a distance their love remains unaltered. In this concrete way, with the action of getting close and pulling away repeated innumerable times, Quirón has managed to safeguard the personal space he needs in order to preserve his relationship with Luisa.

There are four issues which occur repeatedly in the analysis of Quirón: the feeling of being hurt, the predominance of the visual sense, the issue of distance as a regulator of his social relationships, and finally the issue of his argumentative personality, aroused by the permanent threat to his personal space, which leads him to be constantly on the alert in order to protect it. Among all these, and acting as a pivot around which the other issues revolve, he lacks the presence of a paternal figure which can stabilise and hold him on a symbolic foundation, and keep him out of the constant mirror-like and imaginary fight for the dominance of space.

The feeling of being hurt, which is related to disappointment and to a lack of affection in his childhood, leads him into a never-ending search for feminine love in order to heal his wounds. But as this feeling of being hurt is unconscious, he usually chooses women whose wounds he must first heal; however, he fails in the attempt, thus repeating the history with his wife. In terms of the theory of the Ego-skin, we could say that he presents failures in the function of protection against stimuli (which are shown by the wound that will not heal) and in the functions of support and container.

A story by Quirón

Quirón wrote a story, which is reproduced here:

WEEKEND TRIP TO CÓRDOBA

He moved his elbow surreptitiously, almost stealthily over the armrest of his seat. He tried to win the rear as though not really wanting to, while looking fixedly to the front. Then he took a magazine which was inside the seat pocket in front of him and pretended to read, though in truth he was paying attention to what the other man, sitting next to him, was doing.

Marcos thought how he had not been to Córdoba for a long time. Exactly how long? And then he remembered the agony of his friend Nicolás's wife. Her name was Teresa, poor thing. And once again images of her came back to his mind; bedridden in the double bed, no sex since God knows when, and poor Nicolás with his sad, wrinkled face, with no money to pay for his wife's treatment and medications.

What a horrible thing, god! he told himself. And suddenly he remembered he did not believe in god, yes, written with lower case letters because he was an agnostic, that should be understood. He was not an atheist, as the father of Nicolás, his childhood friend, declared himself to be. Nicolás, his dear and close friend. However, he had refused to lend Nicolás the money he had recently wanted to borrow. He had done it so that he would not lose him, he told himself, yes, so that he would continue to be his friend and not feel that interest in money had reached them too.

Suddenly he felt the slight pressure of the other man, who was also trying to win that little piece of armrest with his elbow. Perhaps he had taken advantage of his momentary distraction, in which his own thoughts had occupied him.

It was a wonderful midday that Friday at the airport, and although the plane was small, Miguel had gone up the steps with the renewed enthusiasm that flying produced in him. Yes, he liked to travel by plane. It was not merely a statistical thing. It was not that flying by plane is safer than taking the bus or the old "Rayos del Sol" trains he used to take twenty years ago, when he used to visit his girlfriend at weekends; that was not what this was about. He was excited to feel that tickle produced by the risk of flying, not being safe until the plane lands and the engines are completely turned off.

However, when Miguel reached the edge of his seat, he saw that the man who would sit next to him had that disagreeable look typical of those who want the whole plane for themselves. He did not say anything, though. He merely limited himself to looking at him and, almost with contempt, silently demanded to have his own seat. Window again, he said to himself, even though I asked that stupid secretary of mine to get me the aisle. She knows very well that with these long legs I can't sit comfortably. And even less in these planes, which are so small. Worst of all, it's Friday, the day most planes are packed. Well, we'll see.

Marcos had seen this man standing next to him, quiet, as if incapable of talking to him. I've always hated these stuck up skinny types, he thought. I'm going to wait until he asks me to move. And he sat quietly, unperturbed. But he could not resist much longer, so he suddenly stood up and let him pass, trying to pretend he had not seen him before. That is how everything started.

When the plane started to move, they had begun to fight for their small spaces. It's a matter of dignity, come to think about it, thought Miguel as he tried to win the back part of the armrest with his elbow in order to have a better posture. But he didn't succeed, because Marcos's elbow was already there.

I wonder how my cousins are doing, thought Marcos. I haven't seen them in three years. Lidia separated from Bruno, it's terrible! With four daughters. At least they are older now, I believe the youngest is 16.

But suddenly he felt the pressure of another arm which was smoothly trying to displace him. In consequence, and with an impatient movement, he opened the paper, extending its pages. Who does he think he is, I'll teach him a lesson, he thought, and put at least a third of *La Nación* under Miguel's nose. Miguel almost couldn't resist the temptation to look him in the eye, because he had been looking at him for a while out of the corner of his eye, and so could perfectly measure all his movements.

What a relief that this trip only lasts an hour, thought Miguel. "55 minutes exactly", as the poster on route 9 says when you are approaching the city. It's only done so that you'll be beside yourself with anger after having driven for almost seven hours. I can't put up with this guy any longer. And thinking about this, he stood up abruptly and almost walked over his flight companion towards the toilet. At that instant, the plane fell into an air pocket, and Miguel hurt his hip on the seat next to him. He could see the smile of satisfaction on Marcos's face. It was almost a triumph, because he also saw how he had won all the armrest for himself with his left arm. You bastard! he thought. You'll see.

Miguel stayed in the toilet for quite a while. In fact, only five minutes had gone by, but it was enough to get some relief, in particular from the unbearable man sitting next to him. Then he remembered his several trips to Córdoba, sometimes by bus. He also remembered that he had finally married Claudia, despite the fact that he was actually in love with Irene, her sister. But people from Córdoba are terrible about "convenience", and as Irene was the prettier, her family had destined her for the rich guy, Luis Amenábar, that conceited man who even had a yacht. But in the end he was happy, because he usually went to Córdoba only at weekends, and luckily he had his work in Buenos Aires, where he spent most of his time. And then there was Leonor, pretty and lovable, waiting for him after work in the small flat he had bought for her. But now I have to solve this problem, he thought.

He opened the small door and walked decidedly towards his seat. Suddenly he saw the flight attendant, who was coming in the opposite direction towards him with the drinks trolley. He knew from experience that he would not be able to get to his seat if he didn't hurry. He walked faster and got to his place just in time. The girl looked at him with a smile and asked him, as usual:

"What will you have, sir?"

"Mineral water, that's all."

"Still or sparkling mineral water?"

"Still, thanks," he replied.

And that's when the tragedy occurred. The man sitting next to him looked at him from below, sitting in his seat without the least intention of moving. You'll have to ask me, you poor sod, thought Marcos, looking at him slyly.

Miguel took the small bottle of water, with infinite calm he took the lid off and then, very slowly, he started to pour its entire contents on Marcos's head. Marcos was soaking wet, and couldn't grasp what was going on.

"But, sir, what are you doing?" asked the flight attendant, horrified, as she tried to clean Marcos's head and clothes. Marcos started to say: "But, but, what's going on? Why? Why?" And he suddenly stood up, at the same time trying to dry himself with both hands.

Everything happened in an instant. The fight was inevitable and the space was too small for the fighters to move. Miguel pushed Marcos, who fell back into his seat; when he tried to stand up, the voice of the pilot was suddenly heard through the speakers: "Ladies and gentlemen, this is the captain speaking. I am sorry to inform you that due to an electrical breakdown, we won't be able to land in Córdoba. At present I am communicating with Ezeiza airport to authorise our landing there. Please stay calm, go back to your seats and fasten your seat belts until further notice. Thank you. Cockpit crew, please prepare for emergency landing."

Speechless, the passengers looked at one another. There was an air of surprise and heightened fear. The plane was not as invulnerable as it seemed; nor were they. Then it was all over. What seemed to be an irreconcilable fight became forced solidarity in times of adversity. Miguel extended his hand to Marcos so that he could stand up and return to his seat. Marcos looked at him and in silence fastened his seat belt.

"This doesn't look good. Something strange is going on, don't you think?" asked Miguel, looking him straight in the eye, as if wanting to make up with him after what had happened.

"I don't know, but I don't buy that 'electrical breakdown'."

"Well," said Miguel, "now the idea is to get to Ezeiza, or anywhere. . ."

"Yes," replied Marcos. "The thing is to be able to land." And he looked ahead, very frightened. A few seats behind, the flight attendant was helping a lady who was unwell. Other passengers fretted in their seats. Some of them stood up and looked at the small door of the cockpit.

Suddenly the plane fell forwards again. But this time it continued to fall and it seemed as though it would never stop, until suddenly it stabilised, and after a few moments it climbed again. People started to scream, and some of them were pointing out of the windows close to the wings. Thick smoke was coming out of the port engine. On the right of the plane things weren't any better, because the propeller was cutting out and looked as if it was about to stop. Suddenly the plane started up again, but smoke was still coming out of the other engine.

Then Miguel clutched Marcos's arm, and with the other hand showed him his personal card, which came from nowhere.

"Look, if you make it. . ."

"Stop that nonsense; here either we all make it or nobody makes it. I think we are almost there, luckily."

The laboured sound of the engines heightened and the vegetation of the woods surrounding Ezeiza could be seen far away. The plane started to descend slowly. Come on, come on, Miguel told himself, let's get down once and for all. . .

To the left, a flame emerged from the engine which, amid the thickening smoke, heightened panic among the passengers. The flight attendants could not stand it any longer. They shouted at them to sit, but it made no difference whatsoever. Finally, the runway appeared and the plane touched down. The sirens of the fire engines coming towards the plane could be heard clearly. The plane started to lose speed and then, suddenly, it stopped.

When the two men separated, Miguel squeezed Marcos's shoulder. Marcos, looking him in the eye, in turn said:

"Fortunately we've arrived in one piece."

"Yes, I think we have been very lucky. Well, goodbye." And Miguel walked towards the line of taxis which were eagerly awaiting their cargo.

Analysis of the story: the Ego's fight for space and death lurking behind

In the story, what we can see are two characters in a mirror-like fight. At times it becomes difficult to distinguish them, it is as if it were only one person duplicated. In the setting, as a backdrop against which the fight for space develops, there are references to feminine death and helplessness, as well as to man's impotence to repair that situation.

The place where the scene develops is an unsafe plane which, when Miguel leaves his seat in order to go to the toilet, falls into an air pocket. It is as if the seat were the only safe container and support in which to relax when faced with so much agony, misery and threatening death, in a world where god is written with lower case letters and does not guarantee anything.

The fight for space is complemented with the interchange of looks. Miguel was almost unable to resist the temptation to look Marcos in the eye. However, he had been looking at him for a while out of the corner of his eye. What could the difference be? It would seem that a direct look in the eye is an invasion of the other's image, a violation and an attack on dignity. As will be discussed later, the look transforms the other into a target, as if the eye that looks were the sight of a shotgun, and the observed eye were an object, namely the target that will be shot (see Chapter 12). Only after the threat of a crash, with the sense of imminent death and with a squeeze on the arm, can the look become reassuring: while Miguel squeezes Marcos's shoulder, clinging to someone who only a few minutes before was threatening his own dignity merely by his presence, Marcos looks him in the eye, but this time not to go through him or objectify him, but to acknowledge him.

The real threat of death introduced a hiatus at the exact point at which the Ego-to-Ego fight was constantly disavowing it by means of a series of narcissistic displays. "The plane was not as invulnerable as it seemed", and the Ego was not omnipotent either. That hiatus which cracks narcissism is represented in the story by the air pocket, the flaming wing and the plane that starts to fall.

The Ego is a dual agency. If there is a beautiful Ego, it is because there is another Ego which is ugly. If there is an Ego which is strong, it is because there is another Ego which is weak. In the story, the Ego's narcissistic tendency demands a place for itself, a space in which to expand and dominate. In order to realise this wish, the other can never be an object in the sense of object relations, because then the Ego must recognise a boundary, a limit it does not want to acknowledge as that would involve losing narcissism. (It should be remembered that "when Miguel reached the *edge* of his seat, he saw that the man who would sit next to him had that disagreeable look typical of those who want the whole plane for themselves".) If this edge is not acknowledged by the Ego, when faced with the lack of boundaries that can circumscribe a space, the imaginary Ego-to Ego fight begins: a fight in which space and distance will be defined by means of strength; a fight in which one person's Ego can only find its place if the other's Ego shrinks or disappears. In this fight there are no limits, only the threat of anxiety; and the other becomes another-Ego who cannot be loved. He can only be objectified, that is to say reduced to a thing, to something "given to be seen", a thing helpless before a look that goes through him or gives sense to what he wants without acknowledging him (the person reduced to a thing) at all.

Erga omnes: a feeling of shame in front of everyone. Analysis of the function of the gaze and the skin's response to it

In the story written by Quirón, space, distance and gaze are permanently present. His psoriasis plays an essential role, since it performs the same function that in the story is attributed to the fire which makes the plane go down. Once, when he felt anxious due to the imminent arrival of Luisa, whom he had only known for a short time, Quirón's skin disease started to appear again and nothing had any effect on it. He exercised such obsessive control over the evolution of his disease that he spent a long time in front of his mirrors at home to see if the disease was worse, or if it could be stopped. He was asked to cover all the mirrors he had at home and to refrain from looking at himself for a week, until the following session. His improvement was surprising.

> The way I looked made me feel watched all the time. As if the universe was like an audience, for example the audience at a theatre where one is exposed to its gaze. I have a friend who is a notary and he once told me that there is a legal principle which in Latin is *erga omnes,* which means "in front of all". It seems that this principle is applied, for example, when a document such as a deed is public, or when the State must guarantee the rule of law "in front of all and for all".

These associations were very enlightening. *Erga omnes* is a way of naming the Other, considered as "all-seeing". And in front of an Other who gazes and who transforms the subject into an object of his gaze, which then immediately categorises him as a public object, the subject, denaturalised, becomes something "given to be seen". That is why Quirón's feelings of shame appear not before Luisa or any other woman, but when he exhibits himself on the beach, or at a football stadium, where he remains "in front of all."

The reference to the rule of law shows the symbolic failure and his attempt at restitution. Where the Other as the law, as a boundary, as a function of the interdicting father who establishes abstract and invisible norms which are nevertheless respected by all, does not function properly, there appears a scopic Other who imposes a pseudo-law in which image predominates above all things. The phrase "in front of all" is no longer a product of a symbolic pact, which is accepted because it has become written law, but rather it is a public marking, a stigma, a sentence of aesthetic mutilation, derision, in short: shame.

Distance and limits

When he started analysis, Quirón established a distance, and he resisted accepting the frequency of sessions proposed by his therapist. The analysis began as he wished, until in one session he spoke about his childhood and remembered he had been very lonely. He enjoyed exclusivity, he did not have to share his toys, and he received care in particular from his nanny, Apacible, though she probably clung to him in order to satisfy her own need for affection and contact. In consequence, Quirón was overcome by a feeling of sadness and of loneliness within an environment which had imprecise boundaries. Any child who is cuddled and embraced by a sexually unsatisfied woman, or by a woman who is sad and an orphan, develops a contradictory attitude: on the one hand, he enjoys this soft body which embraces him and gives him warmth, but on the other hand he feels an inversion of roles in which boundaries fade, and this invades him and fills him with fear. In this way Quirón developed a paradoxical pattern of behaviour: he demanded exclusivity, but then resisted receiving what he was offered for fear of being invaded in his narcissistic aspect. It was as if he had said: "I am here! Pay attention to me!—but only up to here, do not trespass beyond this limit, otherwise I will feel overwhelmed and invaded."

I've always felt a particular aversion to anything sugary, to sticky substances. For me, excessive contact ends in a clash, friction or something disagreeable. It is important to keep that distance which is like the protective shell of a relationship.

At the point where he was able to associate his childhood loneliness with his fear of being invaded, he spontaneously asked to increase the frequency of the sessions. The feeling of being hurt and his argumentative attitude are also related to these indefinite boundaries:

I was once humiliated. I believe that when a subordinate makes a mistake and he is humiliated, it is very difficult to heal the wound. At the school I used to go to it was common to be reminded of a mistake one had made. That causes resentment. When I feel someone wants to harm me, I put on the ego, I pick up my sword and go out to fight.

Quirón's dreams and Freudian slips

In contrast with what is usually said about patients with psychosomatic problems, Quirón makes Freudian slips and refers to dreams. In one session, when he wanted to say that the common man is helpless when faced with people who have power, he said instead that he is "unharmed".[2] By using the word "unharmed" he associated the wish to not be harmed and to be immune with all sorts of aggressions.

This slip proves the extent to which he feels hurt unconsciously, and what is more, this feeling of being hurt (which, as I said earlier, acquires in his discourse the figurative idea of a wound) would seem to have consequences in two different aspects of his life. In the behavioural aspect he is always fighting, from a paranoid position, against those who hurt him either in the past or in the present, while in the somatic aspect, the lesions of psoriasis acquire the significance of wounds that cannot heal. The fact that in psoriasis the index of cell reproduction of keratinocytes is accelerated to a speed similar to that which occurs in the healing of wounds was used in analysis as a "bridge" in order to work on this sensation of a wound that is impossible to repair. In this same way, we worked with the idea of a protective shell, an expression taken from his own discourse. After four years of analysis, Quirón told me the following dream:

> It was dawn. I went into the water and it never reached beyond halfway up my legs. Then the sun started to disappear and I was afraid of getting lost in the water and of not being able to go back. I calmed down slowly on seeing that I was going back to where I had started.

Associations:
Fear of getting lost and not being able to go back: I associate this with death.

Search for depth: I thought it was the river (River Plate). With death I associate not being able to go back, drowning, falling into a pit. The River Plate is not deep: you could wade across the river to Uruguay. When we were young and used to sail in a sailing boat, we used to throw ourselves into the river and we could stand on the bottom, but suddenly we would be out of our depth and we would take a step and sink. It is an uneven river.

Darkness within the water scares me. I lose my bearings, the idea of where I am.

The fear of getting lost in the dream I associate with arriving in a country I'm not familiar with.

One of the beaches of Colombia, a place where there is a fortress, and where we go with Luisa, has a gentle slope: you start to get into the water, but it doesn't cover you, they are quiet waters.

The interpretation of the dream connects the history of his childhood to Apacible, his mother and his sister, and to his present situation with Luisa. The idea of water and of depth is related to his need for an envelope that can progressively cover his body. This envelope is associated with two meanings. One is dangerous: "you take a step and you sink", which refers to the character of both his sister and his mother; "you drown", which refers to the supporting and loving, but also smothering embrace of Apacible, as well as to a strengthening and constructive embrace: this is the affectionate and protective embrace he is looking for in Luisa. Luisa condenses the "strength" he wants for himself and the peaceful tranquillity which reminds him of his nanny. The gentle slope could be related to a wish to spend his old age with Luisa. Before he told me his dream, he had said that Luisa enjoys travelling and that she usually travels calmly. In the representation of the water that rises and progressively covers him, we can think of life as a starting point, and in the representation of falling into the water we can think of death, which also appears in the dream through the idea of his not being able to go back.

The dream reflects his wishes and his fears amid the significant women in his life: he has found love and has fantasies of uniting with Luisa. However, these fantasies, which represent the possibility of finding an envelope for his Ego that will embrace him without smothering him, that will strengthen him in order to face life and death, also represent to him the fears of treacherous love, love that suddenly becomes a pit of death, as happened with his wife. The fantasies of uniting with Luisa are accompanied by the idea of travelling with her and spending his old age in Colombia, finding at last a peaceful life without feeling smothered.

The associations that followed the work of interpreting the dream revolved around his feeling of lacking roots in Argentina, of feeling distant from the people who are around him in Buenos Aires and feeling a great insecurity about what is going on "outside him", in contrast to what he feels "inside", such as the need for a warmer climate, something which is probably influenced by Luisa.

In the following session, his discourse revolved around the skin and a new way of living life:

My skin is better. This is getting easier and easier to control. As soon as you detect a problem, the solution is at hand. In a short time you start seeing results.

In the end, you only live once and each moment of life should be enjoyed as unique, because perhaps you'll never get the chance again. I try to watch entertaining stuff because I am too sensitive.

People restrain themselves for lack of money and go out less, and what they don't see is that they are starving themselves of what provides more life: being in contact with others.

When I was a child, I had all the space I wanted in order to move about and enjoy being with my friends. But my friends were not available. I always felt that I was more available for them than they were for me. I am not jealous of women, but I am certainly jealous of my friend's affections. But not any more, that affective jealousy doesn't affect me, doesn't irritate me any more. It's not that I have built a shell. What this is about is accepting the world and others as they really are and not as I'd like them to be. This is not just resigning myself to it or feeling defeated. It's accepting reality.

Last weekend was a long rainy weekend: sometimes I feel a desperate urge to change what is hopeless. But this time I bought myself a book, I gave a book to a friend and I rested a lot. It was like some form of spiritual tranquillity.

After five years of treatment, Quirón still has some small lesions of psoriasis, but they do not affect his quality of life at all. He does not constantly fight with others. He has a very good relationship with his dermatologist, whom he trusts, and the symptoms have remained unchanged now for years.

Notes

1. Apacible in English means "peaceful".
2. In Spanish the words "helpless" and "unharmed" have a similar sound. This similarity is unfortunately lost in translation.

CHAPTER EIGHT

Body image and the psychosomatic patterns of childhood. Medical publicity regarding the skin

Constitution of the body image and reactive psychosomatic patterns in childhood

When a child is born, he receives a series of stimuli with which he will construct his body image. With a pedagogical objective, they will be grouped arbitrarily into three categories:

- Sensoperceptive stimuli
- Interaction with the Other[1] who speaks with him
- Visual images both of himself and of the helpful person

Although the three categories are, all things considered, sensoperceptive stimuli (in which case we could say that the first category in fact includes the other two), here they have been artificially separated since each of these stimuli has a different influence.

SENSOPERCEPTIVE STIMULI

Among the sensoperceptive stimuli, those received by exteroceptors, proprioceptors and interoceptors will be emphasised. We must also add to these the so-called superior sensations (DeMyer, 1976).

Exteroceptors
These receive sensations of vision and of sound, olfactory sensations and cutaneous sensations. The main sensations provided by the

cutaneous exteroceptors are the superficial sensations of the skin: tactile sensations, temperature, superficial pain, and itching and ticklish feelings.

Proprioceptors

These conduct deep somatic sensations from the receptors deep within the skin, muscles, inner ear and articulations, and they make possible the senses of position, movement, internal pain, vibration, pressure and equilibrium.

Interoceptors

These provide visceral sensations: visceral pain and pressure or distension.

Superior sensations

This category includes shape, size, weight and consistency; and tactile discrimination between two points

INTERACTION WITH THE OTHER

In order to understand the influence of interaction with the Other on the constitution of body image, three interrelated subjects be developed:

- The influence of the mother in the development of the child's language
- The experience of satisfaction
- The night-time processes of separation-individuation

The influence of the mother in the development of the child's language

As the child cannot adequately decode all the stimuli he receives, the intervention of language acquires special importance. The mother will say to him: "This is what's wrong with you," and in this way she acts as if she were a translator of the aforementioned stimuli. Then she will put him to bed, feed him, pick him up or rock him according to her own intuition as well as what she is capable of understanding from the signals the child emits, and while she is carrying out any of these activities, she will talk to the child or sometimes sing to him.

When he is being spoken or sung to, the child listens to the sound of the voice and registers what Freud called "sound image". He then associates this sound with an innervation. What does this mean? That if he repeats what he has been told, even if what he repeats does not coincide at all with what he heard, the very fact of repeating involves a motor sensation, a registering of the movement of his mouth. For example, the mother says to him "dummy" or "toy"; the child says "to" and has the sensation of the letter "t". When babies begin to talk, they not only say "to", they also pronounce the "t" many times, because they are repeating the motor sensation of resting the tongue on the palate and on the incisors. The addition of the sound image of the word plus the motor innervation or "feeling of innervation of the word" will produce in the child a *motor representation of language* (Freud, 1915b).

In order to imagine in practice what a motor representation of language is, let us look at the following example. A young girl could not pronounce the letter "r" properly, nor could she pronounce the letters that accompany the "r". For example, she could not say "dry". Her father wanted to teach her: "Repeat with me: Dora, Dora, Dora, Dora, Dora, Dora, faster and faster and you'll be able to pronounce 'dr'." However, it was all no use. Then the mother, who remembered songs and sayings from primary school, asked her to repeat: "Round the rugged rocks the ragged rascal ran". But that didn't help either. So they consulted a speech therapist, perhaps thinking that she would do the same as they had, only with more patience. However, it was nothing like that. They found something that surprised them: the speech therapist told the girl to put a pencil over her lips and hold it, without letting it fall. Then she taught her a game which consisted of sweeping, with the "little broom" that was her tongue, the "little roof" that was her palate, after which she told her to make the sound of an engine, something like "ttbrrrrrrrum", and then she told her to play at imitating the snort of a horse. She told her to practice those sounds and exercises while playing with her mum and dad as homework. And in this way, playing with the sounds of an engine and of a little horse, the girl acquired the notion of vibration, which is essential in order to be able to pronounce the letter "r". She acquired the association between a sound image, "ttbrrrrrrum", and an innervation, that is to say the association necessary to produce a vibration by moving certain muscles. In this way she also learned to combine the "d" and the "r" of "Andrea" (the name of the speech therapist) and with that she constructed the motor representation of language, after which she could pronounce the "r" perfectly well. What is more, she could pronounce "dry" and confirmed that now she realized that some words were pronounced with the "dr" used in sweeping the palate with the little "broom".

The problem is that to begin with the child behaves as if he had a self-created language, because from listening to his mother say, for example, the words "dummy" or "toy", he says "to". Subsequently, he names all the things in the world using the word "to". Everything becomes "to" because the child has learnt that with this word he can recreate, in their absence, the objects he wants. With two or three more words he names the toy, the dummy, any kind of food, and even the names of people. Freud suggests this in the addenda to his paper "The unconscious": when the child acquires the sound image of the pronounced word, he no longer particularly cares if what he says coincides with what he hears, and he uses a single word to name all things (1915b). However, this word may or may not be heard, and it may or may not be translated by the Other. When it is not heard, the child will use other mechanisms of a more primitive nature than the word in order to communicate. The previous experience of having being heard or given attention through non-verbal expression is what Freud called *experience of satisfaction* (1895).

The experience of satisfaction

The experience of satisfaction has a first component called *tension of need,* which does not necessarily have a visual representation. When someone says, "I am hungry", what he immediately thinks about in images is the food that will satisfy the hunger. Yet the food is a visual image of the object that was evoked in order to relieve the tension of need; it is not the tension of need proper. To put it as clearly as possible: when someone is hungry, bread is evoked, but bread is the image of the object, not the image of hunger. The "image" of the tension of need is a sensoperceptive register and not a figurative register. Freud conceived of the tension of need as an increase in charge within the psychic apparatus, taking the latter to be a system prone to discharge. As discharge without the object causes more tension, the child produces what is called the *internal alteration*. This is what Freud called a series of secretor and vasomotor discharges, screaming and the expression of emotions. The helpful person responds to the internal alteration and gives the extraneous help which generally provides the object that will meet this need.

Tension of need (hunger)	→	Object of need provided by the extraneous help (breast, milk, read)	→	Movement of the stomach to assimilate the food

This experience has two consequences which it is important to take into account, the first being that the internal alteration[2] functions as an initial language, although it is a language similar to a code, made of signs. Nevertheless, it is an initial form of communication with the Other because as a consequence of the child crying or having a runny nose or kicking, the Other appears and provides him with what he was looking for. The other consequence is that the experience of satisfaction is an association of mnemonic traces, which are heterogeneous. The tension of need is an interoceptive sensation, such as the ones mentioned at the beginning of the chapter. The object, in contrast, is an object which can be named, represented and seen, that is to say it lends itself more to figuration.

In addition, the experience of satisfaction includes the movements which are later made by the stomach in order to assimilate food, and those movements belong once again to the ambit of sensoperception, in this particular case interoception. This means that within the psychic apparatus *the heterogeneous elements can associate with each other and modify each other*, which gives us some hope of intervening, with words or images, in the proprioceptive or interoceptiove sensations and, through the sensations, of intervening also in the movements and secretions of the organs such as, in this case, the movements of the stomach.

Let us come back to the subject of the child's "only word" or first words: if the Other does not hear or translates wrongly the only word with which the child communicates, distortions in the sensations and registers of the child will be produced, thus altering his internal world. The next stage in children is what is called learning to post-speak, which is when children repeat parrot-fashion, because they learn to repeat what they hear without understanding it very well.

The child can repeat anything. If someone says to him: "Say otorhinolaryngologist", or "Say polyhedron", he will say "otorhinolaryngologist" or "polyhedron" without understanding what those words mean, but despite knowing this, the parents are satisfied with the repetition of the words.

The wishes of the parents progressively begin to over-impress themselves on the confusing and nebulous sensations produced by perception within the child. The mother and father have their own personal histories and also have their own body images, which have been formed with the same elements mentioned earlier: sensoperceptive stimuli, the relationship with language and the image of the helpful person. This family history and the body image of each of the parents will mark the body of the child, privileging certain organs or functions.

The night-time processes of separation-individuation

There is a period of development in the child, generally coinciding with the beginning of language, which generally takes place between eight months and two years of age, in which he begins to wake up at night. He already sleeps in his own room, he can already say "mum", but he wakes up in the middle of the night either crying or calling out. In the beginning he does this every five hours, then every four hours, then he might do it every two hours, and almost every time the child calms down when his mother or his father goes to his room and stays with him until he goes back to sleep.

From then on the following happens: the child goes to his parents' bed: a bad solution that nevertheless brings the problem to an end. In truth, he continues to wake up every two hours, but he soon goes back to sleep as his parents can calm him down almost without waking up, by means of stroking or patting him in his sleep. Unfortunately, it is at this point that many marriages begin to break. Since there is not enough room in the bed for everyone, the sexual life of the couple is altered and the father usually starts to be displaced, or—depending on the dynamics of the marriage—the mother may be the one who is displaced. It could also happen that the child becomes over-excited due to the proximity of his parents' bodies or their sexual activity. Alternatively, one of the parents goes to sleep in the child's bed. This is also a bad solution, although it pacifies the "psychoanalytic superego", because the child has not gone to his parents' bed. The third alternative is to leave the child to cry.

When the child is left to cry, he will replace calling out "mum!" repeatedly with crying, at which point he will cry uncontrollably. But if nobody answers him, he might say: "Mum, snot!" or he might make sniffing noises, begin to sob and cough or have bronchial spasms, at which point the mother might go to him or say to him without getting out of bed:

"Blow your nose."

"I don't have a handkerchief."

"Use the blanket, it doesn't matter."

Faced with this lack of satisfaction of his demand, the child will look for a substitute to snot:

"Mum, wee!"

In this case, she would hardly tell him to wet his bed; however, she might reply:

"You know how to go to the loo, go on your own, nothing will happen to you."

The child might then reply:

"Mum, poo!"

Or alternatively, the noise of breathing spasms might appear, or a compulsive scratching that accompanies eczema and complaints of itching. The series ends when one (or both) of the parents accepts one of the child's proposals and responds to this form of calling. In this way, the child's body comes to the fore. The child will learn that his coughing, his itching, his faeces, his snot, his spots, etc. take the place of the word that names all the things he feels at night: anxiety, loneliness, separation, fears, and so on.

Previously, we said that in the development of language there is a motor representation of language, a self-created language and an association of heterogeneous elements with each other. This development constitutes a kind of basis. Taking this as a starting point, substitute forms of development can take place, in which the following aspects are connected: a) different motor representations (including the vasomotor representations) which take the place of a new motor representation of language; b) other forms of self-created language in which the "only word" is not a word but a physical reaction, that is to say instead of saying "to", for example, the child "names" all things with his coughing or with his allergic reaction;

and finally c) new associations of heterogeneous elements, such that the vasomotor reaction (blushing, for example) takes the place of a word, but is later associated with words of his own or words he has heard. It is as if he were styling himself on one of those children's books in which the text combines not only words and images but also sounds, by way of buttons beside the pages which are permanently in view no matter which page of the story is being read. The text refers to certain pictures which are associated with sounds, but the button can be pushed at any time, and the sound will still be produced regardless of the page. In addition, the same sound can be connected with several passages of the text (figure 8.1).

Figure 8.1
Example of an interactive story. In the psychosomatic reactions of the child, the "buttons" would be coughing, spots, spasms, eczema, etc.

In a similar way, taking the experiences of individuation and separation that take place at night or during sleep as our starting point, ways in which the child calls out for his parents are produced such that, when they succeed in making the parents come to him, they become a form of communication and leave a mark which is part of a complex mnemonic trace constituted by heterogeneous registers that remain connected with each other (the body of the child with all its emissions of fluids and sounds, screaming, the parents' response, sleep, contact with the parents, lullabies, and so on). In this way what could be called a *reactive psychosomatic pattern of childhood* is configured.

The image of the helpful person

The image of the mother or the father who goes to the child in order to provide him with the extraneous help or to act as a hostile object also has a constitutive power over the body image. However, the way in which the image of the helpful person is imprinted depends greatly on the functioning of a symbolic system. This system could be compared to a flat mirror such as those which can swing, generally used by tailors (Peskin, 2003, pp. 105–109). If we call real space the space before the mirror and virtual space that which is reflected in the mirror, we can then see that if the swinging mirror has loose screws, is broken or is too inclined, the image reflected in the virtual space will appear distorted, fragmented, too far forward or further back than it should be. This is what usually happens when we use a slide projector and we lose the notions of left, right, forwards and backwards. In this way, the flat mirror that swings becomes a metaphor for the symbolic system of a subject, for his ability to discriminate Me from Not-Me, internal from external, container from content, and what is his own from what is alien; for his capacity to name things with words and produce a new significance every time he feels anxiety or finds himself in a situation which questions his identity, one which he cannot work through. In consequence, having a good symbolic system at his disposal enables a subject to get out of a tight spot with a new meaning, or to inscribe a new identity on himself when the one he thought he had with some certainty is questioned.

The body image in dermatological advertising and in patients' drawings

If the symbolic system is badly constituted, it is as if the mirror deformed or fragmented the images that should be reflected in it. This means that a bad connection will occur between the three elements mentioned earlier: sensoperception, language and visual images. As a consequence, one of the three elements will be privileged over the other two. In this way a subject will come to feel that his identity exists through pain, thus privileging sensoperception, for example. It would be as if to say: "I'm in pain, therefore I am". Another alternative is for a subject to privilege an imaginary world and possess an identity as a consequence of imposing his own image regardless of the "real world". This would be as if to say: "I'm seen, therefore I am". A third alternative is that identity could adhere indissolubly to a name, as in the case of a woman with vitiligo whose name is Blanca Negri;[3] another example is a person called Florence whose skin shows symptoms every spring.[4] These cases would involve saying: "I'm named, therefore I am".

When one element assumes the representation of all the others, the alterations in the body image are added to the identity problems. The following pictures show medical advertisements or photographs and drawings by patients which show different failures in the connection of the three elements just mentioned. The effects of these failures include experiences of having a fragmented body, symbiotic relationships, problems in constituting the boundaries of the body, the search for distinctive marks, relationship problems, and so on.

In figure 8.2 the body is represented by a once-popular toy consisting of a cube the parts of which could be turned in different directions in order to bring together on each face of the cube the squares of the same colour, or in this case to form a figure that represents the human body. The implicit message is that the disease causes the individual to experience physical fragmentation, as if he had a body which cannot complete its formation, and this difficulty could be overcome by taking the medication.

Many patients with alopecia areata usually say, on referring to their disease, that "they have a part missing", or that they have "a hole in their head". In fact, an area of alopecia is not a hole, and

Figure 8.2 Fragmented body

although there may be one or several areas of the scalp in which the hair does not grow, it does not mean that there is "a part" of the body missing, despite the fact that some patients experience it in this way. In figure 8.3, the advertising of a product for combating hair loss shows the head as if it were a puzzle which lacks many pieces, and then goes on to suggest that the components of the product could be the pieces that the patient lacks.

When the symbolic system mentioned earlier fails, we saw that indiscriminate and symbiotic relationships can be established. Figure

Figure 8.3 Representation of alopecia as pieces missing from a puzzle

8.4 shows a picture of two dancers who are connected and merged at the arms and the feet. As the advertisement is for an anti-perspirant, we can observe that at armpit level on both dancers the limit separating the interior from the exterior is clear and well defined, suggesting that nothing comes outwards from the interior, while other parts of their bodies are merged with the external world and the inside and the outside are thus confused.

Certain symbiotic aspects can also make themselves apparent in the patient's discourse. For example, Pepe, a patient with these characteristics, always says "I adhere" in order to say that he agrees with something. He emphasizes that he bought a "permanent timeshare" to go on holidays with his wife. She wants to separate from him, but he says that "selfishness and stopping breathing are the same". When he was part of a psychotherapy group and one of the members abandoned treatment, he said: "He left because he could neither contribute nor draw from the group's common resources."

The picture in figure 8.5 illustrates the consequences of a failure in the configuration of an interior and an exterior. It is a hospital

Figure 8.4
Advertisement
for a deodorant
depicting two
"symbiotic"
dancers

patient with chronic psoriasis who used to say: "I am the hospital's safe." All the professionals from the Unit gave her their bags, coats and valuables, which she then kept on her bed. These objects took up so much space that she ended up with part of her body hanging over the edge of the mattress. The doctors said that it was far safer to give their belongings to her because the lockers where they used to keep their valuables had been raided, whereas with her nothing ever went missing. However, this was in fact a pathological way for the patient to constitute an interior by extending her body image to the bed, thus alleviating her feeling of lacking boundaries by imagining that she possessed inviolable walls, like those of a safe. The paradox was that when she was discharged from hospital, her symptoms reappeared, and in this way she was never really out of

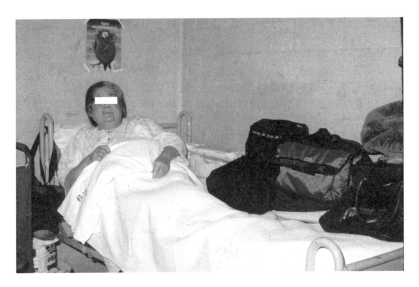

Figure 8.5 Hospitalised patient with psoriasis: "The hospital safe"

the "inside" of the hospital, where she had managed to build an "inside" of herself which included the space of her bed.

Figure 8.6 shows a human figure drawn by a patient originally from Brazil, who was hospitalized due to a skin disease. He called his drawing "Muller em terapia" (woman in therapy). As can be seen, the backward limit of the body is confused with the couch. In this way he shows not only his pressing need to establish thick and protective limits, but also his difficulty in distinguishing himself from external objects, and perhaps even a wish to merge with the analyst.

Another patient with psoriasis who was seen at the hospital, and who was also blind, used to live in a town in the interior of the country when he was young, near an industrial estate which had a power station. He had a game with his little brother which consisted of touching a part of the power station with a wooden stick; this produced an electric shock of such intensity that it threw him violently backwards. The game consisted of competing with his brother to see who could be thrown further away. They used to draw a line with chalk to mark the previous record of where they had fallen, and the big challenge was to pass the line. This idea of tracing a limit from a potentially fatal contact was perhaps connected to the fact that when he went near his father looking for affection, his father

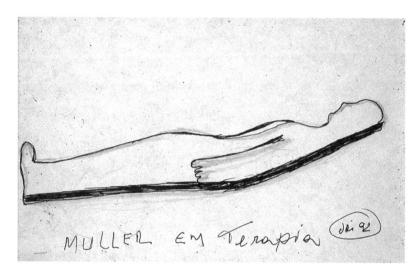

Figure 8.6 "Woman in therapy"

used to say "Air!" as a way of making him go away. What can be inferred from this patient's material is on the one hand his need for contact, and on the other hand the wish to be acknowledged, to have support, to construct a boundary that will contain him no matter what, and to broaden it progressively, even in an almost suicidal way.

As can be seen, contact has different connotations: it can be loving and soft, or it can be deadly, like the *touché* of fencers or the contact of electricity. Indeed, with electricity it is called precisely that: "contact". In the same way as the absence of the mother can be experienced as the presence of a bad mother, the absence of contact can be experienced as the presence of a deadly contact.

Another way of constructing a limit is to build a wall, as shown in figure 8.7. This is sometimes seen in the personality that people intuitively call "hard". A person can also make a muscular shell, for example by body-building, thus building a "second skin" (see Chapters 2 and 3). These are all ways of acquiring a body or an identity and of being its self-container.

Figure 8.8 shows a drawing by a patient with psoriasis who drew a face divided into two: one half of the face has a large eye from which a tear is falling, while the other half of the face has blocks of flats. He called it "Stone sadness".

Onicomicosis

Su tratamiento ha chocado
siempre contra un
muro impenetrable

Figure 8.7
The skin and
the nails as
a wall

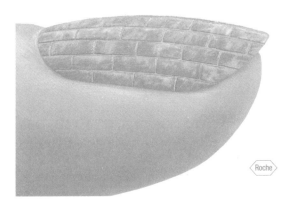

Roche

When a child draws a picture, he generally passes from the configurations of his own body to the spatial configurations of the drawing. For example, he passes from his fingers to a pencil with which he scrawls everywhere, until from the pencil he passes to the paper, and once on the paper, he starts to make configurations which have to do with the ideas he has about his own body. Later, the pictures he draws on the paper will once again have an effect on his body, and in this way both his body image and his drawings will be enriched. When the "to and fro" between the body and the drawings is not dynamic, or when the "tailor's mirror" swings (the mirror we mentioned previously as a metaphor of the symbolic system), projections are fixated and remain stuck, which means they lack the

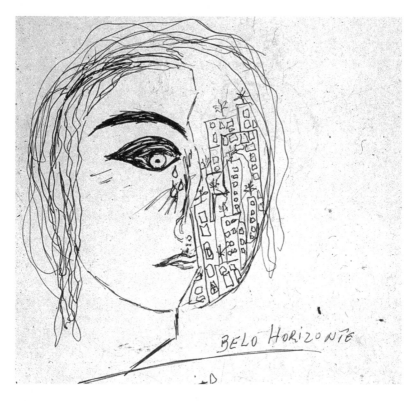

Figure 8.8 "Stone sadness"

sliding that permits creativity. In some cases creativity is nevertheless produced, but a disease develops at the same time. I once had a shocking experience when I attended the exhibition of an artist, and a professor of pathological anatomy who was with me "diagnosed" in one of the paintings a case of poststreptococcal glomerulonephritis. I later learned that the painter had had a renal insufficiency.

In the case of figure 8.8, the drawing shows in a more indirect way something that is actually going on in the patient's body, namely the fact that certain sad impressions he had in life remained imprinted as marks. The lesions of psoriasis were for him like life wounds, and he felt sadness as if it were literally sculpted or cut into his skin.

I once saw a young man who had his hands rendered useless by psoriasis; the disease had started after he had held in his arms the agonised body of his best friend, who had had an accident. He began to heal when he started writing swear words on the wall of his room, and then went on to write on paper. The progression of his feelings, from the hands transformed into claws by psoriasis, through to using his fingers as pencils, then on to writing proper, advanced at the same rate as the disappearance of his lesions.

The difficulty of establishing one's own boundaries as well as adequate discrimination generates mechanisms of projective identification and behaviour sequences such as those represented in figure 8.9. Let us suppose that A is a subject carrying his own lack, his castration, on his shoulders. First he sees someone else, B, who is worse off than he is, meaning that B is more unstable or deteriorated. Then the initial subject, A, projects his lack onto B. Later, he sees that B is not well; he feels sorry for him and gives him his love. Finally, the picture shows that B improves and leaves very happy, apparently without the lack, while A, the "donor", remains in the state B was in when A saw him for the very first time, but with his lack "at boiling point", so to speak.

In some patients with psoriasis, it is very common to observe this under the guise of extreme generosity. In a particular psychotherapy group for psoriasis patients we had agreed that in order to celebrate New Year's Eve, each of us would bring along something to eat and that we would drink a toast. One of the patients, undoubtedly with the intention of attracting love and appreciation, came with an enormous fridge, like those taken for days at a time, and brought everything: disposable glasses, enough food to feed an army, and champagne. What happened then? He had done this in his eagerness to please, but what he actually generated in everyone else was a feeling of being at fault because they had brought along less than he had. As a result, what he received instead of love was criticism and aggression. For example, a disposable glass falling apart was enough for someone to say as a joke: "What rubbish you've brought!" When this was analysed, he referred to the fact that he had once organized a Christmas Eve party for fifty families at his own home. He worked a great deal, preparing everything, and he even had gone to the trouble of making little gifts, an enormous display involving great expense, that none of the guests would have, and what he brought about was the loss of almost all of his friends due to this same mechanism. Another patient expressed this in the following way:

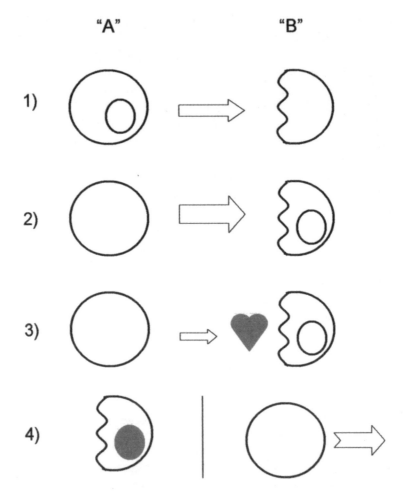

Figure 8.9 The one who gives more than he can afford finds that what he gets in return is never enough

"The one who gives more than he can afford finds that what he gets in return is never enough, while the one who receives more than he asked for, or more than he expects, is prevented by guilt from being thankful."

In figure 8.10, the lesion appears to be the object of the doctor's gaze, but in fact it is the doctor who has become the object of the patient's gaze.

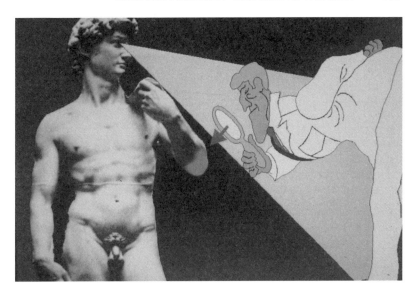

Figure 8.10 Who is the object of the gaze?

When the visual aspect, which is the third of the elements mentioned as being necessary for the constitution of the body image, is considered to be of the utmost importance, we will see that a patient can develop a lesion of any sort as long as it is able to catch the gaze of the other in order to "freeze" it at that point, thus controlling him. When we look at patients, we believe that we are the ones who observe; however, the more masochistic and controlling a patient is, and the more he uses his disease as an identity trait, the more he will be observing the way in which we look at him and arranging his relationship with us according to this.

The disease functioning as a personal name is illustrated in figure 8.11. With the slogan "For the treatment of mycoses, a prestigious brand", the advertising attempts to replace the mark of the disease with the brand of the product prescribed for its treatment.

This is a phenomenon which is becoming increasingly prevalent in our society. At one time sports shirts were identified with brands which had no meaning, but nowadays they are called "Sergio Tacchini", or the name of some sportsman or other. Nowadays brands have proper names, and curiously, football shirts, which used

Figure 8.11 The disease and the treatment as marks of identity

to be like a personal name due to their distinctive colours, now need the addition of a commercial brand.

Figure 8.12 shows a drawing by a boy aged eleven, with psoriasis on his back. It shows a football player scoring a penalty; he has the number eleven on his back, and the brand name "Salicrem" is clearly visible on his shirt. On the exact same spot where the boy has his plaque of psoriasis, he drew the brand name of a cream and a shirt number which represents his own age.

Quino's cartoon in figures 8.13 and 8.14 shows how a disease can acquire the status of an identity. While on all the graves there are symbols and phrases alluding to what each of the people were in their lives, at the last grave there is a photo of the same man who is looking at the graves, and a monument of a bored and listless angel. On the stone plaque we read: "He somatized", meaning that his disease was his life and that his identity revolved around his illness.

Conclusions

The body image is a *gestalt* which is constructed taking the connection of several elements as a starting point. Among these elements,

Figure 8.12 Drawing by a boy aged 11, with psoriasis in the area between his scapulae

sensoperceptive stimuli, the words which come from encounters with the Other, and the subject's visual images of him- or herself and of the Other all stand out.

The parents play an active part, exercising great influence over the connection of these three groups of stimuli. When the communication between the parents and the child is inadequate, a physical reaction can take the place of words and intervene in the emission of messages as though it were a motor representation of language. This process marks organs and functions, thus constituting reactive psychosomatic patterns of childhood.

When the connection between sensoperceptive stimuli, interaction with the Other and visual images is not produced or loosens, each of these stimuli can individually represent a totality and generate a

Figure 8.13 The disease as a mark of identity (part 1): picture 1, "He offered his own blood for freedom"; picture 2, "He offered his life fighting against cruel bacilli"; picture 3, "His wings folded to elevate him to glory"

Figure 8.14 The disease as a mark of identity (part2): picture 1, "He fell for his country"; picture 2, "He somatized"

disarticulated body image, which in turn causes a problem with identity. This badly constituted identity will strengthen itself using concrete elements of an imaginary origin, including marks on the body, the personal name taken literally, massive projective identifications and symbiotic relationships, idealized images of the human figure, affective reactions with compromise of the body, diseases during the first years of life, and so on.

Likewise, alterations in the configuration of the boundaries of the body and of space will be seen: confusions between Me and Not-Me, internal and external, contents and container, as well as spaces of reciprocal inclusions. These alterations are reflected in the drawings and the spontaneous discourse of patients, as well as in advertisements for medical products.

As identity is constantly being constructed; the alterations described can manifest themselves at any time of life, particularly at crucial moments. The appearance of somatic diseases at times when the individual is faced with traumatic conflicts and situations can be related to these alterations in the body image. This leads us to suppose a *psychosomatic tendency* in those who suffer from these diseases, though not necessarily a *psychosomatic personality*.

Notes

1. The "Other" with a capital O is used in order to make reference to the structure of language, which in this case is incarnated, so to speak, by the mother, the father, or both.

2. We have to remember that if the object of need is not available, the child reacts with an internal alteration.

3. Translator's note: This name is very significant in Spanish, as it means White Black. It is as if the patient's name were Blanche Black.

4. Both examples are real, although the names are fictitious due to doctor-patient confidentiality.

CHAPTER NINE

Pathomimias: self-inflicted lesions on the skin

Introduction

In the departments of psychiatry and dermatology, the knowledge, experience and vocational service of doctors is usually structured or compartmentalised in a certain way, as a natural corollary of specialized medical training. Psychiatrists and psychoanalysts face the multiple challenges of promoting mental health in a population assailed by addictions to drugs and alcohol, while at the same time trying to reintegrate mental health patients into society, be they depressive, psychotic, or suffering from any other kind of difficulty in facing reality. Dermatologists always see an enormous number of patients, and they face a vast array of problems ranging from aesthetic preoccupations to cancer. Despite the difficulties each medical speciality experiences, these battles against disease are developed within a predictable framework which does not give rise to misunderstanding.

However, there is a percentage of patients who will see a dermatologist and will also need the help of a psychiatrist or a psychoanalyst. Madhulika Gupta (1996) claims that at least a third of dermatological patients who come for consultation present either undeclared or inadequately diagnosed emotional problems, and that the effective management of the dermatological disorder can only be achieved by including the consideration of associated emotional factors. Many dermatologists acknowledge this fact and accept it, yet they cannot find a way to change their therapeutic behaviour such that it is practical and conforms to the reality of the hospital and the consultations, or the pressure of their workload. In consequence, there is no correspondence between the claims of the scientific community regarding the importance of psychological factors and studies concerning quality of life which are so widespread in psycho-dermatology on the one hand, and the actual reality of the patient-dermatologist relationship or the usual methodology of work (duration of consultations, characteristics of treatment) on the other hand.

Psycho-dermatology

There are two large groups of patients studied by psycho-dermatology: patients with cutaneous problems associated with psychiatric pathologies, and patients with psychiatric problems associated with cutaneous pathologies.

The first group, consisting of patients with cutaneous problems associated with psychiatric disorders, constitutes a special problem. If patients deny self-inflicting the lesions (dermatitis artefacta), or insist delusionally that their disease is produced by non-existent parasites or insects (delusional parasitosis), or frantically scratch themselves, thus fuelling a vicious circle of scratching and itchiness (neurotic excoriations), then clinical judgement and above all therapy becomes difficult, and this inevitably produces a disturbed doctor-patient relationship.[1]

If patients distort the data or if they hurt themselves, the doctor's work is hindered. As a consequence, his investigation becomes police-like and the diagnosis starts to become a sentence. If the sick person self-inflicts his or her lesions and does not admit it, once discovered, he or she becomes guilty of the disease besides being responsible for the failure of the therapy. This problem is posed with differing degrees of severity in a wide range of pathologies, since it happens not only to psychotic patients with coenaesthetic hallucinations, but to obsessional patients with a compulsion to wash, touch, or scratch themselves, and also to dysmorphophobic patients, who do not accept any trait of their physical appearance and want to change it at any cost.

For the doctor who has not specialised in psychiatry or psychology, it is difficult to conceive of such flagrant self-infliction of a disease. In fact, everyday reality is full of examples of irrational behaviour, masochistic traits and attitudes not appropriate to people's age, sex or identity. However, the need to assist, know and treat that characterises doctors can in fact blind them in their capacity to understand and accept these kinds of behaviour, something which threatens these very objectives. As a result, they respond negatively to disappointment, lack of diagnosis and the attitudes of patients who question doctors' knowledge.

In the meantime, as these patients do not consult professionals from the psychological field, the latter do not become familiar with this kind of pathology and scarcely come to treat it assiduously. Thus dermatologists are forced into the role of psychotherapists, a role they do not wish to perform, because these patients do not follow their referral to psychiatry, while the dermatological treatment fails because the patients themselves scupper the process.

The second group, consisting of patients with psychiatric problems associated with cutaneous pathologies, is the more frequent and the more questioned because, as their diseases have an organic aetiology, it is easier to deny the psychological factor. However, we observe daily that the initial stages, the evolution, the outbreaks and even the response to treatment shown by skin diseases are at times affected by consequent crucial facts and emotional states.

Within this second group, a sub-group can be isolated and characterised: that of "self-worsened" dermatoses (Suarez Martin, 1980). This consists of real cutaneous pathologies, where the behaviour of the patient perpetuates the disease due to self-destructive actions similar to those of dermatitis artefacta, or due to vicious circles similar to those of neurotic excoriations. It can be considered a sub-group because although the dermatosis is real, a large part of the pathology is self-inflicted.

Self-inflicted dermatoses and the pathomimic effect

Within the wide range of patients who may be referred to a psychotherapist for treatment, there are those who suffer from so-called "self-inflicted cutaneous diseases". The study of these kinds of patients has always revolved around distinguishing the degree of mental pathology presented by these patients, or the intentionality of their behaviour. This area of dermatology and psychiatry includes the schizophrenic patient with tactile hallucinations and excoriations produced by stereotypical movements, the neurotic patient who will even hurt himself at times of crisis, and even the soldier who self-inflicts ulcerations in order to exempt himself from military action.

Attempts at classification have shown groups which are not always well-defined; however, the manifestations characterised by self-inflicted lesions which try to imitate a disease with the intention of obtaining some sort of benefit have been called "pathomimia". Dieulafoy has used the term "disinterested pathomimia" for a situation where the sick person does not obtain any advantage or material benefit from the lesions but uses them to hide some sort of intimate *jouissance* (quoted by Garzón and Consigli, 1952). The manifestations of pathomimia coincide with what other authors call dermatitis artefacta, which is in fact the term that has earned greater consensus (Gupta & Gupta, 1996, p. 1034). However, for the purpose of this analysis, the term "pathomimia" will be maintained, owing to the trait of "pantomime" exhibited by this kind of disease, that is to say because it concerns a phenomenon that involves acting something out specifically for someone who is looking.

Within the field of dermatitis artefacta, clinical manifestations which from a psychiatric point of view are very different are usually grouped together (Gupta & Gupta, 1996; see chart 9.1). Casalá and others provide an important clarification by dividing these patients into two large groups: those who wish to obtain some kind of benefit, and those who are not seeking a material objective (Casalá, 1955, pp. 159–166). In complete agreement with these authors, this is the first diagnostic distinction that should be made when facing a case of pathomimia, dermatitis artefacta or even neurotic excoriations. The reason for this distinction is the therapeutic orientation, since with patients in the first group the disease will not be cured unless the material benefit is known and eliminated. The second group shows what Dieulafoy called "disinterested pathomimia" and is far more interesting and enigmatic; apart from which it consists of sick people who are genuinely seeking our help. Although they are not pursuing a material objective, it could be claimed that their behaviour has an unconscious motive, which we will try to investigate in greater depth.

Description of pathomimias

Pathomimias have a surprising and unpredictable evolution, and present capricious relapses and a resistance to all therapeutic treatment that is generally successful with other dermatoses. They can imitate a wide range of dermatological diseases, because patients can present oedema, erythema, nodules, blisters, ulcers, bruises, and so on, depending on the means used to cause the lesions (Gupta & Gupta, 1996, p. 1034). However, most of the time they present an abnormal localisation which does not correspond to any known type, and they are sometimes too symmetrical. They generally appear around the tegument areas which are inaccessible to the hands (Rook, 1968).

The lesions frequently resemble geometrical figures, something which is not usual in dermatological manifestations, or they are clearly delimited unilateral ulcers. If a chemical product has been used to provoke them, traces of it can be found in the patient's fingernails and skin. The anamnesis usually reveals a mental state favourable to this disease, and the sick person does not admit to causing his or her own lesions. The following chart shows the characteristics of differential diagnosis of dermatitis artefacta with simulation, conversion and neurotic excoriations (taken from Suárez Martín, 1890, with modifications).

The "intimate jouissance" and the body image: three clinical cases

Taking the study of three clinical cases as a starting point, and focusing on the unconscious intentionality of the patient in the production of his or her disease, I will now try to analyse that "intimate *jouissance*" to which Dieulafoy referred. Although these are not typical cases of dermatitis artefacta, since in all three the lesions are a product of excoriations, they are nevertheless suitable for investigating the pathomimic effect we wish to analyse. First a brief account of the patient's history will be given, followed by a theoretical analysis in which the psychodynamic mechanisms and the alterations of the body image observed in all three cases will be pointed out.

Chart 9.1 Differential diagnosis of dermatitis artefacta

	Dermatitis artefacta	Simulation	Conversion	Neurotic excoriations
Diagnosis	Multiple: Schizophrenia Borderline OCD Munchhausen Depression	Psychopathy Normal	Hysteria	Symptom of OCD Depression Anxiety Hypochondria Others
Aim	To establish limits To acquire identity To ask for help	To obtain benefit	Symbolic expression of an unconscious conflict	Affective discharge
Type of pathology	Dermatological preference. Can imitate other cutaneous disorders.	"Neurological" tendency	Rarely self-inflicts lesions. Neurological and visceral preference.	Always excoriations. Can have previous pathology, but does not imitate other disorders.
Evolution of pathology over time	Chronic and stable; no clear reasons for improvement and relapse	Only at right times	Can change due to external stimuli or the relationship with the doctor	Cycle: itching-scratching-itching; usually at night
Attitude regarding self-infliction of the disease	Does not admit it: disavowal? Foreclosure?	Does not admit it: conscious concealment	Does not admit it: repression	Admits it, but is unable to alter behaviour: compulsion

Case 1: Valeria

Valeria is a 48-year-old single woman, a domestic worker, referred for consultation by a dermatologist who gave a diagnosis of pathomimia. She has presented self-inflicted lesions on her face (figure 9.1), back, buttocks, arms and legs for four years (figure 9.2).

Valeria's disease began when she discovered that her daughter had had a baby girl and that Valeria's parents, who live with her daughter in Córdoba, were planning to give the baby up for adoption because the father refused to acknowledge her and they were unwilling to assume responsibility for her. Up to the time she received the news, Valeria was unaware that her daughter was even pregnant. The similarities with her own history are overwhelming, as she herself had her daughter with a man who deserted her when he found out she was pregnant, and Valeria was forced to leave her daughter with her own parents while she went to Buenos Aires to work.

While Valeria has dark hair and is obese, her daughter is blonde and pretty with straight hair and blue eyes. It is evident that the

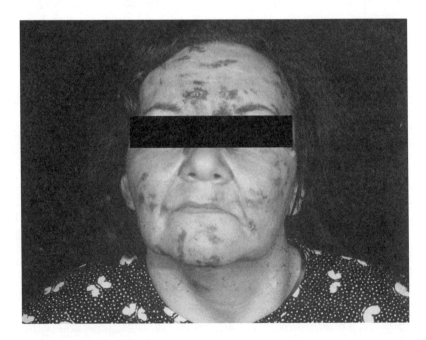

Figure 9.1 Self-inflicted lesions on the face

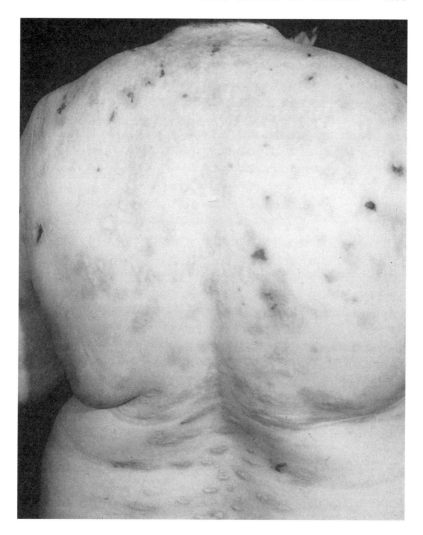

Figure 9.2 Self-inflicted lesions on the back

patient's own self-esteem rests on the image of her daughter, from whom she cannot discriminate herself adequately: in her family photo album she places pictures of her daughter next to those of herself in similar environments and similar contexts, as if she wanted to produce a mirror-like illusion, i.e. that one is the reflection of the other (figures 9.3 and 9.4).

Figure 9.3 Notice the similarity of the contexts: the trees in the background and the diagonal disposition of the road. Valeria is wearing dark glasses.

Figure 9.4 Notice the coincidence in the elements of the scene: the flowers, brick structures in view, and both subjects are seated. Valeria is wearing dark glasses.

It is striking how in another picture (figure 9.5) the patient appears to be the photographic negative of her sister. Valeria, who is wearing dark glasses, is also wearing a white hair band, a white bracelet and a black top. Her sister is wearing a black hair band, a black bracelet and a white top. Both are in the same position.

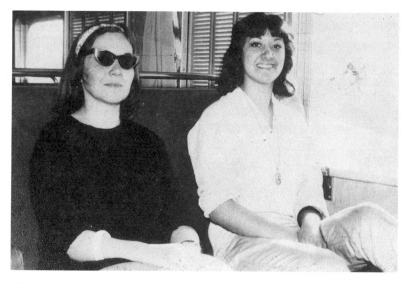

Figure 9.5. Valeria and her sister

Valeria wears dark glasses almost permanently, perhaps with the intention of watching others without being watched herself, and is always dependent on what others might say about her, as her identity depends on others.

Not long ago, Valeria separated from a man with whom she had been in a relationship for 14 years because she discovered him with another woman. When she saw him she told him: "You've got some nerve, you can't even be ashamed of yourself!"[2] Valeria's father has psoriasis on his arms and legs and her mother has allergic reactions to flowers and tomatoes, which are localised on her face. "Her face goes all red," says Valeria.

Case 2: Patricia
Patricia, 66, is an alcoholic and has a paranoid delirium that her daughter-in-law has organised a plot in order to prevent her from having any kind of contact with her son, whom she maintains financially, with the help of the rest of the family. Patricia had a grandfather who was very important to her and who enjoyed "squeezing out her pimples" when she was a young girl. Her mother, a cold and distant woman, used to dress her in furs. She still keeps a photograph in which she was dressed up as a shiny butterfly

Figure 9.6 Patricia when she was a young girl: to the left, dressed in furs, and to the right, dressed up as a butterfly

(figure 9.6). All this converges so that her skin is important as an erotogenic zone and an expression screen for her emotions.

With the deaths of her husband and her father, she began to incubate a feeling of loneliness which reached its crisis the day her mother died, the day on which she started to self-inflict lesions (figure 9.7). She attributed these lesions to the quarrels caused by the family of her daughter-in-law, who on that day of sadness and loneliness refused to let Patricia's son know of his grandmother's death, thus preventing him from accompanying his mother to the wake and the funeral. The disease got worse almost a year later, on Mothers' day, when her son—to whom she had always been extremely close—did not pay her a visit and did not even call her. She then started to feel a tremendous itching on her nose which led her to "tear off a piece of flesh that never healed".

Patricia presents severe personality alterations. She feels the need to constantly name Society people: by means of this contact and by referring to them she attributes importance to herself. She has an invasive attitude during interviews and cannot bear to end the sessions, which is made evident by the fact that she continues to talk

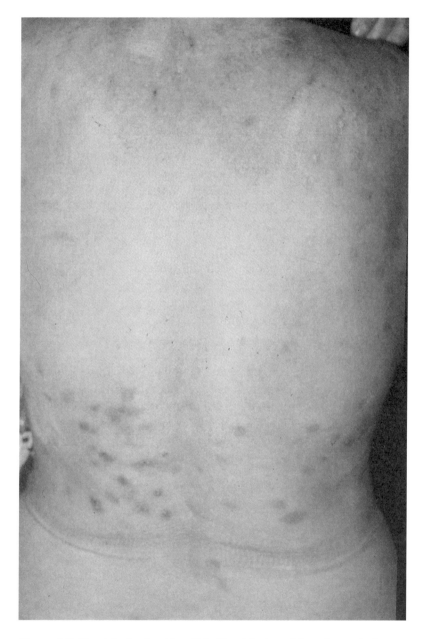

Figure 9.7 Patricia: back with self-inflicted lesions. Note the typical disposition of the lesions, which are present only where the hands can reach and are absent in the middle of the back.

even in the corridor. In addition to this, she does not handle distances with others appropriately. She subordinates her identity to the gaze of others: she describes in detail the "twenty eyes" that looked at her during her first dermatological consultation; what is more, she claims that her son can "sweep her with his gaze" and she constantly uses dark glasses.

Patricia's disease is intimately connected with her inability to mourn and to discriminate between her own identity and that of her loved ones, with whom she feels a need to share the same skin. For example, she sleeps wearing a shirt of her son's whilst wrapped up in her parents' blankets, and she herself says she "seems to be a mummy".

This lack of a body image, with a skin that functions as a boundary, can also be observed in the difficulty she has in confining herself to the boundaries of the paper when she writes (figure 9.8). What is more, a graphic representation of her tendency to self-inflict lesions appears on the back of a sheet of paper which she gave to her therapist deeply scored, explaining that her pen had run out of ink (figure 9.9).

Patricia uses highly-wrought examples which work not as metaphors but as direct displacements of the sign to the referent. For example, about the death of her father she says: "My tears became itching", and about the treatment she receives from the family of her daughter-in-law she claims: "They take leaves from the fallen tree, can that be pathomimia?"

Case 3: Estela

A 56-year-old housewife, Estela was diagnosed four years ago as having a case of "neurotic excoriations", although she claims that she comes out in rashes and does not admit to self-inflicting her lesions (figures 9.10 and 9.11). Her disease began when her daughter suffered a railway accident. After an initial period of uncertainty during which she did not know whether she would find her daughter dead or alive, she found her at a hospital, injured and blood-soaked, but alive.

Very shortly afterwards, her husband left for the South of Argentina to live with another woman and abandoned her with her five children. Despite this fact, Estela wants to show that she has not separated from him. Although she is racked with unease, she tries

Figure 9.8 Front of the sheet of paper

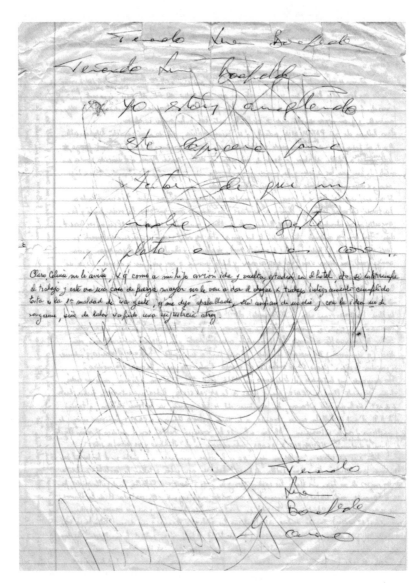

Figure 9.9 Back of the sheet of paper

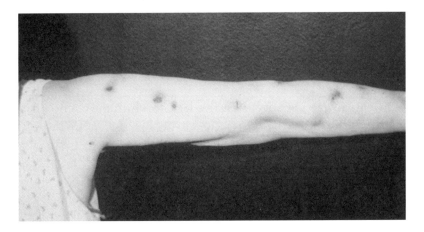

Figure 9.10 Estela (self-inflicted lesions on her arm)

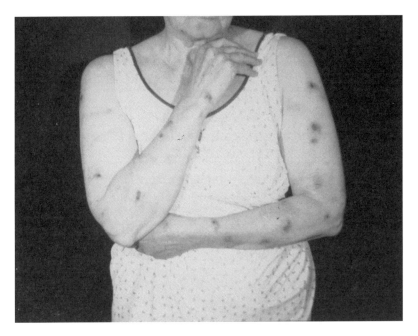

Figure 9.11 Estela (self-inflicted lesions)

to keep up appearances by following the moral precepts of her own mother, a cold woman set in her ways, who refused to accept that a married woman can separate or have a new partner. Her father, a man who barely displays any affection, has never paid any attention to her.

Estela shows a very deep affective lack, to which she refers as "an internal torture". The need to be close to her husband is still present; however, other things have happened that prevent her from going back. Her only daughter, Susy, who consoled her in her loneliness (they used to sleep together in bed, and when Estela spoke about her she would make a rocking gesture), has just moved in with a married man, thus challenging all the moral values of her grandmother. Estela would like to "quarrel with her", but fears she might cause in Susy the same hatred that she has always secretly felt for her parents, and she does not want to lose her permanently.

Estela is angry with herself for still needing her husband (whom she no longer loves), for still depending on the approval of her own parents, and because she has been forced to accept that her daughter has had a life so different from hers. As a result, she has still has a deep and insistent need for warmth and company, which she tries to alleviate by stimulating her own skin.

Pathos and Mimos: the disease, simulation, caressing and the observer

As we shall now see, several common elements have been observed in these case studies, which it is important to emphasise.

A PATHOLOGY OF IDENTIFICATION AND OF THE CONSTITUTION OF IDENTITY

Faced with a mother who, instead of being receptive and cushioning the anxieties of the child, responds with her own anxieties, the child learns to function as a container for his mother rather than the other way round, as would be expected. While the necessary tactile stimuli are not produced, the physical and emotional interior, which produces unbearable experiences of pain, is disinvested. As a consequence, the child tends to privilege the reception of external stimuli over internal stimuli, and a bi-dimensional vision of himself and of others is generated, leading to the notion that the only thing of importance is the external aspect: the façade (Liberman et al., 1982). Thus the identifications necessary for normal development, for working through separations and grief, and for constructing the notion of absence cannot be made except in a "mimetic" or superficial way (Liberman et al., 1982; Guir, 1984).

As the differentiation from the other would produce in the patient a feeling of unbearable loss, he will instead try to erase the notion of absence by means of "seizing" the other, by imitating his gestures or behaving in a mirror-like way towards him, at least in terms of his disease, thus maintaining the illusion of having the other always present. The face is a privileged place for the production of these imitation phenomena.

Instead of constructing an image of the other in his memory, the patient attempts to carry a trait of the other on his skin, like individuals who get tattoos, or like those fanatics who, having touched their idol, refuse to wash the hand with which they touched him. Carrying someone else on the skin or being impregnated with his image creates an illusory symbiotic fusion (Ulnik, 1988).

In the case of Valeria the phenomenon is evident: confronted by the face of a mother who, instead of being receptive, only exteriorised violent emotions ("all red", dark glasses), the patient suffers a process of loss of symbolic identity for which she compensates by identifying, "as in a mirror", with her sister or her daughter. When her daughter repeats her own history, abandoning her baby girl, Valeria feels displaced and abandoned both by her daughter and by her parents (who did not even inform her about what was going on), and tries to "recover them", evoking with her marked face the face of her mother ("all red"), and with her body the body of her psoriatic father. However, in the same way that her mother had the "barefaced shamelessness" to give away a granddaughter in order to present the appearance of a well-constituted family, Valeria also behaves in a "shameless" way: in fact, she avoids showing her true feelings and avoids confrontation. The marks have the effect of attracting and fixating the attention of others, thus allowing her to observe that others are looking at her. "Almost like a blind spot in others, the mark on her face allows her to avoid the interchange of looks and grants [Valeria] control over the image of the others" (Guir, 1984). The phenomenon is reinforced by wearing dark glasses: despite the fact that she attracts attention due to her disease, Valeria remains "incognito".

The same can be said in the case of Patricia, who wears dark glasses most of the time. In her, the "façade-identifications" with an ideal image are produced in a more elaborate way by means of her constant mention of people from "Society".

Valeria was able to exteriorise her feelings when she discovered her boyfriend with another woman, and what is striking is the way in which she directed all her insults and reproaches to his face,[3] thus emphasising the value the face has for her as a representative feature of the body as a whole.

A PATHOLOGY OF THE ATTACHMENT DRIVE

As was explained in Chapter 6, taking Bowlby's work as a basis, attachment can be described as a way of conceiving the proclivity shown by human beings towards establishing strong affective bonds with other people they consider to be stronger, and of explaining the manifold forms of emotional disorder and personality alterations occasioned by the involuntary separation from, and the loss of, loved ones. Attachment is a normal feeling which expresses the need to be intimately united with another and makes it hard to bear separation. When attachment is exaggerated, what occurs in the face of separations is the same as when a person takes off a plaster he has been wearing for too long: it is inevitable that the plaster will take with it a piece of the skin (Ulnik, 1988).

The Spanish word for attachment is "apego". Etymologically, this word comes from the Latin *picare*, which means to smear with pitch. This is a resinous substance used as a revulsive; revulsion being a local or superficial irritation the objective of which is to stop the congestion or inflammation of deeper physical structures.

Metaphorically speaking, normal "revulsion" is obtained by means of caressing, patting or hugging: all stimuli which from the surface ease the most profound sadness and lacks. We can then suppose that these patients, when faced with traumatic separations which expose them to situations of deep affective lack, try to calm themselves by producing, through scratching, a superficial irritation or inflammation the object of which is to stop a deep need for intimate unions. Valeria could not bear the separation from her daughter and her parents; nor could Estela bear being separated from her husband, or Patricia from her son and her mother.

LACK OF DISCRIMINATION BETWEEN THE INTERNAL AND THE EXTERNAL

We are not born with the psychic representations of the internal and the external, but construct them throughout our development (Freud, 1915, 1925b). According to Anzieu, the notions of "inside" and "outside" are acquired from the tactile and coenaesthetic experiences of earliest childhood, and mutilations of the skin try to maintain the boundaries of the body and the Ego, as well as the feeling of being intact and cohesive (see Chapter 2).

Many animals, when faced with situations of danger, replace an action in the external world with an adaptation using the body (for example, instead of fighting they change colour or lose their tail). It is conceivable that these patients displayed similar behaviour when the sensation of identity which had supported them and given them cohesion broke down (and as their construction of the concepts of inside and outside was already weak and confused): they ended up doing "inside" what they should have done "outside" and instead of separating from others, they sought to tear them off their own skin. Or from a different perspective: if we understand the psyche as being "inside" and the skin "outside", they were able to attempt outside, on their skin, the mourning that they could not carry out inside by working through it in the psychic apparatus.

As regards touch, the constitution of the exterior and the interior is simultaneous. As Ong says: "When I touch that something objective which is "outside", beyond the boundaries of my body, I experience at the same time the presence of my own self" (quoted by Montagu, 1971). The other and one's own Ego are felt at the same instant, which fosters confusion and could lead these patients to a need for permanent contact with the other so as not to lose their own Ego.

The incorporation of the other within one's own body by means of the skin can clearly be seen in certain individuals who wear tattoos with that intention (see the reference to tattoos in jail in Chapter 2). There was a time when prisoners and sailors were practically the only ones who wore tattoos, in order to achieve a sense of belonging to a group and of identity, or simply to keep alive the memory of a loved one whom they could not see (see figure 9.12).

The patients described might unconsciously be trying, by means of scratching, to "tear off" people from their own history who have left marks on them. The absence of a feeling of symbolic identity, which can allow them to support themselves with their name, their job or their image, causes identity to come to rest on the presence of loved ones, but working as an "envelope of suffering" (see Chapter 2, section 2.6.3).

We must bear in mind that Anzieu said that in the cutaneous language, the irritation of the skin remains undifferentiated from mental irritation, such that the physical symptom is itself a way of

Figure 9.12 This patient, who had psoriasis, had tattooed the name of her boyfriend on her back. A short while after she separated from him, her father, whose name was Florencio Rossi, passed away. Her reaction was to tattoo her back with flowers (the name of her father) thus covering with them the name of her boyfriend, which she wanted to forget or to "tear off".[4] (By courtesy of Psoriahue Interdisciplinary Medicine, Dr María L. García Pazos and Lic Patricia Mirochnik)

exhibiting frustration, anger and suffering (see Chapter 2, section 2.2). In all three clinical cases the loved one is at the same time hated because of his or her inconstant presence, and the symptoms are the manifestation of the anger produced by the patient's need for the loved one. There may be nothing more "itch-provoking" than loving or needing someone one hates, or the reverse, hating oneself because one loves and needs someone who is "impossible".

PREDOMINANCE OF THE VISUAL AND OF THE IMAGINARY

The Ego is formed not only from tactile experiences but also from images. Virtually no one can perceive his own body as a unit if he does not possess a totalising image with which to look at himself (see Chapter 8). Faced with experiences of fragmentation or disintegration of the Ego, one of the ways of restoring the feeling of identity and cohesion is to try to attract people's attention, and be looked at and known in order to obtain an identification with the image that the other is observing.

In the histories and pictures/photos of the patients we have studied, their dependence on the image they gave to others can clearly be seen. Let us recall with Patricia the "twenty eyes" of her dermatological consultation, and the son who could "sweep her with his gaze". In Valeria's pictures her attempt at managing an identification with the image of her daughter, or that of her sister, is evident, while in Patricia's photos the importance she placed on "showing off" with her furs and dressing-up clothes can be seen. Estela, for her part, made constant reference to "what is noticeable and what is not noticeable". All three families paid close attention to the gaze of others and to what their neighbours might say about them. In fact, pathomimia does have a trait of "pantomime": this is a phenomenon that involves acting something out specifically for someone who is looking.

For a child not to be touched or caressed is as terrible as to go unnoticed. Both facts—not being touched and not being looked at—can create a feeling of non-existence, a deficit in the construction of the Ego and the body image that may well cause difficulty through-out life in the discrimination and separation of the subject and the object, the internal and the external, the Ego and the Non-Ego.

The auto-erotic stimulus of scratching taken to the point of the self-infliction of lesions could satisfy the patient's overpowering need to receive stimuli while at the same time producing an effect aimed at the observer, either of attracting his attention—when his gaze allows the individual to say to him "here I am"—or of making him look away in horror, especially when the gaze, treating him as a pure object, goes through him and dilutes his subjectivity.

The presence of an observer has a lot to do with the name "pathomimia", which etymologically can be divided into *pathos* and *mimos*, which in Greek are related to the simulation of a disease. We read in some texts that the skin is the reflection of the soul; perhaps in these kinds of patient what is fictitious is not only the dermatosis but also the nature of their relationships, their "feeling of self", the boundaries and self-affirmation of identity.

Notes

1. There are many other cutaneous problems associated with psychiatric disorders, but to list and classify them would exceed the limits of this work. This is why only three of them, which are quite representative, are mentioned.

2. Translator's note: the words actually used by Valeria are informal expressions alluding to the face, something like "barefaced" (not feeling ashamed of a bad action), but they are unfortunately lost in translation.

3. See previous footnote.

4. Translator's note: This name conveys the idea of flowers: "Florencio", sounds similar to "flowers" in Spanish and "Rossi" sounds similar to "roses" in Spanish. Unfortunately, all this is lost in translation.

CHAPTER TEN

Franz Kafka's *In the Penal Colony*: Superego and the skin

Summary of the story

In this story by Kafka, a military officer tries to convince an explorer, appointed as a Judge by the Government, regarding the benefits of a perfect machine which has been created by the late commander of a penal colony. As a means of imposing fair punishment on the inmates, the objective of the machine is the maintenance of wellbeing and justice in the colony, beyond the will of men.

The punishment itself consists of writing on the convicts' bodies—with sharp needles protruding from the upper part of the machine—the regulation they have broken. This writing carved into the skin gradually penetrates deeper into the body, ultimately bringing about the convict's death. What is more, the execution is public and constitutes a kind of party, to which everyone in town flocks in order to watch the show.

The explorer must judge if the punishment inflicted by the machine is adequate, in order to sanction a demand from the officer and thus obtain a higher budget for the maintenance of the machine. As the explorer eventually rejects this method of execution, the officer himself submits to the machine and dies pierced by its needles.

The Superego, the need for punishment and somatic disease

In *Inhibition, symptoms and anxiety*, Freud describes five types of resistance: three belong to the Ego, one to the Id, and one to the Superego. The resistance from the Superego

(. . .) is also the most obscure, though not always the least power-ful one. It seems to originate from the sense of guilt or the need for punishment; and it opposes every move towards success, including, therefore, the patient's own recovery through analysis. [1926, p. 160]

In *An Outline of Psychoanalysis*, in the chapter on technique, Freud refers to the unconscious feeling of guilt, which is part of the "need to be ill or suffer":

It is evidently the portion of the resistance contributed by a superego that has become particularly severe and cruel. The patient must not become well but must remain ill, for he deserves no better. This resistance does not actually interfere with our intel-lectual work, but it makes it inoperative; indeed, it often allows us to remove one form of neurotic suffering, but is ready at once to replace it by another, *or perhaps by some somatic illness.* [1938, p. 180]

In "The economic problem of masochism" he says:

(. . .) a neurosis which has defied every therapeutic effort may vanish if the subject becomes involved in the misery of an unhappy marriage, or loses all his money, *or develops a danger-us organic disease.* [1924, p. 166]

The somatic disease, as it satisfies the need for illness or suffering, soothes the feeling of guilt and pacifies the Superego.

If the patient finds himself facing his Superego and discovers that he is incapable of distancing, denying, getting wrong or displacing what his parents and teachers ordered him to do, he is exposed to the cruellest form of superego, and might literally incorporate those orders by materialising them or embodying them, as if he could feel them "in his own flesh", so to speak, or as if they were written on his skin, as in Kafka's story. Thus the somatic disease will be able to substitute neurosis for some form of physical symptom and the organ selection will have some traceable meaning. This is because the physical symptom will appear in the areas where the subject was punished, or on those parts of the body which were the object of threats, reprimands or criticism. However, the problem here is that this meaning will resist analysis, as there is no subject able to respond.

The "physical superego"

Sami-Ali called the superegoic agency "physical superego" when it acts as a set of normative rules and modes of conduct which are expressed in the body, as, for example, in the education of a person, when the demands to conform to a certain moral principle coincide with physical restrictions.

Schreber is a paradigmatic example, as his own father was a doctor who developed a series of orthopaedic devices which he used in the education of his son, and which he proposed—following a Nazi ideology—for the training of all children. Thus it was that later, in his deluded state, Schreber imagined that his body was directed and manipulated by the rays of God. Schreber himself considered pain as a way of stopping *jouissance*, but at the same time pain itself formed a part of it. In Schreber's delusion the outside world comes to embody the agency which rewards and punishes with the darts of its rays, dictating the laws of behaviour. This agency is first and foremost physical in its effects, as if all action could only be exercised over the body and through the body.

When the superego has these characteristics, the body is acted upon as in childhood and the subject constitutes only a body with demands that inflict violence upon him while at the same time allowing him to exist. It is as if an irrational will were realised in concrete, being written on his body.

Although Schreber is not an example of a somatic patient, I have had the opportunity to see many cases in which the predominating symptoms were of this nature. The most illustrative case is that of Ceferino, the patient with generalised psoriasis to whom I referred to in Chapter 1, pages 35–36. During his childhood, Ceferino's father forbade him to sweat because he thought that sweat caused the skin to become cold, and that could bring on disease. He used to subject Ceferino to harsh corporal punishment if he perspired, and when Ceferino came home after having been out playing, he used to check him by introducing his hand between Ceferino's clothes and skin in order to see whether he had sweated or not.

The example used by Lacan explaining the Superego is paradigmatic of the subject we are trying to develop. Lacan's example was a patient who had been brought up a Muslim but had then renounced the Koran and was suffering a series of symptoms affecting his hand. His previous analyst had interpreted a hypothetical relationship between these symptoms, the desires linked to infantile masturbation and the consequent punishment of those desires. However, this interpretation had not been successful. The foundation of his symptoms was in fact in his Superego and was transmitted through the concept of the law.

During his childhood, this individual had been involved in a public furore in which his father had been dismissed from the public office he held, at which point he heard people say that his father was a thief and that his hand should be cut off. As we know, Islamic law is totalitarian in character and its judicial and religious aspects cannot be separated. Indeed, it is this very law which states that thieves should have their hand cut off, and it was this statement which then appeared in the symptoms of the patient.

I am not certain whether this case mentioned by Lacan was neurotic, and hence whether the hand symptoms presented by the patient could be considered of a "hysterical" nature. However, the aspect I do consider to be of the utmost importance is the action upon the body of "(. . .) a discordant statement, which is ignored within the law. A statement that becomes manifest due to a traumatic episode, which reduces the law to an emergence of an inadmissible character, that cannot be integrated (. . .) a blind, repetitive agency which we generally define with the term Superego" (Lacan, 1954, p. 292).

Freud says that "the ego ideal opens up an important avenue for the understanding of group psychology. In addition to its individual side, this ideal has a social side; it is also the common ideal of a family, a class or a nation" (1914, p. 101). The individual's cultural and ethical representations are not part of an intellectual body of knowledge; they seem rather to be of a normative nature, that is to say demands to which the individual subjects himself.

The normative ideals which patients construct within themselves also function as written codes or matrices, as mentioned by Lacan with regard to animals. However, unlike animals, in man these ideals are not at the service of the survival of the species, but are used in the service of business, character, ways of eating or of marrying, or any other kind of structure within a family clan. The individual is born "dead" as far as the eternal life demanded for family ideology is concerned, because the important thing is not him as a subject, but rather as a link within the "family plasma" that survives him. Thus any manifestation that he is in fact a subject unleashes unconscious feelings of guilt, which appear under the guise of a need for punishment or for suffering. [Ulnik, 1993]

The ideology of the clan operates as a categorical imperative, that is to say an imperative that orders something as if what has been ordered were good in itself, quite independently from any end, and the patient receives his punishment in a way similar to the convicts of *In the Penal Colony*.

The Superego, the skin and the scopic drive

Kafka's story deals with the function of the Ego-skin which Anzieu called "inscription of traces" (see Chapter 2). The law is "written" on the body and is inscribed through the skin and the wounds by means of which the convict "reads" his sentence. In this way the story exemplifies the close relationship which exists between the Superego, the skin and the gaze.

> After looking at the Condemned Man the explorer merely asked, "Does he know his sentence?" "No," said the Officer. (. . .) Then he said, "It would be useless to give him that information. He experiences it on his own body."
>
> He went on to explain: "The basic principle I use for my decisions is this: Guilt is always beyond a doubt." [Kafka, 1919]

The lack of distance between the symbol and what has been symbolized is evident in the officer. Despite the fact that he is wearing a uniform which is too heavy for the tropical location of the colony, and that he is feeling tired and short of breath due to the hot climate, he does not take it off since for him his uniform means his home country, which he does not want to lose. As in the other texts we have analysed, once again dress—in this case the uniform—assumes the representation of the entire Ego and acts as a second skin for someone who, through the death of his superior and the lack of support from the government for his machine, has lost his own support as well as his identity. The description the officer provides of the torture is horrible:

"For the first six hours the condemned man goes on living almost as before. He suffers nothing but pain. After two hours, the felt is removed, for at that point the man has no more energy for screaming. Here at the head of the bed warm rice pudding is put in this electrically heated bowl. From this the man, if he feels like it, can help himself to what he can lap up with his tongue. No one passes up this opportunity. I don't know of a single one, and I have had a lot of experience. He first loses his pleasure in eating around the sixth hour. (. . .) The man rarely swallows the last bit. He turns it around in his mouth and spits it into the pit. (. . .) But how quiet the man becomes around the sixth hour! The most stupid of them begin to understand. It starts around the eyes and spreads out from there. A look that could tempt one to lie down under the harrow. Nothing else happens. The man simply begins to decipher the inscription. He purses his lips, as if he were listening. You've seen that it's not easy to make out the inscription with your eyes, but our man deciphers it with his wounds. True, it takes a lot of work. It requires six hours to complete. But then the harrow spits him right out and throws him into the pit, where he splashes down into the bloody water and cotton wool. Then the judgment is over, and we, the soldier and I, quickly bury him." [*ibid.*]

What is remarkable in the description of the torture is how the condemned man gradually loses his condition of subject until he becomes nothing but an object and finally falls next to the machine, as if he were merely the remains of the same operation of inscribing the broken law. At the beginning he is capable of speaking and screaming. Then a regressive process begins in which the oral aspect is the predominant feature, and the man spits out the felt which has been introduced into his mouth to stifle his screams, and eagerly eats warm rice pudding. At the sixth hour of torture the transformation from subject to object begins with the eyes, as the condemned man is transformed. He begins to form a complete union with what is being written on his body and to decipher the text through his wounds, which is what the officer wants from him and what he achieves by means of the machine.

The public gawks at the scene, as if the wish to watch actually penetrated the skin and the body of the condemned man, who is reduced to a bloodied corpse after having calmed the savage drives of men, women and children who, like a family clan, wish to watch the sentence being "embodied".

> "You should have seen the executions in earlier days! The entire valley was overflowing with people, even a day before the execution. They all came merely to watch. (. . .) In front of hundreds of eyes—all the spectators stood on tiptoe right up to the hills there—the condemned man was laid down under the harrow by the Commandant himself. (. . .) Well, then came the sixth hour. It was impossible to grant all the requests people made to be allowed to watch from up close. (. . .) How we all took in the expression of transfiguration on the martyred face! How we held our cheeks in the glow of this justice, finally attained and already passing away!"[Kafka, 1919]

The condemned man whose punishment is to be witnessed by the explorer is to have the sentence "honour your superior" written on him. After his speech, the officer expects the explorer's approval. In this way he will obtain a higher budget for the adequate maintenance of the machine, which lately has not been working properly. However, the explorer replies:

> "I am opposed to this procedure (. . .); however, I find your conviction genuinely moving, even if it cannot deter me."
> "So the process has not convinced you," replied the Officer, smiling the way an old man smiles over the silliness of a child.
> "Well then, it's time," he said finally, and suddenly looked at the Traveller with bright eyes which contained some sort of demand. [ibid.]

The officer sets the condemned man free, and at the point where we expect him to subject the naïve explorer to the machine's torture, he merely makes him read a complicated papyrus: one of those inserted into the machine for inscription onto the bodies of the condemned men, as if they were posthumous commandments. The papyrus—like all the rest—cannot be properly read with the eyes; . however, it contains the maxim: "be just". All of a sudden, the officer undresses and subjects himself to the machine, which, on being put to work, turns out to be defective and kills him immediately.

Final reflections

Pierre Benoit (1988) says that every man has a secret life hiding from itself, meaning that it is dominated by an unconscious representation, but this sometimes, through certain processes of analysis, comes to light. This unconscious representation can lead the individual to question the integrity of a certain part of his own body. Moreover, this unconscious representation can be a part of the Superego which, like a categorical imperative, must be obeyed if punishment is to be avoided. If this imperative were to be written on a part of the body, the skin would be the ideal parchment.

Many patients experience their disease as a punishment and the diagnosis as a conviction. It could perhaps be an important task to establish whether what has been written is a demand that must be obeyed or rather the punishment for not having obeyed. The therapeutic behaviour that should be followed, as well as its eventual meaning, will often depend on the particular way we "read" what has been written. And the possible meanings are absolution, commutation of the sentence, or a curative balm so that the inevitable wounds do not become deeper.

CHAPTER ELEVEN

The relationship between what the psychoanalyst hears and what the dermatologist sees

The encounter between psychic and somatic

In "Pathways of mutual influence", Freud suggests that every modification in the field of biological needs and functions can have an influence on the erogenicity linked to the particular organ that carries out these functions. And likewise, every alteration in an organ's erogenicity can also affect its biological functions (1905a, pp. 205, 206). If we were to take the skin as an example, we could say that dry skin which has not received the necessary hydration, or sunburnt skin which has not received the necessary solar protection, could both participate in different ways from normal skin in what Freud calls the general current of sexual instinct. And vice versa, highly erotized skin, or in contrast, minimally stimulated skin could become ill in different ways: generating itching, becoming infected with herpes, showing blisters or even eczema (see Chapter 3, section 3.3).

> A patient who had a strongly eroticised pharyngo-nasal area used to say that he liked grappa, an alcoholic drink which produced in him a feeling of warmth on the palate that rose up like fire to his nose. In addition, he had nasal polyps and used to snore at night. He had a laser operation to burn away part of his soft palate in order to allow him to inhale more air through the respiratory tract and thus stop snoring. The result was a large inflammation in the area, which later became infected, causing his throat to ache and sting. The snoring persisted. Additionally, he found it

very difficult to enjoy life, in particular the things he liked most, as if he were unable to find what brought him pleasure "palatable". The bucco-nasal mucus, the need to breathe and to swallow, and the erotogenic difficulty of tasting things all followed pathways of mutual influence.

In the epicrisis of Elizabeth R's case history, Freud establishes a relationship between the verbal expressions referring to the body and the somatic sensations linked to them, and he comes to the conclusion that "the hysteric is not taking liberties with words, but is simply reviving once more the sensations to which the verbal expression owes its justification" (p. 180). But he also claims that they re-establish the primitive verbal sense for their strongest innervations. This is not the case only in hysterical conversions: when he studies the relationship of the dream to the somatic sources of stimulus, although he quotes many authors to criticise their hypotheses that the dream is generated by somatic stimuli, he nevertheless admits that they are right in claiming that the body is represented in different ways in the dream. He emphasises that in cases of serious somatic disease (for example, a pulmonary or cardiac disease with feelings of shortness of breath) the somatic anxiety can be psychically interpreted, and dreams fulfilling strenuously suffocated wishes can appear, which could thus have caused anxiety, or dreams which take advantage of the somatic sensations in order to manifest themselves, since in any case the anxiety was already present.

> But there is no difficulty in reconciling these two apparently different groups. In both groups of dreams two psychical factors are involved: an inclination towards an affect and an ideational content; and these are intimately related to each other. If one of them is currently active, it calls up the other even in a dream; in the one case the somatically determined anxiety calls up the suppressed ideational content, and in the other the ideational content with its accompanying sexual excitation, having been set free from repression, calls up a release of anxiety. [Freud, 1900b, p. 236]

For Freud, physical pain and psychic affect are naturally intertwined, to the point where he says that if someone were to find this linking affected, it would be as unjustified as showing surprise at the fact that it is precisely the rich who have more money (1883–1895).

With his idea that in every hysterical conversion there is a basis of "somatic compliance" owing to a previous somatic disease, Freud suggests that the boundary between the psychic and the somatic is not well-defined, inasmuch as both fields find, intersect, articulate and lend each other the aforementioned "compliance". In fact, the term "somatic compliance" is the translation of the German expression *somatisches Entgegenkommen* (Freud, 1905d) which, more than "compliance", would seem to suggest an "encounter" between the somatic and the psychic (Ulnik, 2002). The encounter between the psychic and the somatic is also produced by the fact that any somatic disease, whatever it might be (whether it has already manifested itself or it is latent, as a hereditary predisposition) is suffered by a particular individual with a complex history, who belongs to a society and moves in a family, object and discursive interweaving that transcends and determines him or her.

Once the "encounter" has taken place, both the psychic and the somatic modify each other following the "pathways of mutual influence" to which we referred previously. The result is a new and more complex unit the components of which are heterogeneous and cannot be detached from each other, because the new entity they constitute is equal to more than the sum of its parts.

Taking these ideas into consideration, psychoanalytic interventions and psychotherapeutic frames could be created which could affect the evolution and the prognosis of somatic diseases. Likewise, it could also be considered that medical interventions, ranging from the words uttered by the physician to the actual medical examination, could have an unconscious meaning for both doctor and patient. Thus an interdisciplinary approach was developed, the aim of which was the integrated treatment of chronic skin diseases; this approach will now be described.

Experience of an interdisciplinary approach to patients with psoriasis

After seeing, together with the dermatologists, the patients hospitalised in the Dermatology Department of the José de San Martín Clinicas Hospital, I started treating, in private practice with

Dr Javier Ubogui, patients suffering from psoriasis who visited the Copahue thermal centre in the province of Neuquén. There I was able to observe that the mythology surrounding the Copahue volcano and the curative properties of the waters, the seaweeds and the mud used there all interacted with the personal history of the patients and affected the development of their disease, probably due both to the actual therapeutic power of these elements and to the self-modifying power that the Unconscious can have over the body. The therapeutic power is directed and boosted by the patients' beliefs and by their articulation with their archaic world and their subjectivity (see figure 2.7). The experience at Copahue served only to confirm this previous conviction I had acquired at my hospital and in private practice, when I was conducting psychoanalysis with somatic patients. These considerations led me to put into practice an experimental joint (dermatological and psychoanalytical) treatment of patients with psoriasis, utilising the following methodology.

The patient attends the first consultation with the dermatologist; however, this is conducted in the presence of a psychoanalyst who, when the medical examination is over, carries out a semi-directed questioning on the life of the patient, which includes family constellation, life circumstances in which the disease appeared, new outbreaks of the disease, traumatic experiences, migration and, if the necessary confidence is attained, questions concerning the sexual life of the patient.

In general, the skin patient and the dermatologist become allies: one of them shows a problem and the other examines it. That is why it is frequently the case that the dermatologist says at the beginning of the consultation: "*Show me* what's going on" instead of saying: "*Tell me* what's going on". With the intention of changing this habit and widening the channels of communication with patients, the dermatologist was encouraged to ask the patient to *tell* us what the matter was with him or her. If the patient tends to "show" or to speak only about his or her psoriasis, the dermatologist begins the questioning and then performs the physical examination. If, on the contrary, the patient decides to speak initially about his or her other problems (as was the case with a patient who, coming into the consulting room and putting her bag on the desk, exclaimed: "I've come here because my life is a mess"), then the psychoanalyst is the one who starts with the semi-directed questioning, after which the dermatologist carries out the physical examination. The most important thing about this first stage is that as the patients "show", they also "speak", and the psychoanalyst listens to them.

In "On psychotherapy" (1904), Freud says that the physician cannot easily discard psychotherapy because the other person interested in the therapeutic process—the patient—has no intention of discarding it. In this way, it is in fact usual for the physician, by means of his words, advice, comfort and prescriptions, to practice psychotherapy without the intention of doing it, and without even being aware of doing it. Even the physical examination and certain procedures such as extracting moles (nevus) or taking biopsies can have reassuring or threatening effects which modify the patient's psyche.

From the psychoanalytic interview the most important elements are sometimes obtained for an interpretation that will be offered later. However, the psychoanalyst also observes the patient, which is important, when we take into account Freud's words:

> When I set myself the task of bringing to light what human beings kept hidden within them, not by the compelling power of hypnosis, but by observing what they say and what they show, I thought the task was a harder one than it really is. He that has eyes to see and ears to hear may convince himself that no mortal can keep a secret. If his lips are silent, he chatters with his finger-tips; betrayal oozes out of him at every pore. And thus the task of making conscious the most hidden recesses of the mind is one which it is quite possible to accomplish. [1905d, pp. 77, 78]

If the patient accepts treatment and is admitted by the treatment team, he or she joins a psychoanalytically oriented psychotherapy group on a weekly basis. The groups are made up of patients with psoriasis and are co-ordinated by the psychoanalyst. The dermatologist takes part in the sessions as an observer. All the patients have a dermatological check up once a month with the dermatologist. The kinds of patients who come to be treated say that their psoriasis is the consultation motive and that they are not specifically seeking psychoanalytic treatment. We work with interpretations from the unconscious material produced by the patients. These are not "self-help groups", nor are they groups based on the charisma of the co-ordinator or social meetings to offer information.

Over the course of ten years we have worked with six groups, three of which lasted approximately five years, the other three lasting between one and two years. Of the six groups, two are currently running. The groups had between five and eight members each. The best results were obtained with groups which were heterogeneous regarding age, cultural background and personality type. The two homogeneous groups (one of teenagers and the other of young mothers) dissolved quickly and did not represent a good experience for the patients, the reason being that as they were groups of people suffering from the same disease, they were already homogeneous. When the ages or the life circumstances coincided as well, cross-identifications occurred which were so massive that they made it impossible for each of the members to work through what the other was experiencing without suffering it themselves (on their own skin). The group of teenagers dissolved when the father of one of them became ill with cancer and she would tell the rest, with high levels of anxiety, the agonies she had to witness daily. This generated in the others greater anxiety and more outbreaks of the disease, in addition to defence mechanisms that did not allow them either to help and support the fellow member or to work through the situation on their own. Something similar happened with the group of young mothers when one of them told the rest that two of her three children had psoriasis, something the rest of the group could not listen to for fear of the same happening to them.

In contrast, in the groups which were heterogeneous apart from the fact that they shared the same disease, the stark differences between the members allowed them to cope with similar anxiety-provoking or mourning situations experienced by some members of the group. The experience of being similar in some respects and different in others helped them a great deal in developing processes of discrimination, as well as in building or asserting their own identity without the psoriasis being a stigma or an identity mark in which to find refuge. On the other hand, the possibility of sharing certain kinds of suffering, such as rejection and lack of social understanding, allowed them to be tolerant with regard to other differences and to accept them, in some cases even going so far as to learn from them.

The groups begin as psychotherapy groups of patients with psoriasis or "psoriasis groups", but as they evolve they become group psychoanalysis of individuals, with their own singularities, in whom psoriasis ceases to be the axis of their lives even before their disease goes into the long awaited remission.

Group psychoanalysis turned out to be a very useful resource for the analysis of many patients who did not have previous experience, and even rejected the possibility, of analysis. Those patients with alexythimic traits or dissociative defensive mechanisms benefited greatly from the group by sharing experiences and working through in the group various affective situations that one member or another always found words to express.

As time went by, many patients began individual psychotherapy, and at present the offer of group psychotherapy is only one of many at our Centre. The last two groups which were formed no longer include the dermatologists: this would have been very difficult to keep up taking into account the demands put on them by work. However, it is crucial that referral to psychotherapy be done within the institution and that the institution maintain a time for clinical sessions as well as the exchange of interdisciplinary experiences and information (which is sometimes trans-disciplinary), in order to prevent the psyche-soma dissociation which tacitly operates within the patients from appearing within the professional team as well. Often this interdisciplinary work basically consists of integrating within the team of professionals what is split within the patient. For example, a patient may decide to stop consulting the dermatologist for a while and may consider trying just "the psychic part". Or he may give up his psychotherapy but continue to be a patient of the same dermatologist who suggested it. He may also give different and contradictory information to each professional, or when talking to one professional he may even say a bad (or a good) word about the other, without this showing in his behaviour. Only joint work in clinical sessions, in addition to the exchange and discussion of information, will allow the professional team to maintain a coherent line of treatment as well as the cohesion necessary in order not to succumb to affective reactions (depression, anger, burnout, etc) or to "psychotic" reactions (confusion, ambiguity, paranoia, narcissistic retraction) when faced with the patient's multiple splitting.

What the psychoanalyst hears

What does the psychoanalyst hear?

While telling the doctor about the history of his illness, while taking off his clothes, while paying the fee, the patient makes comments and has patterns of behaviour which the dermatologist "discards", but which the psychoanalyst can understand and take advantage of in the subsequent treatment. It is not common for the patient to remain silent while the dermatologist examines him. He generally makes comments about his body, his lesions and also his "defects", which are exposed with his nakedness. The same happens when a treatment is prescribed: the patients who show resistance to it usually comment on its side-effects, its physical characteristics (odour, colour, consistency), its cost or its lack of effectiveness.

In all these comments, fantasies manifest themselves: they are sometimes conscious and sometimes unconscious; they interact with the disease, determining the patterns of behaviour and irrational attitudes which make each case different from the rest and are of extraordinary value in psychotherapy. What the psychoanalyst hears in the doctor's consulting room allows him to infer that there are unconscious factors which have a part in

- The motive for and the time of consultation
- The self-destructive patterns of behaviour that make the disease worse
- The kind of complaint or suffering that will be privileged by the patient
- The acceptance or rejection of a treatment or of a medicine
- The location of the lesions.

Even at the risk of presenting them in a somewhat oversimplified form, each of these inferences will be described with the help of clinical vignettes, explaining in each case the clinical situation, a brief history of the patient and the corresponding interpretation.

This interpretation is merely a first step, similar to the one carried out by the clinician when he performs a dilated eye examination: he can diagnose a brain tumour or a systemic disease by means of this practice; however, this does not mean that the dilated eye examination explains everything or that the origin of the problem lies in the retina. Moreover, for the subsequent treatment other resources will have to be used, and perhaps standing between the dilated eye examination and the diagnosed tumour there might be vital structures which cannot be passed through and which make access impossible.[1] In the same way, from the initial interpretation to definitive psychotherapy there is a lot of ground to cover.

PSYCHOLOGICAL FACTORS WHICH DETERMINE THE MOTIVE FOR AND THE TIME OF CONSULTATION

Every patient has a manifest and a latent consultation motive. The manifest motive is the disease, which in this case is psoriasis. The latent motive is always a conflict in his or her life, often unconscious, which takes advantage of the disease to manifest itself hidden behind it, in a way similar to opportunistic mycosis, which takes advantage of a debilitated immune system.

Case 1: male, 32 years old

Consultation motive: "A very small thing, which is growing, appeared in my navel."

History: He comes from a disadvantaged background; he is the eldest son of a large family. His family situation caused him to feel orphaned at the birth of each of his siblings. At the time of consultation, his wife is pregnant with their first child. The unconscious motive for consultation is his wife's pregnancy and not psoriasis.

Interpretation: The patient is feeling anxious because his son's birth rekindles the feelings of being orphaned back when his siblings were born. He is afraid of his wife devoting herself to their son in the same way that his mother did with his brothers and sisters. He has identified with his wife as a defence mechanism: the area of psoriasis is located in his navel and it is growing on to his stomach, in the same way as his son is growing within his wife's womb.

Case 2: female, 14 years old

Consultation motive: She comes with her mother, who does not allow her to speak and says: "The lesions are small in size but then they grow. What I want is *for them not to grow*. That is what worries me the most: I don't want them to grow."

History: She was born premature and was very small. She was raised in an over-protective environment and treated as if she had a mental handicap. In consequence, she is quite immature and dependent. At the time of the consultation she is growing up and developing sexually.

Interpretation: The mother is used to seeing in her daughter a small, weak, premature girl whom she over-protects. Her concern about her daughter's growth and sexual development has been displaced to the lesions of psoriasis. Her desire is to prevent her daughter from growing up.

Case 3: male, 52 years old

Consultation motive: "What I want is to break free from the ointment, because due to this disease I can't be without it. I would like to eradicate the problem."

History: He wishes to travel and visit other parts of the world, but his wife "lives tied down to the children" and does not want to go with him. As he does not dare leave his wife's side, he stays in Buenos Aires, feeling resentful.

Interpretation: The patient has displaced on to the ointment his dependence on and need for his wife. He wishes he could break free from *her*. The verb "eradicate" is apt to refer to his true wish: to pull up roots and leave the country. And the problem is not only the psoriasis, but his inability to leave, owing to his dependence and fear of loneliness. The expression "I can't be without it" alludes to the ointment, but also to his wife, from whom he does not dare separate.

Case 4: male, 49 years old

Consultation motive: "10- and 20-cent coins fall off" (referring to the big, rounded scales of epidermis that fall off the sacrum).

History: As a child he lived through situations of extreme poverty and his mother, who was domineering and miserly, used to send him to do the shopping and forced him to demand all the change from the shopkeepers down to the last coin. At present he has economic conflicts with his wife.

Interpretation: He has displaced onto his scaling his concern about the money his wife makes him spend. His comparison of the scales of epidermis with 10- and 20-cent coins is apparently an attempt to point out that his scales of epidermis are large in size, but it simultaneously condenses the sad history he suffered because of his mother's economic worries. In this case, two kinds of erogenicity have united: the skin erogenicity and the anal erogenicity, as the "coins" gain the significance of faeces he cannot control and which fall off the posterior part of his body.

PSYCHOLOGICAL FACTORS DETERMINING
SELF-DESTRUCTIVE BEHAVIOUR WHICH IN TURN
WORSENS THE DISEASE

Case 5: male, 32 years old

History: This patient was a guerrilla in the armed faction of a left-wing political party during the time of the military dictatorship. When the Berlin Wall was destroyed and the Soviet Union suffered political and economic changes, he suffered an ideological crisis, and from being an atheist he went on to join a religious sect. During the process of change the psoriasis appeared, accompanied by severe excoriations.

Interpretation: Although this process of change fulfilled his fantasies of belonging to a group of enlightened people and of changing the world, it invalidated his violent impulses, which, having no acceptable mode of discharge through the religious movement to which he belongs, were reverted towards himself. Thus as he hurts himself, his psoriasis worsens and his violence finds a vent without hurting other people, which would be unacceptable to his new belief system.

PSYCHOLOGICAL FACTORS WHICH DETERMINE THE KIND OF
COMPLAINT OR SUFFERING PRIVILEGED BY THE PATIENT

Case 6: male, 58 years old

Kind of complaint: "The psoriasis has stayed to live with me; it has found in me the ideal candidate."

History: The psoriasis broke out when he separated from his wife, who left him because he was too possessive. At present he is living with a woman who is very cold, will not give in to his repeated requests for company, and who is always rejecting him.

Interpretation: The patient personalises his disease and attributes to it what he cannot obtain from his wife: that she stay at his side forever. This patient, when his disease finally went into remission after 36 years, would anxiously try to touch the lesions on his leg under the blankets to make sure that "they were still there and hadn't gone permanently". He confessed he used to ask in a whisper: "Are you there? Are you still there?"

PSYCHOLOGICAL FACTORS WHICH DETERMINE THE CHOICE OR REFUSAL OF A TREATMENT OR MEDICATION

Case 7: Male, 18 years old

Consultation motive: Serious psoriasis on his hands, for which he would not accept any treatment other than cyclosporine. As his disease was confined to his hands and he had not yet tried local treatment with high-potency topical medication, no dermatologist would agree to his request.

History: His parents are separated, and the father, a nephrologist who was emotionally distant, had formed a new family and dedicated himself almost exclusively to his work and to his new wife's children. He specialised in renal transplants and was an authority on the use of cyclosporine with his patients.

Interpretation: As the youth could not obtain the love he wanted from his father, he was trying to obtain at least the drug with which his father cured his patients.

Case 8: Male, 44 years old

Consultation motive: He arrives at a group psychotherapy session suffering from conjunctivitis and says that he has interrupted his PUVA therapy,[2] explaining that the dark glasses couldn't have been clean. He accuses the substitute nurse, who had seen him because the nurse who usually treated him, and whom he liked very much, was away.

Interpretation: The problem was clarified during a group psycho-therapy session, starting from a series of childhood memories which came out while the therapist and the other members of the group were exchanging questions and opinions with him. The initial interpretation put to him was that he had felt abandoned by his nurse, who could not treat him because she was away on holiday. This fact had certainly reawakened feelings of abandonment in relation to his mother.

The patient rejected this interpretation, but remembered that when it was his turn to go in for PUVA therapy, he had found scales of epidermis from a previous patient on the floor. He found this unbearable. He accused the substitute nurse and, most surprisingly for the rest of the group, claimed that looking at the scales of epidermis was the cause of his conjunctivitis. Subsequently, and with great emotion, he associated the scales of epidermis on the floor with the memory of his mother, who had suffered from psoriasis and whose walks around the house were easily traceable because of the scales she left behind and never bothered to clean. This memory was deeply difficult, not so much because of the scales of epidermis but because his mother would never complete any course of treatment and refused to be helped by her son. After this session the patient went back to the PUVA therapy he was on the verge of abandoning just as his mother had done with all her treatments. To sum up, the scales of epidermis on the floor were added to the absence of the nurse and the whole impression activated a complex of memories related to his mother. The difficulty in working through the situation generated an *act* (interruption of treatment) and a kind of "organ dialogue" between the eye (conjunctivitis) and the scale of epidermis.

Case 9: Male, 64 years old

Consultation motive: The patient is a typical "entitled demander" with chronic psoriasis which has not gone into remission for 25 years. He behaves as if he were a "Doctor of Psoriasis" but is as demanding as a child. When it came to choosing a treatment, he emphasised the factor of lubrication: "Doctor, I prefer creams that lubricate. If you prescribe something that does not lubricate properly, I will not put it on."

History: He is very attached to his wife, although she only demonstrates her affection towards the children and not towards him. However, he does feel desired by her and is certain that he is loved by her because of the way she becomes lubricated during their sexual relationship. Although she tells him nothing, as long as she becomes lubricated, he is certain he is doing things properly in bed.

Interpretation: The request for lubricant creams is a way of expressing to his doctor the need to feel loved, as he feels he is by his partner.

PSYCHOLOGICAL FACTORS RELATED TO THE LOCALISATION OF THE LESIONS

Although in this case the psychological significance would seem to explain the localisation, I would not dare state categorically that this is the case, because I would not be able to explain the mechanisms by which this is produced, and because there is always the doubt as to whether the patient's story is a myth, so to speak, constructed after the appearance of the lesion. Moreover, there are cases of psoriasis in which the zone affected is fixed while in others the lesions "migrate" from one place to the other and then converge in outbreaks, thus configuring bigger plaques. However, if we distance ourselves from the focus of cause and effect, there is no doubt that whether we are dealing with myths or with realities, the patient has established signification links between his lesions, the area of the body where they appear and the history of his life. These links are absolutely singular for that patient and hence they should not be generalised.

Case 10: Male, 40 years old

Localisation of the psoriasis when it started: "The psoriasis began on the penis."

History: He is married to a frigid woman. They maintain long dialogues of great intellectual profundity, which they both enjoy. The relationship with her reproduces his infantile experience with a cold mother, but he corrects that experience with the warmth of the dialogues. In fact, it is the patient who has a passionate and unbridled sexuality, and the relationship with this woman fulfils the repression of his sexuality. One day he decided that in order to live with her without conflict, he had to forget that sexuality existed and convince himself that he had no needs or desires regarding it. In this way, life with his wife would be perfect. That week psoriasis appeared for the first time on the glans.

Case 11: Male, 48 years old

When the psoriasis began and localisation: "The psoriasis began on the right big toe. I discovered it during a very special circumstance: I was with my present wife at a 'Love Hotel'" (where people rent a room by the hour to make love).

History: He had been in love with his first wife and was by her side during the five dramatic years that she survived breast cancer. As he could not bear feeling lonely, he was already seeing his present wife shortly after the death of the first. They made love at a 'Love Hotel' because he considered that doing it in his own home was disrespectful to his late wife. That day, after the sexual relationship, the woman told him he had to forget about his previous wife and he felt a strong desire to "give her the boot". He looked at his foot and noticed the psoriasis for the first time.

As we can see, the significance a patient gives to his disease is not merely an epiphenomenon of it for many reasons: in the first place because the interaction that is produced dynamically modifies both disease and significance; in the second place because the disease can disappear and its significance can remain, as is the case with a disease which acquires the significance of a "punishment" and which disappears with a treatment the patient takes on as a new form of punishment, as in a case of "the solution being worse than the problem". And finally, because the aforementioned significance can explain why the disease appears at a certain moment in life and perhaps in some cases may even be related to a certain part of the body. We can add to the examples mentioned previously the cases of "anniversary diseases", which occur at the same age, or in the same month (and sometimes even on the same date) as the death of a significant other, or those examples in which a skin lesion appears in the zone of the body where the patient used to be punished as a child by his parents.

What the dermatologist sees

When the psychoanalyst asks questions and the patient speaks, the dermatologist learns to listen, and discovers a singular and un-imagined world in what until then was just "a new case of psoriasis". What is remarkable is that far from simply being an anecdotic learning process, what the dermatologist hears modifies his therapeutic criteria.

How does the dermatologist modify his therapeutic criteria when using the methodology proposed here?

Psoriasis is a chronic inflammatory disease of the skin which is very hard to treat. Difficulties in the doctor-patient relationship are common, and as a consequence, patients tend to wander from one doctor to another and finally to abandon treatment, after which they look for magical solutions with quacks and various "healers". If and when a patient returns to traditional medicine, his disease has often worsened, the analysis and prescriptions then multiply, and it all ends up in rising costs for the patient and for the health system, as well as in an increasing level of distrust for traditional medicine and the exhaustion of the home environment. The difficulties seem to be insurmountable due to several possible considerations which are a product of the disease being chronic and evolving in outbreaks, of the powerlessness of medicine to achieve the patient's well-being, of the minimal duration of improvements, of the side-effects of certain medications, and so on.

However, although all this is true, it is also true that psoriasis is a disease which improves with a wide variety of treatments, and it is up to the dermatologist to decide which to use. In order to do this, he will take into account factors such as age, sex, work activity, the general condition and the capacity of the patient to receive, accept and follow the prescriptions. He will also record the type, location, extension, degree of inflammation, itchiness and scaling of the lesions and the evolutionary development of the disease. He will also need to know the broad spectrum of available medications and all the ways in which they are applied: creams, pastes, ointments, lotions, shampoos and emulsions for cases in which he chooses a topical treatment, as well as capsules, pills, phototherapy and injections of biological agents for when he chooses systemic treatment.

For many patients suffering from psoriasis, topical treatments turn into daily routines, "jumping from plaque to plaque" as they improve, get worse or even new lesions appear. This therapeutic routine can acquire the characteristics of a rite in which the patient carries out his treatment in a progressive way, for example product A + cap for the scalp, product B for the genital area and product C for the torso and the limbs. All this happens in private; the patient is wearing his "therapeutic uniform" (old clothes which can get stained) in order to avoid exposing his body or invading with unpleasant smells the lives of the people he lives with.

In some cases, psoriasis is so intense and has extended so far that it is appropriate to propose a systemic therapy. In these cases the available medications are normally used for the treatment of other diseases far more serious than psoriasis. Methotrexate, for instance, is a drug used for treating cancer. Cyclosporine is an inmuno-depressor used on transplant patients. Phototherapy can be prescribed for cutaneous lymphoma, and biological agents are used for the treatment of arthropathies and for certain conditions with immunological compromise. In all these cases, the potential adverse effects are many and the risk is higher.

If the cure obtained with medical treatment is not definitive, the dermatologist faces different options, and the wider the variety of medications and the less he knows about his patient, the more difficult the decision becomes. On the other hand, both the favourable and the adverse effects will have a "symbolic efficacy" (Lévi-Strauss, 1958b) which a psychoanalytic interview could determine. For example, the odour of a product is not considered an adverse effect; however, it could be if the patient to whom it has been prescribed feels dirty and contemptible in advance, or if he is an obsessional neurotic who is concerned with cleanliness. Likewise, it has also been seen that some patients only obtain the caresses they want from their wives by asking them to apply the creams.

It is not the function of the dermatologist to offer any inter-pretations. However, during the psychoanalytic interview channels of expression are opened that allow him to better anticipate a possible rejection of corticoids, future non-compliance with a scheme (product A+ B+ C) in certain types of patients, or, for example, when itching seems to be more an equivalent to anxiety or depression than the direct expression of an inflammatory state.

His usual experience is that he has to obtain quick and visible results so as to ensure that the patient comes back to see him. But in working together with the psychoanalyst, links beyond what is visible are developed, and they maintain continuity and allow the dermatologist to opt for schemes which, despite not promising immediate or spectacular effects, are far safer and more feasible, and are very effective when the cure is understood as *a process* and not merely as a result.

Unconscious factors, as well as personality traits, can have an influence not only on better acceptance of a particular medication but also on a better therapeutic response. Caresses can increase a cream's curative power, not just make it more tolerable. It is not the same to tell a patient that his lesions will be erased, that they will disappear or that they will be cleaned. Words maintain some of their ancient power even today and "physicians practise psychotherapy without the intention of doing it, or even without being aware of it" (Freud, 1904, p. 258).

It was seen that patients with a higher degree of masochism subjected themselves to, and even seemed to need, highly aggressive treatments, as in the case of a man who went to see a Chinese quack who burned him with incense symmetrically on both sides of his spinal cord (two burns for each dorsal vertebra) without using any kind of anaesthesia. Although he did not get any results, the patient invited the "healer" to a barbecue at his weekend home. The relationship between the burns and the barbecue could not be investigated in this case.

In another case, which will be developed in detail in Chapter 12, a woman had an outbreak of erythrodermic psoriasis after her little son suffered a febrile convulsion. She felt guilty about not having looked after him enough because she had gone to sleep, leaving her son in a fever alone in his own room. She said she wished that the fever had happened to her instead of to her son (she even thought the boy was dying of a fever). She described the pain caused by her psoriasis lesions as that of burning in an oven, probably because the representation of burning herself in her unconscious was put on the same level as her son, who was "burning" with fever.

A clinical case: Mr Rojo[3]

Mr Rojo is a 72-year-old patient. He attends the interview elegantly dressed in a suit and a tie, but wearing sandals and socks. When he was asked his date of birth in order to fill in the medical chart, he replied: "I was born with psoriasis," emphasising that on the calendar, the date "was put in red" due to the fact that he was born on a holiday, "but then it was taken off". This is an indication of a projective tendency which will display itself in all its magnitude during the interview. It is obvious that due to his psoriasis, it is he who was "put in red", so to speak. From birth he has had a mark—red—the meaning of which we still do not know.

Although he knows he is being seen by a dermatologist and a psychoanalyst, he says from the very beginning, referring to the psychological aspect: "I don't want to do the other part." By calling his internal psychic world "the other part", he is showing us the dissociation resulting from the aforementioned projective tendency. The typical medical scene plays out, but while the patient takes his clothes off, he talks about his lesions by personifying them:

The first lesion was stuck to my leg. . . the one that comes out stays to live there forever. . . I usually pick them a lot. . . there was a new outbreak of the problem after I was the victim of a fraud, I was angry back then, and they were angry with me.

The main problem is on the feet; that's where I've got most of them and where it's harder to take them off.

Normally, the dermatologist rejects these comments as he considers them improper. As he looks at the morphological characteristics of the lesions, the references to "anger" or "fraud" sound like background music, which at most is categorised—and neutralised—as stress. This is not the dermatologist's problem. We psychoanalysts, while we are listening, make the same mistake when we think that an "actual" lesion about which the patient does not spontaneously speak is a problem beyond the field of analysis. This is how we let the images of the lesions pass, as if we were carelessly channel-hopping.

While he is being examined, the patient continues with his discourse, and what over the course of the examination were dissociative traits and a tendency to personalise the lesions gain the characteristics of a passionate, concrete struggle with his internal objects.

> One day I was angry with her [a wart], I got a red-hot iron and
> I stuck it on her.

The patient shows scar lesions due to burns on both hands, with small
psoriasis plaques added.

> When you rip her off it hurts. Sometimes they come off dead,
> sometimes alive. If they are bleeding, they are alive, if not, they
> are dead. I chase them to see if they will go. They do go, but
> then they come back stronger.
>   My testicles are absolutely full [of lesions].
>   Psoriasis is not a psychosomatic disease; I was born with it
> and I don't think a newborn baby can have psychosomatic
> problems.

All these comments are made while the patient is being questioned
and examined by the dermatologist. When the "psychological part"
is about to begin, the patient says:

> You do the psychological part, you are my enemy. I have a
> computer which is sometimes out of order, it's shut down. So
> you'll never get inside me.

This is how he expresses how invasive and intrusive he finds the
psychological consultation and perhaps also certain homosexual
fears which are very far from his consciousness. But fundamentally,
this shows us how his internal psychic world is defensively shut and
inaccessible. This does not mean that his psychic world is non-
existent or deficient. As Freud said, "betrayal oozes out of him at
every pore" (Freud, 1905d, p. 68). The patient exhibits himself and
speaks using a plethora of messages which are so concrete that they
are nearer to hieroglyphics or tattoos than to words.

Is it possible to translate them? Contrary to what we expected,
Rojo gave docile and exhaustive replies to the psychological
questioning:

> My mother was very rash, anything could make her angry. She
> used to slam doors; her bouts of anger were interminable.
> Temperamental people tend to fly off the handle. I am an only

child. When you are an only child your parents control whatever you do. If I moved my hand twice, my mother would ask: Why did you move your hand twice if you were only supposed to move it once? She didn't want women to suffer for a man and she was more concerned with me not ill-treating a woman, not making her suffer, than with my happiness. When I was four, she used to dress me up as a girl, she would have me wear my hair in ringlets. I am certain that she would have liked to have a daughter. She used to blame me because when I was born, they had to "empty her out".

My father was a pain. I liked to play the guitar, so he bought me a guitar, and when I was playing, he would go past and pretend he wasn't paying attention and tread on my feet.

Like all our patients with psoriasis, Mr Rojo has a long history of unsuccessful treatments, but he recalls a time when most of his lesions had disappeared. A friend of his advised him to put a grain of salt on each of his lesions, then wrap the grain in paper, screw the paper up into a ball and throw it away when an old lady walked past saying: "There you go, this is for you", but then he was not supposed to go past the same place again.

It was very successful, but the problem was that I used to go past the same place. As for you, I'm doing this as a hobby. I don't expect you to cure me.

Listening to Rojo during the medical examination as well as in the questioning concerning his family constellation and his life, we came across two parallel histories. We had initially detected in him a tendency to projection: a patient with a disease which he has suffered from the beginning of his life, and which is characterised by the colour red, claims that the calendar date was made red when he was born. However, then he tells us that his mother considered him guilty because they had had to "empty her out" when he was born. Moreover, she would have liked to have a girl.

In consequence, when Rojo says, "I was born with the lesion", we wonder: with whose lesion? That of the emptied out mother, who didn't want men to make women suffer and who accused Rojo of having made her suffer—castration—from the moment of his birth.

That is why "if mum could cut off my balls, she would, so that I would be a girl"—with which comment it makes sense to us that Rojo's testicles are "absolutely full" of lesions.

These lesions, to which he refers as if they were women living with him, women who get angry and with whom he in turn gets angry, are treated as imaginary reduplications of his mother (who was always angry), and of himself with a feminine identity. This phenomenon of imaginary reduplication was exhaustively described by Sami-Ali (1986), and was considered the result of a projective alteration, the consequence of which is the configuration of spaces he called "reciprocal inclusion spaces". In a previous paper (Ulnik, 1993) this was compared to being in a vestibule with two mirrors facing each other: one can see oneself reflected an infinite number of times, as a product of the reflection of images which include each other.

Surely the success of the therapy suggested by the friend (throwing the grains of salt at an old lady) is related to a feeling of giving back to his mother all the marks she left on him when he was born; and the relapse of the disease is related to the impossibility of breaking free from the symbiotic union with her, as well as the impossibility of identity being about something other than this symbiotic union. "I used to go past the same place".

As regards the feet, "the main problem" no doctor would have missed on performing the examination is that for such an elegant man to be wearing sandals is an indication of the havoc this disease is wreaking on his limbs. The same havoc that an ambivalent and sadistic father would wreak, whose way of loving consisted of treading on his son when he was happy, surely to make him suffer (as he made his wife suffer? As men made women suffer?).

The mutual influence of the doctor and the psychoanalyst

Many patients come to see us saying that they know we will not cure them, and yet they still come. We believe that this attitude corresponds to a repetitive compulsion: what is repeated with the doctor is the hope of receiving the love promised in childhood followed by the subsequent disappointment of abandonment, indifference or cruelty. One patient put this in a very graphic way: "The doctors don't pay attention to me. They appear on television, but they just give me a quick look, open the door and say: 'Come back next week'. If I am lucky, I might get a free sample of some product. . . but I'm still trying."

To the pathways of mutual influence between the psychic and the somatic corresponds the reciprocal influence of the doctor and the psychoanalyst, each of them in his own field, so that "the other part" ceases to be something that is unknown to each of them. Perhaps the use of working as a team—something which is already being seen in many hospitals—is that the words of the suffering being who inhabits the body are heard, while the body of the speaking being who will not speak will open up its pores to reveal its secrets to us.

Notes

1. This metaphor was provided by Dr Leonardo Peskin (personal communication).

2. This therapy consists of the application of ultraviolet A light after having taken a psoralen, which is a drug that makes the skin more sensitive to light. The therapy requires patients to protect their eyes, for example with special dark glasses.

3. "Rojo" in English is "red", so we should read Mr Red.

CHAPTER TWELVE

Psoriasis: Father, don't you see I'm burning? (The skin and the gaze)

The gaze and its structuring function

As we have seen in previous chapters, loving caresses, holding, thermal stimuli, pressure and pain, and the care of cleaning the child leave behind traces which are important in the psychic evolution of the individual. In addition, punishments received and infantile dermatitis contribute to augment and to lend meaning to the particular erogenicity that the skin has par excellence. However, we should not forget that the skin is characterised by being visible and photo-sensitive. This characteristic determines a function of communication and affective expression which is highly important in social relationships.

The descriptions of the mirror stage proposed by Lacan and the theory of the face proposed by Sami-Ali are both examples of how the acknowledgement—and the alienation—of an image has a structuring function. What is more, the image is greatly determined by the condition of the skin and the way in which the subject is looked at. In this chapter, therefore, I intend to develop certain aspects of the relationship between the image, the skin and the gaze.

Acknowledgement and reciprocity

Whatever their appearance, race or condition, when in front of fellow humans we acknowledge them and in this way we know what to do and who we are by taking them as a reference. Thus we obtain a reciprocal acknowledgement. However, the field of reciprocity of the gaze is conducive to deception, due both to the concealing action of the *mask*—teenagers nowadays in Argentina use the term "mask" to refer to those who live for appearances—and to the presence of the *bait*, which attracts and confiscates the gaze. Animals, which live in an imaginary plane, use this resource of bait in mimicry as well as in mating or preparation for conflict. In each of these three situations, the animal manifests itself by means of a separate form of itself (Caillois & Lacan, 1964). In human beings there is also a function that we could call the function of the *veil* or of the *appearance*, which consists of representing something in the imaginary aspect, tending to the concealment of the true self which escapes any representation.

A patient with a serious case of psoriasis offers to the gaze of others an image of someone who is not a "fellow human"; a "raw" image which causes anxiety and horror in the one who is looking, as well as consequent rejection because the one looking finds it impossible to recognise him- or herself in this image. The dermatologist faces this horror by translating into a well-known domain that which cannot be represented. To do so, he nominates and classifies the lesions according to their shape and localisation. This often has a diagnostic and therapeutic objective, but at other times it merely attempts to avoid anxiety by presuming to see lesions shaped as coins, spots, medals and so on, precisely in the place where the stain emerges as an alteration of what is normal. In fact, the dermatologist believes that the patient is his object and that he is the subject looking at it. However, while his eyes are captured by the lesion, he is, in turn, an object of the patient's gaze. The lesion, as it were, "looks at him" and the patient observes this (Guir, 1984; Ulnik, 1994, 1998a, 2000; see figure 8.10). The disease acts as *bait*.

Scopic self-support, the function of the stain, and the real

Zeuxis and Parrhasios were competing to see who was a better painter. On a wall, Zeuxis painted a bunch of grapes which looked so real that it acted as bait and a flock of birds rushed towards it. However, the winner was Parrhasios, as he was able to paint on the same wall a veil so like a real veil that Zeuxis impatiently said to him: "Come on, show me what you have painted behind it." Unlike the birds,

(. . .) when someone wishes to deceive a man, he is presented with the painting of a veil, that is to say, of something beyond what he asks to see. (. . .) Only the subject—the human subject, the subject of desire which is the essence of man—is not completely imprisoned, unlike animals, in that imaginary lure. In it he finds his bearings. How? Only if he can isolate the function of the screen and use it. [Lacan, 1964]

The body image[1] is constructed by way of a complex nexus of many elements, the most prominent being tactile and proprioceptive sensitivity, the allusions of language that refer to one's own body and to the bodies of others, and the mirror-like image in which we recognise ourselves, which is in turn related to the images imposed upon us by culture (Schilder, 1958). This subject was developed in detail in Chapter 8.

When this connection is not produced adequately, identity may attempt to support itself on one element, independently of the others (Ulnik, 1996). For example, a subject might feel he exists only through his image. The less subjectifying the gaze of the parents has been, the more anxiety will manifest itself in the scopic field, and the predominance of the image can cause failure in the mediating function of the screen.

When a child is not recognised, when the gaze of his parents goes through him as if he were transparent, or when they look at him as though he were an inanimate doll, or when the image of a dead relative is over-imprinted upon his image, the child becomes a curtain, as if behind or through him there existed the scene that the Other wished to see. He then offers, like the painter, his function as a stain: "Do you want to see beyond me? Well, look at this! And while you look at the nothing that I am, I will observe you." For Lacan, the stain is the paradigm of the gaze as object a, that is to say, the presence of the real in the scopic field (1964).

Clinical cases and problems

THE BLIND GAZE

The eyes are an object of attraction because they give back, as does a mirror, the image of the one looking at them, who in turn recognises him- or herself in those eyes. Something quite different takes place with the gaze of a blind person or the eyes of a corpse; they too are eyes, but they give nothing back. The "gaze" of the eyes of the blind makes us anxious precisely because it tears off the imaginary field and reveals our condition of beings "given to be seen". It is for this reason that blind people are so frequently regarded as "seers".

Maria's parents are blind, and though she can see perfectly, she has never been seen by them. She has not been able to play hide and seek, nor cover her eyes in order to carry out the presence-absence dialectics present in a game of Peekaboo. In contrast, when she hides, her parents can find her by guiding themselves with the sound of her breathing. The notion of absence is a problem for Maria because, paradoxically, her blind parents are "omnivoyeurs". Maria has psoriasis with punctiform lesions and her mother, who is an expert in translating texts into Braille, "reads" the evolution of her disease by touching her skin. In this way, Maria has found not only a way of being seen through touch, but of hiding at the same time, as her lesions, which appear and disappear, are beyond the aural control of her parents.

FATHER, DON'T YOU SEE I'M BURNING?

At one time an economics student, Mariana[2] is now a housewife, and was in fact on the verge of completing her degree when she decided she "wanted to be a mum". She had never previously thought she would get married and have children. She has been ill with psoriasis for five years and presents rashes that extend over her entire body. The way she refers to her disease is remarkable: "as if I had been burned all over".

Her psoriasis began when her son was a year and a half old. "My son had a fever. My husband was about to go away on a trip and I didn't want to wake him up, so I went back to sleep. When I woke up, my baby was having a febrile convulsion, he was burning with fever; I thought he was going to die. (. . .) For five years I've lived with the feeling of being burned in an oven." Since then, she has had outbreaks of the disease every year in July, which coincide with the anniversary of her child's fever and her father's acute heart attack. The symptoms also appear in February and March, coinciding with a miscarriage and with the death of her grandmother.

Mariana did not want to dedicate herself to her children; however, she decided to do so in compliance with a family demand: "When a woman has children, she gives up work and dedicates herself to them." This is what her own mother had done, and it was also what her husband wanted. Watching her son "die", a wish of hers was fulfilled: "If my son dies, I can go back to how I was, I can get a job as an accountant and go back to work with my father."

Mariana reproaches herself for not having looked after her child in the same way as the father in the dream related by Freud (1900a, p. 509). As a result, she now offers herself to her father, for she is identified with the child "burning" with fever and receiving the punishment of psoriasis which "burns" her because she was not a good mother. "I always say this, before anything bad happens to my son, I'd rather it happened to me."

The Book of Job: Father, don't you see . . .?

The behaviour of displaying one's own suffering, appealing to the gaze of the Other in order to call his attention and ask for love or clemency is described in the Bible in the Book of Job. God puts Job to the test by offering him to Satan so that he will deprive Job of all prosperity and inflict upon him a terrible skin disease. Job, exhibiting his virtue, does not let himself be beaten and continues to be faithful to God. However, what his virtue proves is that during his utmost suffering, when Job rips his clothes and shows to those who might have said that he was so alienated he could not feel anything, that he was in fact suffering and showing it "through external signs" (Fray L. De León, 1985).

Faced with impossibility, être peau-cible

In a scene in the film "Cliffhanger", a young woman has to cross an abyss between two mountains supported by a harness hanging from a rope. On one side is Gabe, played by Sylvester Stallone, a self-assured man who offers the girl support to keep her calm while she is crossing, while on the other side her boyfriend is waiting for her. The harness comes away and the girl is left hanging by her harness, which starts to break. She manages to grasp Gabe's hand, which he is holding out to her, but the gloves she is wearing make her hand slip. While she is falling into the void with her gaze fixed on Gabe, she cries out for him to save her, but gets no answer. The girl's boyfriend accuses Gabe of not having done enough, to which Gabe replies he will never be able to get rid of that gaze.

Who is the one who really falls in this scene? Is it the young girl, whose body is already a dead weight thanks to gravity and the void, or the athletic body of Gabe-Stallone, the "father" who, in the desperate gaze of his "daughter", is no longer the hero who guarantees life but has become, instead, the mirror of her despair? In fact, this muscle-bound man has become an object given-to-be-seen for eyes he will never be rid of because they can no longer see.

A psoriasis patient once told me, "When I was watching the film I realised that no matter how strong he was, if the girl slipped, there was nothing to be done. The girl depended on him, and when she is falling she looks at him. Stallone will never be able to get that gaze out of his mind; he will remember it all his life. It must be awful to live with that gaze fixed on you." Frayed attachment remains hanging from the invisible thread of the gaze that replaces it.

Misfortunes, separations, bereavements, disappointments in love and powerful emotions face the patient with an abyss he has to cross. In order to do this, he needs a change, at least a partial change, of the scene in which he is and which he believed he inhabited. These kinds of changes do not take place without pain, and to make them, each person clings to whatever he can. However, when this abyss needs to be crossed, attachment is inconsistent and the hands slip.[3] If the patient supports himself essentially on his image, if he cannot feel pain in an abstract way, and if he cannot represent separation at all, pain might then materialise and become (physically) evident.

One patient, exhibiting a lesion on her hand, used to say: "As I cannot tell my son that I love him, I show him my sacrifice," while another patient claimed: "My little scabs are the tangible, visual presence, making my problem evident before others."

The screen, the veil, the mask have become confused with what is behind them. Misfortune or love literally begin to tear themselves to pieces. Perhaps Ascher's question in his paper "Être peau-cible?" (1980) expresses the main theme by means of this subtle play on words:[4] the person who cannot be or exist by himself will attempt some sort of existence by becoming "eye-catching", "given to be seen", becoming skin-bait for the gaze of the Other and losing part of his subjective existence.

A clinical case: Mrs Sol

This is a 39-year-old patient whose psoriasis began on her scalp when she was 11. Her parents are Spanish immigrants with little education, who deposited their hopes for a better future on her, their first daughter. When Sol was only 11 months old, her mother noticed a spot in her eye, and the ophthalmological consultation found the existence of a retinoblastoma, as a result of which her eye was removed and a prosthesis inserted. From this point she had to undergo frequent ophthalmological examinations due to the ever-present threat of developing a tumour in the other eye.

Her parents' behaviour towards her was of alarm and of expected doom; they saw her as someone who could fall ill at any moment from something similar to a spot in the eye, and consequently go blind or even die. Her parents did not imagine that she would be able to develop a normal sexual and affective life, since they thought that with her eye prosthesis, no man would ever love her. They expected her simply to dedicate her life to accompanying her mother. Sol defended herself initially with her intellectual development and then with her professional development, which caused an idealisation of study and work and a postponement of her emotional development and the attributes of her femininity.

Her mother, who suffered from depression due to having had to leave Spain and separate from her family, devoted all her time to looking after some infirm uncles who lived in Argentina, and she expected her daughter to devote her life to accompanying her in her own suffering. When Sol was 15, the same age as her mother was when she had to leave Spain, her psoriasis got worse, turning into erythrodermia. All treatments failed, and cyclosporine only prevented the disease from extending further; the existing lesions could not be eliminated.

Rebelling against her mother, Sol managed to get married. Nevertheless she would divide her life, her clothes and all her activities into two groups: "things of being well"; namely the clothes she wanted, the hairstyle she wanted, trips to the beach whenever and with whoever she pleased, gym, swimming, freedom of movement; and "things of not being well"; namely going from doctor to doctor, uncertainty (will the disease remain quiet? Will it start up again? Will the psoriasis be beaten?), not being able to dress, to go out, to move, to establish a relationship with others and, most particularly, to have children, as she was taking systemic medication. It was clear that the division of her life into two groups—apparently due to the cyclic evolution of her psoriasis—in fact responded on the one hand to the type of person her parents had imagined she would be (i.e. someone who had to accompany her mother in her suffering, who was not attractive to anyone, who had to resign herself to developing only the intellectual and professional aspects of life), and on the other hand to the type of person she herself would like to be: a normal woman, attractive, affectionate and sensitive, dedicated to motherhood and at the same time to her professional tasks.

When she consulted us,[5] Sol had been taking cyclosporine for three years without any satisfactory results. As a result of her distrust and of the scepticism that commonly characterises chronic patients, she no longer paid attention to the doctor's orders and self-administered her medications irregularly; nor did she follow palliative measures such as the necessary hydration of her skin. As a result, she was prescribed frequent dermatological check-ups and she began a psychoanalytically oriented therapy. Due to the fact that she suffered strong resistance to treatment and refused to attend frequent sessions, she began with an individual session and a group session weekly.

During therapy Sol was surprised to remember that when she was 11—the age at which her psoriasis had appeared—the severe alcoholism that at present still afflicts her mother began. As she began referring to her oedipal constellation, she was able to express her resentment because she felt that her mother had dedicated more to the older members of the family than to her, and that her father had never done anything to change this situation. What was also interpreted for her was the fact that her chronic disease and the psoriasis treatment were being used as excuses for her not to have to face the changes that becoming a mother and developing the postponed aspects of her female identity would involve for her life. She found it difficult to assume this female identity because her mother was not a good model for identification, and had also attacked her so that she would not be able to have a home of her own and in order to force her to stay close to her mother.

Sol made steady progress and was able to stop taking cyclosporine after three uninterrupted years of taking this drug. She was then prescribed topical treatments until only one lesion remained on her hip, a lesion she used to call "the old one, around which all the other lesions grow" (in Argentine Spanish, *la vieja*, "the old one", means the one that has been there the longest; however, it is also an endearing term for "the mother"). In this way, she was saying that she could not yet free herself completely of her disease, in the same way that she was unable to free herself of her mother. In addition, her mother also lived over her with "the old one", who was one of the aunts she had to look after. As Sol had recovered from most of her lesions except "the old one", the dermatologist wanted to complement the treatment with the prescription of a high potency topical corticoid to be applied only on that particular area. However, Sol's life history was taken into account in order to decide on a different therapeutic criterion: if she could not separate from her mother, then it was not yet convenient for the dermatologist to treat this lesion ("the old one"). This criterion is based on a need detected in many patients for an incomplete healing process, as if they needed "a bit of psoriasis" in order to continue to project onto the skin either an attachment figure or a certain punishment, stigma or identity mark. If this need is respected until the patient evolves psychologically, then the global response to treatment and the continuity of the relationship with the doctor will be better than if, in contrast, the unchecked urge to cure leads to an immediate attempt to eliminate all the lesions.

Sol later became pregnant and had a child, and during the first three months of pregnancy suffered a new outbreak of disease. Due to her condition, she could barely take any medication, and her anxiety level increased, making her skin worse and preventing her from speaking and fantasising about her future baby. The outbreak got better when, during the fourth month of pregnancy, it was decided that the evolution of her pregnancy should be highlighted rather than the evolution of her lesions. At the same time, in the psychotherapy group she was encouraged to speak about her fantasies, expectations and anxieties regarding her pregnancy, instead of about her fears of losing control of the disease and of the impossibility of receiving medication due to her condition.

When her child turned two, and Sol had already reached a state of happiness and harmony with her own body, with her child and with herself, she started to entertain the idea of having more children, at which point a new outbreak appeared. During this outbreak a melanoma was diagnosed, study of which revealed a micrometastasis in the armpit. When Sol received the news of the melanoma, without any new medication, her psoriasis began to improve until it almost completely disappeared once again. The patient herself attributed her improvement to the bad news about her melanoma, saying that now she really had a serious reason to worry and so no longer needed her psoriasis.

When the melanoma was treated with interferon, she had a new and extremely serious outbreak of psoriasis which did not respond to any medication, deteriorated following the use of methotrexate, and could not be treated with immunosuppressants due to the history of melanoma. When there were no alternatives left, it was decided that a placebo would be prescribed. Sol was given a daily whole-body topical treatment at a centre for intensive dermatological care, as well as physical therapy with a technique called eutony. The analyst also included the family in the psychological treatment.

The result was highly positive: a 50% reduction in the psoriasis and a subsequent favourable response to methotrexate. The mother accepted treatment for her alcoholism (which she later abandoned), and the father, who had been accused by the patient of not assuming a protective role, took responsibility for making the members of the family attend psychotherapy. Although this situation only lasted for a short time, the patient was able to keep her psoriasis under control and decided to work less and to start taking a course in humanities.

CONCLUSIONS

From the real, objective point of view, this patient had three different illnesses: 1) retinoblastoma; 2) psoriasis; and 3) melanoma. Later she even discovered a "small mark" on her ankle, which turned out to be a leiomyosarcoma and was immediately removed; this proved to be inconsequential as it had been detected very early. In the opinion of some oncologists and geneticists whom she recently consulted, there might be a genetic association between these illnesses. Independently from the medical diagnosis and the genetic studies, however, in the unconscious the disease is represented by the threat of a stain.

The attitudes of the patient and of her parents, as well as those of the doctors from different medical specialities who saw her have been influenced by the idea that there is something dangerous, invading and uncontrollable that manifests itself as a stain which not only threatens to spread but also threatens her existence or her development as a woman. She herself describes the sensation as like a grey cloud that follows her everywhere and does not allow her to think ahead. She does not imagine reaching old age, which for the unconscious means that she despairs at the thought of being looked after by her mother. What threatens her and prevents her from living in peace today is the melanoma; before that it was the leimyosarcoma ("the mark"), earlier it was psoriasis, and first of all it was the retinoblastoma. That is to say there is always a stain which must be controlled by an insistent gaze that sees Sol as potentially seriously ill; a gaze that immobilises her. What is more, it is a gaze from which, throughout her life, she has attempted to set herself free without success.

COMMON CHARACTERISTICS AND LESSONS FOR MULTI-DISCIPLINARY TREATMENT OF PATIENTS WITH CHRONIC SKIN DISEASES

This patient shows paradigmatic features of patients with chronic psoriasis:

The personalisation of lesions
It is common in the patient's attitude to her psoriasis to reproduce her attitude towards some member of the family. In Sol, anxiety about the evolution of the disease reproduced her anxiety regarding the evolution of her alcoholic mother. Will she stop? Will she start up again? Will they be able to control her? Is she going to invade me?

The reproduction of patterns of behaviour found in the family in the relationship with the doctor
The attitude of Sol's parents to her because of the tumour she had had in her eye was reproduced in each doctor-patient relationship Sol went on to establish. First with the ophthalmologists regarding

her other eye; then with the dermatologists regarding the danger of new erythrodermic outbreaks; and finally with the oncologists who, despite being used to dealing with patients' anxiety regarding the appearance of metastasis, were extremely anxious and alert to the danger not so much of the evolution of melanoma, but of the psoriasis that could be awoken by the interferon.

The association of the skin problem with significant life events

In this case, the appearance of the disease coincided with Sol's sexual development, and most particularly with the start of her mother's alcoholism, in addition to dramatic episodes of abandonment and even of violence along with the alcoholism. The development of erythrodermia occurred at the same age Sol's mother was when she had to sacrifice herself for her family, and was forced to emigrate, alone and helpless, to Buenos Aires. If we take into account that the destiny mapped out for Sol was to accompany her mother in her suffering, then we realise that the worsening of the psoriasis in fact fulfilled that demand and made her repeat a similar history of sacrifice at the same age.

The channelling of feelings through the disease

When the patient started treatment, she seemed akin to a computer. She looked structured and sought to work everything out by means of logical sequences of thought, i.e. "If. . . then. . .", as if she were programming herself. She even made "little noises" with her mouth, similar to those of a computer, when thinking to try and remember events from her childhood. In many sessions, she did not want to start talking, saying that she had nothing to say. However, she always worsened every time something dramatic happened at home, or at her parents' home. What did not appear to hurt her in her emotional life caused her visible pain on her skin.

The association between the field of the gaze and the skin problems

We cannot prove that the loss of her eye had an influence on the choice of the skin as the organ where her disease would be located. However, what we can certainly claim is that this patient was looked at differently from other children, at the very least because she was periodically subjected to extensive ophthalmological examinations, to which the worried look of her parents was added. The development of her psoriasis perpetuated this gaze long after the risk of bilateral retinoblastoma had ceased to be a problem.

Regarding treatment and a multi-disciplinary approach, the case of Sol teaches us many things:

The importance of reconsidering therapeutic habits (and bedside manner)

Doctors are used to certain schemes, fixed according to protocol, which do not always adjust to the particular circumstances of the patient. For example, they believe that they must progressively prescribe treatments ranging from the most harmless to the most toxic, and so when they reach the most potent treatments without obtaining the desired results, the use of topical or milder treatments appears to lack sense. In addition, they believe that a placebo only acts in cases where the patient feels ill without actually being so, or suffers from trivial pathologies, and will not work with severely ill patients. However, with the patient we presented, when the most aggressive treatments proved to be unsuccessful, it was found that the application of mud, the stimulation of her skin through contact used as an excuse for applying her moisturising creams, and ultimately what amounted to immersing her in an atmosphere where she received care and attention produced the desired remission.

Reconsideration of the placebo effect

It is usually thought that the term "placebo" should only be used for inert substances; however, we forget that there is a placebo effect which accompanies that of any medication. This effect is produced by the doctor's words, the nurse's massages when she applies a topical substance, the name of the medication, its colour, smell, and so on. In consequence, as we said in Chapter 5, the placebo effect should be defined as the difference between the effect expected from the pharmacological action and the real effect which is obtained.

The importance of communication within the doctor-patient relationship

Although the lack of response to treatment is sometimes due to unknown factors of a biological nature, at other times it is due to not following medical prescriptions adequately. The patients does not take the medication in the way the doctor prescribed, but does not dare admit this for fear that the doctor will be angry. As a consequence, he continues with the treatment but feel guilty for deceiving the doctor, and in addition no longer trusts him because in truth the doctor does not know what he is really doing. Faced with each new change in the treatment, a doubt arises: "Would he give me the same prescription if he knew the truth?" This distrust increases and finally he ends up abandoning treatment.

The patient begins to wander around doctors' surgeries, and in so doing starts to accumulate knowledge. Within a part of his mind, he feels he knows as much as the doctor, or even more. However, there is another part of his mind in which he feels the need to see in the doctor a superior, "clean", omnipotent and protective figure. This ultimately generates confusion because the doctor receives this expectation while simultaneously facing the patient's disobedience and mistrust.

Hence the importance of communication. The doctor must be able to plan the treatment along with the patient and he must know how to determine what kind of attitude each patient needs. Although modern medicine asks researchers to base themselves on evidence, the other interested party in the process of curing—the patient—asks his doctor for something that only becomes evident if he knows how to listen, namely the recognition of the fact that "simple moderation, a simple suspension of medical activism is enough to create an empty place that the patient will come to occupy by spontaneously taking the floor" (Benoit, 1988).

Notes

1. Please notice that the concept of body image which is used here is that of Schilder, not that of Dolto; Schilder's concept includes the notion of biological body while Dolto's concept does not.

2. This case was briefly mentioned in Chapter 11, when alluding to masochism and the search for punishment.

3. A psoriasis patient represented this in a dream in which she put magnets on her best friend's fridge, but they slipped and fell off.

4. "To be possible" in French is "être possible"; "être peau-cible" is pronounced in the same way but it means "to be skin-bait" or "skin-target".

5. In the Psychosomatic Section of Psoriahue Interdisciplinary Medicine.

References

Anzieu, D. (1987a). *El Yo-piel*. Madrid: Biblioteca Nueva [*The Skin Ego*. New Haven, CT: Yale University Press, 1989].

Anzieu, D. (1987b). La concepción del Yo-piel. *Actualidad psicológica, 134*: 11–13.

Anzieu, D. (1995): *El pensar. Del Yo piel al Yo pensante*. Madrid: Biblioteca Nueva.

Ascher, J. (1980). Être Peau-Cible. *Psychologie Médicale XII, 2*: 439–444.

Balzac, H. de (1831). *The Wild Ass's Skin*. London: Penguin, 1977.

Benoit, P. (1988). *Crónicas médicas de un psiocoanalista*. Buenos Aires: Nueva Visión, 1990 [*Chroniques medicales d'un psychanalyste*. Paris: Editions Rivages].

Bick, E. (1968). The experience of the skin in early object relations. *International Journal of Psychoanalalysis 49*: 558–566.

Bleichmar, H. (1997). *Avances en psicoterapia psicoanalítica*. Barcelona: Paidós.

Bowlby, J. (1986). *Vínculos afectivos. Formación, desarrollo y pérdida*. Madrid: Morata [*The making and breaking of affectional bonds*. London: Tavistock, 1979].

Bozal, V. (2002). *Goya: pinturas negras*. Madrid: Fundación amigos del museo del Prado.

Calvino, I. (1959). *The Nonexistent Knight*. New York: Harcourt, 1977.

Canteros, N. (1981). Nuevos aportes al significado de la alergia. Unpublished presentation to C.I.M.P., Buenos Aires.

Casalá, A. M., Pomposiello, I. M. & Saubidet, R. A. (1955). Dermatosis provocadas. *Archivos Argentinos de Dermatología, 5*: 159–166.

Castoriadis-Aulagnier, P. (1988). *The Violence of Interpretation: From Pictogram to Statement*. Hove: Brunner/Routledge, 2001.

Chiozza, L. (1991). *Los afectos ocultos en* . . . Buenos Aires: Alianza [*Hidden Affects in Somatic Disorders: Psychoanalytic Perspectives on Asthma, Psoriasis, Diabetes, Cerebrovascular Disease, and Other Disorders*. Psychosocial Press, 1998].

DeMyer, W. (1976). *Technique of the neurological examination*. New York: Mc Graw-Hill.

Dolto, F. (1984). *L'image inconsciente du corps*. Paris: Seuil.

Eco, U. (1973). *Signo*. Barcelona: Labor, 1988.

Fernández, R. (1978): La piel como órgano de expresión. Upublished presentation to C.I.M.P., Buenos Aires.

Foks, G., Aperovich, J., Navedo, R., Rodriguez, F. & Satke, R. (1972). La piel: observaciones sobre una fantasía específica. In: 3rd Symposium of C.I.M.P., Buenos Aires. Unpublished.

Fonagy, P. (1999). Transgenerational Consistencies of Attachment: A New Theory. http://www.dspp.com/papers/fonagy2.htm

Fray Luis de León (1779). *Exposición del Libro de Job*. Colleción Jorge L. Borges, Biblioteca Personal, Hyspamérica, 1985.

Frazer, J.G. (1922). *The Golden Bough*. New York: Macmillan.

Freud, S. (1883–1895). Studies on Hysteria. *SE 2*.

Freud, S. (1894a). Neuropsychoses of Defence. *SE 3*.

Freud, S. (1894b). On the Grounds for Detaching a Particular Syndrome From Neurasthenia Under the Description "Anxiety Neurosis". *SE 3*.

Freud, S. (1895). Project for a Scientific Psychology. *SE 1*.

Freud, S. (1896). The Aetiology of Hysteria. *SE 3*.

Freud, S. (1900a). The Interpretation of Dreams. *SE 4*.

Freud, S. (1900b). The Interpretation of Dreams. *SE 5*.

Freud, S. (1901). The Psychopathology of Everyday Life. *SE 6*.

Freud, S. (1904). On Psychotherapy. *SE 7*.

Freud, S. (1905a). Three Essays on Sexuality. *SE 7*.

Freud, S. (1905b). Psychical (or Mental) Treatment. *SE 7*.

Freud, S. (1905c). Jokes and their Relation to the Unconscious. *SE 8*.

Freud, S. (1905d). Fragment of an Analysis of a Case of Hysteria. *SE 7*.

Freud, S. (1907). The Sexual Enlightenment of Children. *SE 9*.

Freud, S. (1909a). Analysis of a Phobia in a Five-year-old Boy. *SE 10*.

Freud, S. (1909b). Notes on a Case of Obsessional Neurosis: The Case of the "Rat Man". *SE 10*.

Freud, S. (1911). Psychoanalytic Notes on an Autobiographical Account of a Case of Paranoia (Dementia Paranoides): Case History of Schreber. *SE 12*.

Freud, S. (1912–1913). Totem and Taboo. *SE 13*.

Freud, S. (1914). On Narcissism: an Introduction. *SE 14*.

Freud, S. (1915a). The Unconscious. *SE 14*.

Freud, S. (1915b). The Unconscious. Appendix C: Words and Things. *SE 14*.

Freud, S. (1916–1917). Introductory Lectures on Psychoanalysis. *SE 15–16*.

Freud, S. (1917). Mourning and Melancholia. *SE 14*.

Freud, S. (1915). Instincts and their Vicissitudes. *SE 14*.

Freud, S. (1920). Beyond the Pleasure Principle. *SE 18*.

Freud, S. (1921). Group Psychology. *SE 18*.

Freud, S. (1924). The Economic Problem of Masochism. *SE 19*.

Freud, S. (1925a). A Note upon the "Mystic Writing Pad". *SE 19*.

Freud, S. (1925b). Negation. *SE 19*.

Freud, S. (1926). Inhibitions, Symptoms and Anxiety. *SE 20*.

Freud, S. (1927). Fetishism. *SE 21*.

Freud, S. (1938). An Outline of Psychoanalysis. *SE 23*.

Garzón, C. (1952). Exito del narcoanálisis en un caso de patomimia. *Rev. Arg. Dermatosif. 36*: 280–285.

Gombrich, E. (1950). *The Story of Art*. Phaidon, 1995.

Guillot, C. F. & Cruz, S. (1972). Tatuaje carcelario; experiencia en una prisión bonaerense. In: *Temas de Dermatología*. Buenos Aires: Eudeba.

Guir, J. (1984). *Psicosomática y Cáncer*. Buenos Aires: Catálogos-Paradiso.

Gupta, M.A. & Gupta, A.K. (1996). Psychodermatology: An update. *Journal of the American Academy of Dermatology 34*: 1030–1046.

Hall, E.T. (1951). *The Silent Language*. Garden City, NY: Doubleday.

Hall, E.T. (1966). *The Hidden Dimension*. New York: Anchor.

Hyppolite, J. (1966). A spoken commentary on Freud's *Verneinung*. In: *The Seminar of Jacques Lacan, Book I: Freud's Papers on Technique*. New York: Norton, 1997.

Kafka, Franz (1919): *In the Penal Colony*. Translated by Ian Johnston. http://www.kafka.org/index.php?id=162,167,0,0,1,0

Korovsky, E. (1978). Aportes para la comprensión de la psoriasis. In: 9th Symposium of C.I.M.P., Buenos Aires.

Lacan, J. (1954). The nucleus of repression. In: *The Seminar of Jacques Lacan, Book I: Freud's Papers on Technique*. New York: Norton, 1997.

Lacan, J. (1964): *The Four Fundamental Concepts of Psychoanalysis*. London: Karnac, 2004.

Lacan, J. (1971): The mirror stage as formative of the *I* function as revealed in psychoanalytic experience. In: *Écrits*. London: Norton, 2007.

Lévi-Strauss, C. (1958a). The sorcerer and his magic. In: *Structural Anthropology*. Eudeba, New York: Basic Books, 1999.

Lévi-Strauss, C. (1958b). The effectiveness of symbols. In: *Structural Anthropology*. New York: Basic Books, 1999.

Liberman, D., Grassano de Piccolo, E., Neborak de Dimant, S., Pistiner de Cortiñas, L. & Roitman de Woscoboinik, P. (1982). *Del cuerpo al símbolo.* Buenos Aires: Kargieman.

López Sánchez, J.M. (1985): Exploración en psicodrama de pacientes alopécicos. *Resúmenes de patología psicosomática 1.* Granada: Circulo de Estudios Psicopatológicos.

López Sánchez, J.M. (2002). Aspectos clínicos: alopecías areatas. In: *Monográfico de medicina psicosomática.* Granada: Virgen de las Nieves.

Marrone, M. (2001): *La Teoría del Apego: un enfoque actual.* Madrid: Psimática.

Marty, P. (1958). The allergic object relationship. *International Journal of Psycho-Analysis 39*: 98–103.

McDougall, J. (1989): *Theatres of the Body*. London: Free Association Books.

Meltzer, D. (1975): Adhesive identification. *Contemporary Psycho-Analysis 11*: 289–310.

Montagu, A. (1971). *Touching: The Human Significance of the Skin*. New York: Columbia University Press.

National Psoriasis Foundation (2000). *The Best of It Works For Me.* Portland, Oregon.

Pichon-Rivière, E. (1971). Aspectos psicosomáticos de la dermatología. In: *La Psiquiatría: Una Nueva Problemática* (2nd ed.). Buenos Aires: Nueva Visión, 1980.

Rook, Willkinson, Ebling, Champion & Burton (1968). *Textbook of dermatology* (7th ed.). Oxford: Blackwell, 2004.

Rosenfeld, D. (1973). Trastornos en la piel y el esquema corporal. *Rev. de Psicoanálisis 2*: 309–348.

Sami-Ali, M. (1979). *Cuerpo real, cuerpo imaginario. Para una epistemología psicoanalítica.* Buenos Aires: Paidós.

Sami-Ali, M. (1984). *Lo visual y lo táctil. Ensayo sobre las psicosis y la alergia.* Buenos Aires: Amorrortu.

Sami-Ali, M. (1991). *Pensar lo somático. El imaginario y la patología.* Buenos Aires: Paidós.

Schilder, P. (1958). *The Image and Appearance of the Human Body*. New York: International Universities Press.

Schur, M. (1955). Comments on the metapsychology of somatization. *Psychosomatic Study of the Child 10*: 119–164.

Suarez Martín, E. (1998): Síndrome de Groves. *Piel 13*: 63–68.

Suarez Martín, E. (1980). *Introducción a la patología artefacta.* Unpublished monograph.

Tustin, F. (1981). *Autistic States in Children*. London: Routledge & Kegan Paul.

Ulnik, J. (1986). Observaciones sobre la psoriasis. In 17th Symposium of C.I.M.P., Buenos Aires.

Ulnik, J. (1987a). Algunas ideas sobre la piel. In: 18th Symposium of C.I.M.P., Buenos Aires.

Ulnik, J. (1987b). Observaciones sobre la piel. In: 18th Symposium of C.I.M.P., Buenos Aires.

Ulnik, J. (1988). Aspectos psicológicos de la relación médico-paciente en dermatología. *Archivos Argentinos de Dermatología, 38*: 37- 46.

Ulnik, J. & Chopitea de Fontan Balestra, M. (1991). *Alopecía areata: la ilusión de volver a crecer*. Paper presented at the 11th IPSO Precontress, Buenos Aires.

Ulnik, J. (1993). Narcisismo y enfermedad somática. *Actualidad psicológica XVIII*, 196.

Ulnik, J. & Ubogui, J. (1994). La escucha del psicoanalista y la mirada del dermatólogo. *Actualidad Psicológica XIX, 207*: 16–19.

Ulnik, J. (1996). Constitución subjetiva y tendencia psicosomática: El cuerpo y el lenguaje. *Cuadernos del C.E.P.A. 6*: 1–20. (Centro de Estudios Psicosomáticos de la Argentina).

Ulnik, J. (1998a). Psychological Factors affecting Psoriasis. In: 5th. European Congress on Psoriasis and 7th. International Psoriasis Symposium (Milan) Joint Meeting Abstract Book.

Ulnik, J. & Ubogui, J. (1998b). The Placebo effect in Psoriasis. In: 5th. European Congress on Psoriasis and 7th. International Psoriasis Symposium (Milan) Joint Meeting Abstract Book.

Ulnik, J. & Ubogui, J. (2000). Psoriasis as affective expression means. In: *Dermatology and Psychosomatics: abstracts of the 8th International Congress on Dermatology and psychiatry 1*: 39–40.

Ulnik, J. & López Sánchez, J.M. (2002). *Monográfico de psicosomática*. Granada: Virgen de las Nieves.

Updike, J. (1989). At War with My Skin. In: *Self consciousness*: New York: Knopf.

Updike, J. (1962). *Trust me. Short stories*. London: Penguin, 1988.

Updike, J. (1963). *The centaur*. London: Penguin, 2007.

Zukerfeld, R. (1992). *Acto bulímico y tercera tópica*. Buenos Aires: Paidós.

Zukerfeld, R. & Zonis de Zukerfeld, R. (1999). *Psicoanálisis, tercera tópica y vulnerabilidad somática*. Buenos Aires: Lugar.

Index

Numbers in *italics* refer to figures and illustrations

275